T0298600

THE
AUSTRALIAN
TV BOOK

edited by
Graeme Turner and Stuart Cunningham

Routledge
Taylor & Francis Group

LONDON AND NEW YORK

First published 2000 by Allen & Unwin

Published 2020 by Routledge
2 Park Square, Milton Park, Abingdon, Oxon OX14 4RN
605 Third Avenue, New York, NY 10017

Routledge is an imprint of the Taylor & Francis Group, an informa business

Copyright © this collection Stuart Cunningham and Graeme Turner 2000
The copyright in individual pieces remains with the authors

All rights reserved. No part of this book may be reprinted or reproduced or utilised
in any form or by any electronic, mechanical, or other means, now known or
hereafter invented, including photocopying and recording, or in any information
storage or retrieval system, without permission in writing from the publishers.

Notice:
Product or corporate names may be trademarks or registered trademarks, and are
used only for identification and explanation without intent to infringe.

National Library of Australia
Cataloguing-in-Publication entry:

The Australian TV book.

Bibiography.
Includes index.
ISBN 1 86508 014 4.

1. Television—Australia. 2. Television broadcasting—Australia.
3. Television—Australia—History. 4. Television broadcasting—Australia—
History. I. Cunningham, Stuart. II. Turner, Graeme.

384.550994

Set in 10/12.5 pt Arrus by DOCUPRO, Sydney

ISBN-13: 9781865080147 (pbk)

Contents

Figures and tables

Figures

Tables

Contributors

Frances Bonner lectures in Communication and Cultural Studies in the Department of English at The University of Queensland. Her current research concerns non-fiction television, health in magazines (with Susan McKay) and the production of celebrity in Australia (with David Marshall and Graeme Turner).

Kate Bowles teaches in the Communication and Cultural Studies Program at the University of Wollongong. With Sue Turnbull, she edited *Tomorrow Never Knows: Soaps on Australian Television* (AFI, 1994).

Stuart Cunningham is Professor and Head, School of Media and Journalism, Queensland University of Technology and an author or editor of several books and monographs on Australian media, cultural policy, global television and 'borderless' education, including *New Patterns in Global Television* (with John Sinclair and Elizabeth Jacka, Oxford, 1996), *Australian Television and International Mediascapes* (with Elizabeth Jacka, Cambridge, 1996), *The Media in Australia: Industries, Texts, Audiences* (with Graeme Turner, Allen & Unwin, 2nd edn, 1997) and *Floating Lives: The Media and Asian Diasporas* (with John Sinclair, University of Queensland Press, 2000).

Terry Flew lectures in Media Studies and is Director of the Centre for Media Policy and Practice, School of Media and Journalism, Queensland University of Technology. He is the author of over 30 book chapters and articles in academic journals, on media policy, media and citizenship, new media technologies, media and globalisation, and the impact of media on education. He is the author of *New Media Technologies: An Introduction* (Oxford University Press, forthcoming).

Jock Given has been the Director of the Communications Law Centre since 1995. He is the author of *The Death of Broadcasting? Media's Digital Future* (University of New South Wales Press, 1998).

John Hartley is Dean of Arts at Queensland University of Technology. He is editor of the *International Journal of Cultural Studies*, author of *Uses of Television* (Routledge, 1999) and co-editor of *American Cultural Studies: A Reader* (Oxford University Press, 2000).

Elizabeth Jacka is Professor of Communication Studies and Dean of the Faculty of Humanities and Social Sciences at the University of Technology, Sydney. She has published widely on film and television history and policy, and is the co-author of *Australian Television and International Mediascapes* (with Stuart Cunningham, Cambridge, 1996) and of *The Screening of Australia* and *The Imaginary Industry* (both with Susan Dermody, Currency Press, 1987).

Alan McKee is the editor of *Continuum: Journal of Media and Cultural Studies*, and has published widely in journals including *Cultural Studies, Screen* and *Brother/Sister*. He lectures in Communication and Cultural Studies at The University of Queensland and is currently writing a book entitled *Great Moments in Australian Television: A Genealogy*.

Tom O'Regan is Professor of Cultural and Media Studies and Director of the Australian Key Centre for Cultural and Media Policy, Griffith University. He is the author of *Australian Television Culture* (Allen & Unwin, 1993) and *Australian National Cinema* (Routledge, 1996).

David Rowe is Associate Professor in Media and Cultural Studies at the University of Newcastle. His books include *Popular Cultures: Rock Music, Sport and the Politics of Pleasure* (Sage, 1995); *Tourism, Leisure, Sport: Critical Perspectives* (edited with Geoffrey Lawrence, Cambridge University Press, 1998); and *Sport, Culture and the Media: The Unruly Trinity* (Open University Press, 1999).

Christina Spurgeon is Deputy Director of the Centre for Media Policy and Practice in the School of Media and Journalism, Queensland University of Technology; a member of the Australian Key Centre for Cultural and Media Policy's National Research Network; and is on the Editorial Board of *Media International Australia incorporating Culture and Policy*. She worked from 1988–95 in media and communications policy, research and advocacy at the Communications Law Centre.

Sally Stockbridge was a media academic for many years prior to joining the Commonwealth Film Censorship Board where she was a Board member for five years. In 1996 she became the Chief Classification Officer at Network Ten and has published several articles on content regulation. She has a PhD from Murdoch University.

Sue Turnbull is a Senior Lecturer in the Department of Media Studies at La Trobe University. She is the co-editor with Kate Bowles of *Tomorrow Never Knows: Soap on Australian Television* (AFI, 1994), and her current research interests include Australian screen comedy and the representation of crime on television.

Graeme Turner is Professor of Cultural Studies and Director of the Centre for Critical and Cultural Studies at The University of Queensland. He is editor of the journal *Media International Australia incorporating Culture and Policy*, and the author of a number of books on media and cultural studies. His most recent book (co-written with Frances Bonner and David Marshall) is *Fame Games: The Production of Celebrity in the Australian Media* (Cambridge University Press, 2000).

The beginning

One

Graeme Turner

Studying television

INTRODUCTION

After work and sleeping, Australians spend more time watching television than on any other activity. Not all of this time is felt to be profitably spent, of course. Most of us probably spend more time grumbling about television programs, channel surfing in the hope of finding 'something on' or just plain yelling at the set than we do in silent, pleasurable attention. Nevertheless, television has become essential to us; at certain moments in time—the Bicentenary in 1988, the funeral of Princess Diana in 1997, Millennium Eve 1999—it is irresistible in its capacity to address the national audience. Australian television program-ming remains one of the key means through which we can imagine ourselves belonging to a nation of common interests and experiences. This is true across the range of programming; from special event spectaculars such as *The Millennium Live* through drama series such as *Water Rats*, soap operas such as *Home and Away* and high-profile sporting events such as *World Series Cricket*, Australians watch Australian-made programming avidly. Imported programming, too, feeds its own form of nourishment into the cultural diet of Australian audiences, offering us the seductive American paranoia of *The X-Files*, the dependable post-Thatcher conservatism of *The Bill*, the Generation X obsession with teenage angst in *Party of Five*, or the rich variety of national cinemas in SBS's *World Movies*.

This book presents a detailed account of Australian television—the industry and the programs, the local and the imported, the past as well as the future.

3

It is written in a way that will make it accessible to the general or industry reader as well as the student taking formal subjects in television in colleges and universities. Given the centrality of television to Australian popular culture, it is hoped that a wide readership will find it useful and enjoyable. This chapter provides a short history of how television has been studied by academics and cultural commentators, while Chapter 2 provides an historical overview of the medium's development in Australia, together with an introduction to enduring policy issues about television. For those who are most interested in those chapters which deal with the television industry, it might be best to go straight to Part II of this book, and for those interested in specific genres or their favourite programs, feel free to begin with Part III.

THE DEVELOPMENT OF TELEVISION STUDIES

There was a time, perhaps thirty years ago, when to suggest that television was an appropriate object of study for school and university students could only have been motivated by the need to protect them against it. The possibility that television might be worth studying in its own right would not seriously have been considered. Even today, there are regular complaints about changes to school curricula which focus on media analysis rather than more traditional forms of knowledge: a familiar strategy is to represent such changes as the replacement of Shakespeare with *Neighbours*. While it is now widely studied in schools and universities, television—the quintessential technology of a modernised, commercialised and globalised popular culture—still finds it difficult to command respect.

One reason for this, as John Hartley (1992) has suggested, is that television's populism and immediacy make it an unreflective—even 'scandalous'—medium. Television finds itself routinely developing programs, circulating gossip and representing everyday life in ways which are a constant provocation to liberal ethical and moral concerns about its representations of the social world and about the cultural value of the generic forms and entertainment values it seems to prefer. The responses to television's provocations can be contradictory. On the one hand, television is blamed for violence, depression, social dysfunction, educational disadvantage, racism and sexism; on the other hand, it is regarded as so trivial and meretricious that subjecting it to close analysis is to commit a kind of category error.

Nevertheless—and while it retains the capacity to generate reactions such as these—television today is increasingly the object of academic study. The importance of the political, social and cultural functions now performed by television is widely recognised. Institutional inquiries into television content, such as those of our various broadcasting authorities into violence on television, routinely recommend that greater efforts should be made to educate the community about the operation of the media generally and television in particular. Although generations of studies have failed conclusively to establish causal connections between patterns of behaviour and television viewing, community concern about the social implications of what we see on television continues to propose the need for a better understanding of the relation between television and the society which consumes it. There are now highly reputable international academic journals devoted solely to the analysis of television; 'television studies' is taught in universities in Europe, North America and Australasia, and it feeds into a significant commercial market for publishers.

This realignment of the study of television has had little to do with television itself. Among the significant shifts in focus and attention within the humanities and social sciences, internationally, over the last twenty or thirty years, has been a reassessment of the class-based division between elite and popular cultural forms. Where the traditional humanities, in particular, once defined whole disciplines partly through a principled exclusion of popular culture—literary studies, for instance, but also in many cases film studies—the new humanities which evolved through the 1980s ultimately came to accept and then enthusiastically embrace the notion that popular culture was fundamentally important and deserved to be better understood. The new areas of study which developed over this period—media studies, cultural studies, area studies, and newly theorised versions of literary and historical studies—all defined themselves against the traditional disciplines through, among other things, their commitment to extending the purchase of their methods of analysis into the textual forms consumed within, and the practices of, everyday life. As a result, we began to encounter sophisticated analyses of (for instance) popular cinema, popular music, shopping centres, the suburban home, youth subcultures and, most comprehensively, television.

The appeal of television as an object of study lay, initially, in its usefulness as a convenient means of studying something else—advertising or ideologies, for instance. In such inquiries, the television text became the site where the process of meaning production could be uncovered. However, even rudimentary analysis of television texts eventually required that the analyst knew something about the specificity of television as a textual domain. As the interdisciplinary fields of media studies, communications studies and cultural studies began to develop to the point where areas of specialisation became possible, so too did the concentration on television as a medium to be studied in its own right.

STUDYING TELEVISION

Of course, the history of television studies goes back further than this. Research into the persuasive effects of all media forms took on a high profile during the Cold War in the 1950s, and was reinforced by American military interest in the processes of brainwashing which emerged from the Korean War. As a result of such interests, there are research traditions within the social sciences which have taken television seriously for more than forty years. From the 1960s on, US research into mass communication (not television, *per se*, but often dealing with television as the exemplary process) focused on issues of media influence—so-called 'media effects' research—through the investigation of behavioural or attitudinal change. The objective for much of this work was to describe the means through which media messages, themselves regarded as unproblematically decipherable, could influence viewers' conceptions of the world and their conse-quent behaviour within it.

Accompanying, and to some extent complementing, this tradition was an anti-populist critique of television which represented the medium as the nadir of popular culture's textual forms: the epitome of a trashy culture which was sweeping more valuable forms before it. Adding weight to this critique were the warnings carried by political economies of the media industries. These questioned the effects upon the access to, and supply of, information likely to result from the increasing consolidation of the commercial and political power invested in the large international media organisations. It is in this tradition that we see intellectual trade across the Atlantic, with the media research of Graham Murd-ock and Peter Golding (1973), for instance, being influenced by American mass communications traditions. Unlike the more psychologistic tradition which had examined media effects in individuals, the political economies tended to mount principled political critiques of the broad social distortions produced by the concentration of media power and influence.

The American mass communication tradition (cf. McQuail 1972), with its emphases on political economy and behaviourist approaches, dominated media research until the 1970s, when it was challenged by arguments from a new quarter: the neo-Marxist critiques developing in what was to become British cultural studies. The approach taken by Raymond Williams' *Television: Technology and Cultural Form* (1974) is sympomatic in its exploration of two critical directions. First, it was critical of what it regarded as an ahistorical view of the relation between new technologies and the uses made of them by the culture ('technological determinism'). Second, it insisted that we should attempt to understand more about the specificity of television as a textual regime (television genres as 'cultural form'). Ultimately, what we now think of as the fields of media and cultural studies displaced much of the American mass communications tradition within the United Kingdom. In its place developed a more textual, more interpretatively critical and more political account of television as the contingent production of a dominant culture. Within this tradition we find the bases for what we now think of as conventional approaches to the study of television in Australia.

A key text in this development was John Fiske and John Hartley's *Reading Television* (1978). The title of this book perfectly encapsulates the shift in approaches to television that had taken place over the previous decade. Fiske and Hartley's project was to change the way in which television viewing was understood and evaluated. For them, the consumption of television was active and interpretive—reading, not watching. Furthermore, in a precursor to Fiske's later discussion of 'the cultural economy' in his *Television Culture* (1987) and Hartley's outlining of the 'postmodern public sphere' in his *Popular Reality* (1996), television was placed at the centre of contemporary culture: it stood in place of 'the bard' as the culture's storyteller, oral historian and entertainer.

The process of 'reading' outlined in *Reading Television* employed the methodology of semiotics. Semiotics offered two great advantages to television studies. First, it provided a means of describing the relationship between the visual image and the culture, thus enabling the analysis of the complex mixture of visual, aural and contextual information that comprises the television message. Second, semiotics enabled television studies to break with analytic methods which had derived primarily from literary studies, and were thus tied to evaluative strategies aimed at aesthetic judgments. Television studies could now distance itself from the aesthetic criticisms that led to dismissal of the medium, and focus instead on the medium's social and cultural function. Consequently, in the semiotic textual analyses which followed, the emphasis fell upon the cultural production of meaning—a direction entirely in accord with Fiske and Hartley's proposition of the 'bardic function' of the television message.

For about a decade, the elaboration of the semiotic analysis of the television text overwhelmed all else. The mid-1970s to the mid-1980s saw an eruption of textual analysis of television programs, formats and genres in the United Kingdom, the United States, and in Australia and Canada. The dominance was not complete, however, nor was it aimed solely at producing clever textual analysis (although certainly some of it did). The work of Charlotte Brunsdon and David Morley (1978), for instance, which started out as textual analysis of the construction of social meanings within the British evening magazine television program, *Nationwide*, ended up as an inquiry into the ideological positioning of the audience by the codes and conventions of the genre before leading on to a major program of research into the consumption of television within the home (Morley 1986, 1992), which is still providing insights today.

At some point, though, the question always asked of the textual critics had to be answered: how do you know that audiences will read the text in the way you suggest? A group of highly influential inquiries into audience readings of mainstream popular texts, commencing with Dorothy Hobson's (1980) participant observation studies of the producers and audiences of the British soap, *Crossroads*, and achieving international prominence with Ien Ang's (1985) study of the audience of an American prime-time soap, *Watching Dallas*, turned the attention of television studies away from the text and towards the audience. From the mid-1980s until the mid-1990s, audience studies were the engine room of television studies worldwide, fracturing some of the critical assurance which had marked the semiotic textual analyses and undermining the elitism implicit in the growth of the academic textual critic of television. They also opened up a space for a rapprochement between American social science approaches and the British interpretative approaches to television. New political interventions became possible too, specifically around issues of gender, ethnicity and race, as audience studies helped us understand the differing uses to which the television text would be put by different sections of the community. Much of the most important work in audience studies over this period, for instance, dealt with the female consumer of the television message, while much of the importance of the continuing tradition of audience studies has focused on the consumption practices of particular ethnicities or minority communities.

A product of semiotics' disinterest in aesthetic values and the recognition of the importance of the high degree of contingency and specificity with which television plays its part in the culture has been a reversal of the critical habit of routinely disparaging the medium of television. A key factor in the development of television studies from the mid-1980s to the present has been the more positive assessment of the cultural role played by television as a medium, and of the ways in which it is consumed by its audiences (cf Fiske 1987; Jenkins 1992; Hartley 1999). While some saw the late 1980s as a period when the democratic potential of television was probably overplayed—there have been many accounts of the role of cultural populism in, usually, the work of John Fiske (cf McGuigan 1992)—it is clear that a strongly celebratory strain of television studies was established over this period. It has maintained its relevance to discussions of television, particularly since the elaboration of theories of postmodernity which have precisely suited the nature of the television message and its customary modes of consumption. Certainly, these days, television studies is inhabited by people who seem to enjoy a lot of what they watch on television for a variety of reasons.

The analysis of television has become a familiar part of media studies, communications and cultural studies degree programs, and as these programs have established themselves within schools and universities, they have accommodated more pluralistic and varied bodies of approaches than was the case when it was just beginning. Nevertheless, in her contribution to Geraghty and Lusted's *The Television Studies Book* (1998), Charlotte Brunsdon makes the point that, compared with the television studied in the social sciences and mass communications traditions, the television studied by what she describes as 'television studies' (in the Northern Hemisphere, at least) remains 'textualised':

> The concentration was on programmes and genres rather than industry and
> economy. This was not, in general, a television discussed in relation to issues
> of working practices, labour relations, exports and national and international
> legislation. In contrast to the emphases of literary and dramatic criticism, it was
> a television of low and popular culture. A television of sitcoms, soaps and crime
> series, rather than a television of playwrights, a television of ideology rather than
> aesthetics. (Brunsdon 1998: 105)

As a result, Brunsdon argues, the academic literature of television studies has effectively concentrated on three areas of interest: 'the definition of the television text, the textual analysis of the representations of the social world offered therein, and the investigation of the television audience' (1998: 105). Of these, she suggests, the debate around the definition of the television text has been the most influential and productive because it is here that we find debates which are fundamentally specific to the medium.

In Australia, while the concentrations Brunsdon describes have certainly developed, there have been additional—but centrally important—streams of inquiry which have focused on issues of regulation, ownership and control. As is the case with media and cultural studies generally in Australia, cultural policy issues—particularly those around government regulatory regimes—have been extremely influential in Australian television studies. Significantly, while Brunsdon might feel entitled to talk about 'television' without any qualifying indicator of national location, Australian writers are much more likely to talk about 'Australian television'. Australian television studies has been fundamentally defined by consideration of the specific local or national contexts within which Australian television is produced and consumed.

STUDYING AUSTRALIAN TELEVISION

So far I have been using the terms 'media studies', 'cultural studies' and 'television studies' interchangeably. This could lead to a misunderstanding of the historical relation between the terms. It should be pointed out that television studies has developed as a specialisation from within the broader fields of media or cultural studies and shares its dominant theoretical assumptions and methodologies with those fields. This is why the following section begins by introducing a highly encapsulated account of the growth of media and cultural studies in Australia (for an extended account, see Turner 1993).

The growth of media and cultural studies in the Australian university system is the product of more than academic or theoretical developments. The federal and state governments' investment in a local film industry which commenced in 1969 and grew through the 1970s provided the impetus for academic interest in Australian film and in the formation of an appropriate cultural framework to assist and direct local production. Initially, television was not included within the funding arrangements that supported film production. Many of the cultural nationalist arguments which motivated support for a local film industry, however—the resistance to cultural imperialism and the recognition of the importance of a nationally inflected popular culture—were equally applicable to television. They influenced changes to local content regulations for television which were installed in the early 1970s, and the consequent increase in drama and documentary production helped to place television in the centre of public as well as academic debates about national culture and national identity. Policy initiatives such as these have ensured that media studies adopts a politically engaged stance in much of its work. In order to comment on the media industries, media studies academics have often sought to play a role in the formation of cultural policy (cf Cunningham 1992) and as a result this interest has contributed to the elaboration of the distinctive nature of media and cultural studies in Australia.

A second set of conditions which enabled the development of interdisciplinary academic programs dealing with the media was the establishment of the Colleges of Advanced Education (CAEs), also in the early 1970s. These tertiary institutions were expected to contribute directly to vocational training and to establish a different, more socially engaged, academic profile than the established universities. As a result of this brief, the CAEs (which became universities in the early 1990s) became the prime location for the development of interdisciplinary programs in the humanities and social sciences, particularly those aimed at more specific and practical career outcomes than was common with the generalist Arts degrees of the time. Degrees in media studies, communications and journalism were among the products of this period. At just the moment when the enabling disciplinary frameworks were evolving, then, the expansion of the higher education sector (as well as the abolition of tuition fees) provided the opportunities for these new interdisciplinary formations to establish themselves with a new cohort of students, many of whom were the first generation of their families to attend university and occupied less elite orientations to popular cultural forms.

The result of this combination of conditions was an increased investment in programs offering training in media studies and media practice. A consequence of this, in turn, was the increased professionalisation of media studies academics. They began to research and publish across the field: media histories; critical analyses of the politics or ideologies of media representations; arguments about the appropriate policy regime to deal with the regulation of local content and the control of patterns of ownership; and critical political economies of the commercial television industry.

In our organisation of this book, we have attempted to acknowledge many of the variety of different approaches to television which have proven useful in the Australian context. In the second chapter of this introductory Part I, Stuart Cunningham provides an overview of the place of Australian television within an increasingly international mediascape. While it offers a general history of the medium in Australia, it also discusses both new and enduring policy issues and the politics driving them. After Part I, the structure of the book divides Australian television into three primary categories: the industry, the text and the audience. Part II deals with the history and structure of the television industry in Australia by focusing on the major industry sectors: the commercial television networks, the public broadcasters, and the emerging or alternative regimes of community television, pay television and digital television. Chapter 3, written by Jock Given, provides a detailed nuts-and-bolts account of the operation of the commercial sector, supported by a case study of how the market leader, the Nine Network, has constructed its commercial identity. In Chapter 4's account of the operation of the ABC and SBS, Elizabeth Jacka focuses on the public service obligations of the public broadcasters and the ways in which they are managed against contradictions within their charter, recurrent funding cuts and a decline in the political support for public broadcasting. In Chapter 5, Terry Flew and Christina Spurgeon examine the alternative sectors through the concerns with issues of access and equity which have underpinned virtually all critiques of the history and structure of the television industry in Australia, and much of the regulatory interventions as well.

Part III focuses on the primary genres or program formats currently seen on Australian television. In Chapter 6, I review developments within news and current affairs, particularly over the last decade, in order to discuss the issues of tabloidisation and media responsibility. Frances Bonner, in Chapter 7, provides a much-needed account of lifestyle programming on Australian television. Despite the importance of lifestyle and information programming across the commercial and public sectors over the last decade—from *Burke's Backyard* to *Gardening Australia*—there has been very little attention to the development of this format on Australian television. In contrast, the success of Australian soap operas overseas has been the subject of a great deal of media and academic discussion in recent years and Kate Bowles, in Chapter 8, provides a critical analysis of these debates. Sport, too, has been a long-standing and commercially successful category of Australian programming. In Chapter 9, David Rowe summarises the key factors behind this success, as well as discussing the recent extension of sports programming into 'variety' programming through, for example, the various configurations of Roy and HG and *The Footy Show*.

The history of drama on Australian TV is a history of funding structures and regulatory requirements as well as genres or key programs. Alan McKee, in Chapter 10, surveys this history while also discussing the importance of certain kinds of imported drama (particularly at prime time) to the viewing habits of Australians. And in Chapter 11, John Hartley deals with a less easily controlled category of texts: the televising of the live event, the moments when television operates as the place where the public—particularly the national public—is gathered together and where its authority as a medium is at its most incontestable.

Part IV deals with the audience. As Ien Ang has pointed out in *Desperately Seeking the Audience* (1991), the search for 'the audience' has been the great chimera of commercial television as new methods of research and analysis have been developed, tried and discarded. Studies of the television audience have been significant components of television studies since the mid-1980s. Within the industry, of course, the use of various methods of ratings, focus groups and 'product testing' of new progams has been routine for decades. In Chapter 12, Sue Turnbull reviews the major research traditions in audience studies, both from the industry and the academy, before considering the likely futures of television audiences within an environment which now includes pay TV and within which there are much greater possibilities for interactivity than ever before.

For many years within Australia, the commercial television networks competed for the 'same' audience, achieving market dominance through the attraction of a major share of the available audience to their channel. In a significant departure from this commercial strategy in recent years, the Ten Network has decided to refocus away from competition for the mass audience and pursue instead a particular segment of that audience. In Chapter 13, Sally Stockbridge describes the construction of the Ten audience and the programming it was thought to require, in a unique 'insider's account' of how the television industry produces its audiences. Finally—and as we have seen already—among the developments within audience studies in recent years has been a shift away from mainstream or mass audiences to the examination of the specific desires or cultural needs of particular audience fractions or community groups. Chapter 14 looks at those fractions of the media audience which are, for one reason or another, marginal to the commercial operators' and even to the public broadcasters' conceptions of their audience. In this final chapter, Stuart Cunningham and Tom O'Regan review the question of the status of marginal audiences for popular media.

There are many other things that could be said about Australian television, many other approaches which could be taken. The convergence of television with other media forms, and the growing critical interest in media as the form through which the public now communicates with itself—visible in the academic journalism of Catharine Lumby (1999) or Ken Wark (1999)—means that the elaboration of our understanding of the medium and its implications has only just begun.

Two Stuart Cunningham

History, contexts, politics, policy

Television has been called 'overwhelmingly the most pervasive contemporary mass medium' (Collins 1990: 22). Across the industrialised world, and now almost universally throughout the developing world, television's centrality is bearing out Collins' point. Television is both an intensely local and at the same time an inherently and increasingly global cultural technology. This book will trace many aspects of this Janus-faced nature; here, I will be stressing frameworks for studying the international, historical and policy dimensions which impact on our understanding of Australian television.

HISTORY

What is the history that laid the basis for the contemporary status of television? Television history in Australia can be broken into periods according to a variety of elements of television culture (see Figure 2.1). The television culture, in Tom O'Regan's terms:

> consists of distribution and broadcasting strategies, institutional structures, and the
> different activities involved in creating, regulating, screening, criticising and
> otherwise producing and watching television in Australia . . . The interaction and
> non-interaction, the cohesion and lack of cohesion of these different aspects of the
> service gives Australia's television culture its particular shape (O'Regan 1993: xix).

13

Figure 2.1 Four phases of Australian television

Phase/date	Industry	Government/regulation	Technology	Programming	Audience
Cycle 1 1940s *Innovation* 1950s *Diffusion*	• 1956 TV begins – Sydney and Melbourne • 1959 TV begins – Brisbane, Adelaide, Perth	• 1949 Australian Broadcasting Control Board • 1950 Decision on dual system • 'two-station' rule • 1953 Royal Commission • 1956 *Broadcasting and Television Act* • 1960 amendments to Act • 1962 Vincent Committee	• Live programming • Imported film → TV → film (kineying)	• Imported fiction • Local 'live' news, variety • US/UK dominance	• 1944 ratings start (radio) • Rapid diffusion • Ratings show US dominance
2 1964–74 *Establishment*	• 1964–65 third 'network' starts • Free-to-air system expands to completion by 1968 • Relative ownership stability	• 1964 amendments to Act • 1973 Senate Select Committee	• Third network—signal conversion for Channel 0/10 • Growth of simultaneous programming (landlines and international satellite feeds)	• Local drama production • Growth of local production diversity (current affairs, comedy, drama, sports) • Shift from Melbourne to Sydney as production centre	• Near-total audience reach • Growth of audiences for local production • 1972–74 audience viewing decline
3 1975–87 *Maturity*	• 1980 SBS starts	• 1976 Green Report • 1977 Australian Broadcasting Tribunal • 1982 CSTV (ABT) Report • 1984 Oswin Report • 1985 SBS (ABT) Report	• 1975 colour TV • Domestic VCR technology	• Packer cricket • National TV advertising • Convergence of film/TV	• Increase in audience levels • Colour—fastest take-up in the world • VCR rapid growth

Government timeline: Liberal/Country Party (Menzies) — 1972 — Labor (Whitlam) — 1975 — L/CP (Fraser) — 1983

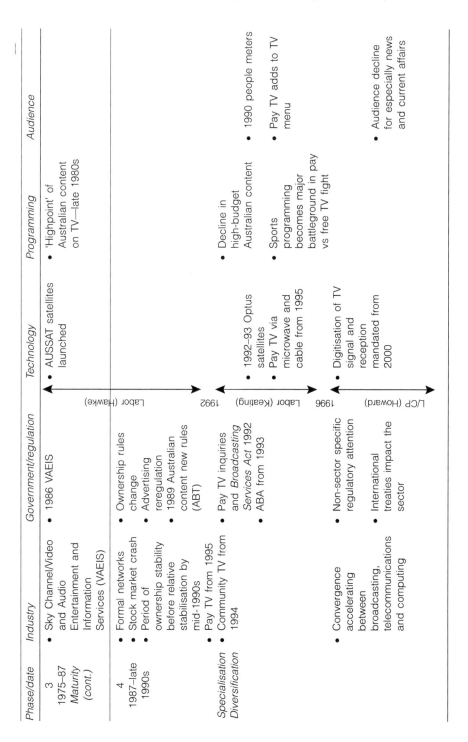

Phase/date	Industry	Government/regulation	Technology	Programming	Audience
3 1975–87 *Maturity* *(cont.)*	• Sky Channel/Video and Audio Entertainment and Information Services (VAEIS)	• 1986 VAEIS	• AUSSAT satellites launched	• 'Highpoint' of Australian content on TV—late 1980s	
4 1987–late 1990s	• Formal networks • Stock market crash • Period of ownership stability before relative stabilisation by mid-1990s • Pay TV from 1995	• Ownership rules change • Advertising reregulation • 1989 Australian content new rules (ABT)			
Specialisation *Diversification*	• Community TV from 1994	• Pay TV inquiries and *Broadcasting Services Act 1992* • ABA from 1993	• 1992–93 Optus satellites • Pay TV via microwave and cable from 1995	• Decline in high-budget Australian content • Sports programming becomes major battleground in pay vs free TV fight	• 1990 people meters • Pay TV adds to TV menu
	• Convergence accelerating between broadcasting, telecommunications and computing	• Non-sector specific regulatory attention • International treaties impact the sector	• Digitisation of TV signal and reception mandated from 2000		• Audience decline for especially news and current affairs

Labor (Hawke)   1992   Labor (Keating)   1996   L/CP (Howard)

There are a number of ways of periodising this history—Moran (1993), for example, creates six stages by including a long prehistory from 1920 during which television was invented, debated and developed elsewhere. He also adds an indefinite epilogue in which television travels into the future. I will shape the present outline of Australian television history using the concept of the long-term 'business cycle', a cycle that moves from the innovation and diffusion of a new technology, to its establishment and system growth as a communications industry, then to a period of maturity and popularity followed by indicators of specialisation and diversification. (For a similar treatment of US television from this perspective, see Comstock 1991; and for a more detailed outline, see Cunningham and Turner 1997: 90–111.) While concentrating on the most recent phases, we can focus on an anatomy of television in economic, technological, industrial and cultural terms.

Immediate prehistory

The years leading up to the introduction of television were preoccupied with political and stakeholder differences over the type of television service appropriate for the country. The federal Labor government in the immediate postwar period had definite plans for the adoption of the British television model for Australia—a system of publicly (or state-) owned television. Like most social democratic reformist governments during postwar reconstruction in the Western world, the Labor government viewed the powerful new medium of television as of central social, cultural and political significance and wished to see it proceed as a publicly owned enterprise. Television's perceived role in moulding social and cultural attitudes and in educating the populace was too important to be left to capitalists and the market.

However, the Labor Party lost power in 1949 and the new Menzies conservative government rapidly set about changing the ground rules. In 1953, it established a Royal Commission to inquire into the introduction of television, after having made an in-principle decision that Australia's would be a 'dual' or 'mixed' television system. This meant that Australia should take the best elements of the systems in the United States (which was overwhelmingly commercial in orientation even after a small public sector was added in the 1960s) and Britain (which was wholly public in nature before a commercial sector was added in the mid-1950s). The practical effect of this decision was to skew the Australian system toward the commercial sector: there would be two commercial stations in each major metropolitan market, along with one public (or 'national') sector station. This system was enshrined in the *Broadcasting and Television Act* of 1956.

First phase: 1956–63

In 1956, television began with what would become the Nine and Seven network flagship stations in Sydney (TCN 9 and ATN 7) and Melbourne (GTV 9 and

HSV 7) and with one ABC station in each of those cities. The ABC's national network expansion kept pace with that of the commercial sector in the major metropolitan areas. In 1959, two commercial stations began in Brisbane and Adelaide and one commercial station began in Perth. In subsequent years through to the late 1960s, commercial stations were added in Darwin, Hobart and regional centres, all after detailed licence hearings by the Australian Broadcasting Control Board (ABCB) (for dates of each of these, see Jones and Bednall 1980).

The prime principle guiding the allocation of licences was 'localism'. Television stations were licensed to service particular local areas, be they metropolitan or regional. Therefore, television was expected to reflect local concerns and be owned by local interests on the model of the 1950s newspaper or radio station. There was no formal provision in the legislation for national networks—it was only in the late 1980s, through changes in the 'audience reach' rules, that a form of de facto recognition was finally achieved. Consequently, the great unofficial story of Australian television is the development of de facto networks: how they have evolved, despite their absence from the systems of regulation, and the way principles of localism and networking have competed, more and more to the detriment of localism (see O'Regan 1993).

The first owners of commercial television stations were, by and large, press proprietors in the regions to be licensed: Consolidated Press won the Nine stations; Fairfax the Seven station in Sydney; and the Herald and Weekly Times group the Seven station in Melbourne. This pattern was repeated elsewhere (Moran 1985, 1993). A system of de facto networking emerged around program sharing and similarities of scheduling and station identity, based on the stations' strengths in news, sports, drama and/or variety. In the development of television, we can see an inherent tension between the legislated principle of localism, and the commercial principles of cost minimisation, economies of scale and maximising audience reach.

The program content of the first phase exhibits the derivative characteristics of a period of establishment. There was overwhelming US dominance in all drama material on commercial television, together with British dominance on the ABC. Stylistically, it is a phase of 'radio with pictures'—a distinctive style of Australian television had yet to emerge (see Jones and Bednall 1980; Moran 1993). The first phase can be presented in stark relief: in prime time up to 1963, virtually all program material was of foreign origin, of which 83 per cent was American and the rest British. While this was cheaper than supporting a local production identity, the prices paid for these programs were already 15 to 25 per cent higher than elsewhere in the world, a trend that was to increase markedly when the third network came onstream in the early to mid-1960s. Ninety-five per cent of television revenue derived from advertising for predominantly transnational companies, although the actual advertising was Australian made, because of legislation, and this constituted the bulk of filmed output in Australia in the early 1960s.

Second phase: 1964–75

This was a period of establishment and growing maturity—of structural completion of the system as it appears in the contemporary period, and of the beginnings of Australian drama production. During this time also, and taking confidence in the success of indigenous drama, Australian programming diversified across a range of genres: comedy reviews, variety and sitcoms showed up the lighter side of television entertainment. Current affairs and quiz shows provided a forum for early achievement in investigative journalism and provided the first models of 'interactive' television. Australian content established itself in this period as a consistent ratings success, and its growth into the present has been one of the main themes of Australian television history. Its story is not simply the outcome of market forces, however. It was demanded first by the ABCB and then by Australian Broadcasting Tribunal (ABT) regulations, together with legislative principles in the *Broadcasting Act* encouraging the use of Australian creative resources and requiring stipulated levels of local content to be reached, and also by a resurgent interest in Australian cultural identity from the late 1960s to the 1988 Bicentennial.

A more directly commercial reason for the growth of local content was the beginning of the third commercial network. This was the other major factor which inaugurated the second phase. With the commencement of the 0 and 10 stations, first in Sydney and Melbourne during 1964–65, and then subsequently in other capitals, the basic structure of Australian terrestrial or free-to-air television as we know it today was in place. (The only major addition to the free-to-air system was the beginning of the Special Broadcasting Service (SBS) in 1980, although community TV, on notice that it may not have continuing access to the UHF band, commenced during the 1990s. Pay TV to domestic households began in 1995.) Sandra Hall (1976) and others have argued that this third network skewed the system too far towards the commercial end, creating too much competition too early for limited programming sources, resulting in three networks triplicating styles, identities and audience targets.

Third phase: 1975–87

The third phase has a clear technical marker with the introduction of colour television and a social marker in the great leap forward in the cultural and industrial importance of local product. Opposition to the dominance of American programming had started to become a public issue by the late 1960s, and the growth in popularity of Australian programming had become very marked by the early 1970s. Two, three or four Australian programs—and not only perennial high scorers such as news programs—were consistently in the top ten most popular programs in each market. The worrying decline in audiences in the early 1970s, the advent of the new network and the institution of a regulatory regime which privileged Australian content all contributed to establishing a climate which encouraged the development of Australian drama production.

Other major defining characteristics of television in this period include new patterns of ownership, the high point of the profitability of television (the British media magnate Lord Thompson's dictum that a television licence is 'a licence to print money' was also borne out in Australian conditions) and the beginnings of the effects of internationalisation in program production which grew apace in the 1980s (and has become a defining mark of policy and practice in the fourth phase). New technologies of distribution and exhibition such as satellite transmission and the introduction of domestic VCR technologies were also of crucial importance.

Another clear marker of the third phase was the establishment of the Australian Broadcasting Tribunal. The differences between the ABT and the ABCB are instructive: it was a more open statutory body developing specific expertise in the field, with provisions for extensive public inquiries that could be triggered by members of the public. Whereas the ABCB was often perceived to be the creature of the long-running conservative government, the ABT was born out of the sweeping administrative reforms initiated during the Whitlam Labor years in power (although it did not begin until a year into the Fraser Liberal government in 1977). It attempted to maintain an independent line— with spectacular lack of success at times such as the notorious 'Murdoch amendments' in the early 1980s (see Windschuttle 1988)—and developed a more coherent approach to regulation that responded to social and cultural as well as commercial imperatives. That it was abolished in 1992 is indicative of contemporary trends that made the 1990s a decidedly different environment for television than the 1970s.

At the cusp of the third and fourth phases was a significant technological innovation: the launch of the first generation of AUSSAT (now Optus) satellites in 1985–86. With this development, the formal recognition of networking, and the revised audience reach limits for single networks (as part of the legislative changes of 1986, owners were no longer restricted to two stations in Australia, but could broadcast to 60 per cent of the population), new possibilities for simultaneous programming and the realities of networking were consolidated.

One of the cleverest remarks made about Australian television (leading commentator Phillip Adams claims it as his own) and repeated often at various anniversaries is that we haven't had ten, twenty or forty years of television, we've had one year ten, twenty (and so on) times. But as a description of television content during the third phase, this is surely unfair. Sports programming, especially that of the Nine Network, has been innovative and of world-class quality. The achievements of Australian mini-series—more than a hundred of them from their inception in 1978 to the early 1990s, with their high point from the early to mid-1980s—were second to none. New format diversity, a trend that becomes more pronounced by the 1990s, began to be evident by the late 1980s. 'Tonight'-style shows, catering to a more sophisticated adult viewing audience, multiplied in format and content. Equally sophisticated comedy spanned the generation gap, drawing large and dedicated audiences from across the demographic spectrum. And during this phase, the dynamic base for Australian production contributed to programs becoming attractive in solid numbers to international buyers.

During the 1980s in Australia, the television system reached structural maturity. By this I mean that what one might expect as possible, within the organisational, economic, policy and production parameters of a country like Australia, was being achieved. A complex confluence of factors occurred to produce this. By the 1980s, an organisational structure of de facto and then formally recognised national networks was delivering sufficient return on revenue to underwrite the acquisition of significant levels of high-quality Australian programming. Fundamentally, this was undertaken because there was stable, longitudinal evidence that indigenous product was popular and successful. Another contributing factor was a regulatory system that was successful in building into the programming decision-making processes of commercial networks a genuine acceptance of local product in the face of the economic disincentive of their high cost relative to foreign acquisitions. These factors would have had little effect without highly creative input. The convergence of film and television in the 1980s—through personnel cross-over, funding mechanisms and outlets—brought a new wave of creativity into Australian television of a quality, popularity and volume unparalleled before or since.

Fourth phase: 1987–late 1990s

While the core business of the system—networked free-to-air television—has only started to shift at the margins in this current phase, there is significant emerging evidence of specialisation and diversification to point to a distinctive fourth phase in Australian television. What ushered in this fourth phase was the single most important change in ownership provisions since the beginning of television. Until late 1986, the so-called 'two-station' rule had been in place. This meant that television licensees were restricted to two television stations anywhere in the nation and one in any one service area, while press and other media interests in a service area could own television and radio stations in that area in accordance with the principle of localism. With the introduction of new cross-media ownership laws—the then federal treasurer Paul Keating said that owners could now become 'princes of print', 'queens of the screen' or 'rajahs of radio'—it was forbidden to own press and television interests in the same service area, while the possible audience reach for any one owner grew strongly from two stations (in, say, Sydney and Melbourne) to a maximum of 60 per cent of the Australian population (it was originally going to be 75 per cent).

As a consequence, almost all the television and radio stations in the capital cities changed hands over a short period during the late 1980s and early 1990s. This contrasts markedly with the long period of relative stability of ownership patterns to this point. The interests of the press in owning television was a *sine qua non* of Australian television before the cross-media ownership changes. The new owners—Alan Bond (Nine), Christopher Skase (Seven) and Frank Lowy (Ten)—who took centre stage for a brief incandescent time were property and beverage magnates with little understanding of the medium, and who fell foul of their massively inflated purchase prices, the record high interest rates of the late 1980s and a deep recession.

Ownership patterns during the 1990s have taken some time to stabilise. The experienced Kerry Packer regained control of the market-leading Nine Network, and has taken it to new heights of dominance. Both Seven and Ten, after periods of being in the hands of receivers, have had significant foreign stakeholder influence, especially Ten under the CanWest organisation. Relations between the three networks were destabilised in the post-1987 period. During the 1970s and the early 1980s, the three networks enjoyed approximate parity in ratings, although typically the Nine Network has been dominant, but not to the degree that it is now. The broadly similar advertising rates able to be charged by the three have changed, perhaps permanently.

The new *Broadcasting Services Act* 1992 rewrote the ground rules for broadcasting that essentially had been in place since the 1942 *Broadcasting Act* and its major update in 1956. It legislated for expansion of the television system (including the addition of pay TV and community TV) and for significant deregulation of program standards, attempted greater clarity in the ownership and control provisions, further liberalisation of networking limits, and the creation of a new authority to oversee broadcasting: the Australian Broadcasting Authority (see Craik et al. 1995: Chs 1, 3). Just as the creation of the ABT signalled the start of a new approach to regulation, so the ABA's brief is significantly different to that of its predecessor. It provides for far less direct public participation in regulatory processes; seeks to regulate with a 'light touch'; and works to push back to the industries the responsibility for self-regulation. The blueprint for the ABA is very much a product of the economic rationalist enthusiasms of the late 1980s and early 1990s.

A harbinger of things to come, and a function of accelerating convergence, is non-sector-specific review and regulation. General regulators like the Australian Competition and Consumer Commission (ACCC) and expert competition policy research and review bodies like the Productivity Commission have begun to look closely at broadcasting in Australia, with the latter conducting the most thorough inquiry (into the competitive structure of broadcasting and its overarching legislation) seen for most of the 1990s. More worrying is the decline of audiences, especially for commercial news and current affairs in the early evening, and the longer-term issue of whether current 'youth' audiences, comfortable with such television substitutes as computer games, video and the Internet, will age without 'returning' to broadcast television.

There have been several system stresses during this period. The imperative for the public broadcasters, the ABC and the SBS, to supplement their government appropriations with sponsorship, advertising or profit-making enterprises has been a constant for most of the time. Indeed, Australia has perhaps begun to share the sense in the post-industrial West that the public service ethos in broadcasting is under extreme pressure from governments unwilling to underwrite an independent and often critical voice. The increased cost differentials for locally produced and imported programs, together with decreased overall profitability, have led to growing funding difficulties for the high-budget television drama which was such an outstanding feature of the 1980s landscape. There has been a significant drop in expenditure by commercial broadcasters on local drama. While network profits and revenues have fully recovered from the deep recession of the late 1980s and early 1990s, Australian content is increasingly being achieved with cheaper programming.

Localism, as we have seen, was traditionally a fundamental plank of Australian television policy, but is everywhere in decline. The financial imperatives of networking work against localism. The only real limitation to nationwide networking is government policy and the variable perceptions of and responses to local needs and audience interests. The beginnings of digital television broadcast and reception, mandated by legislation to start in 2001, may address this to some extent because digital TV allows for many more channels to be broadcast within the bandwidth 'envelope'. Certainly the ABC has prioritised this as part of its digital future.

Finally, the system has begun to expand and diversify, as well as to internationalise more extensively. It is to the latter trend that we shall now turn—new types of television will be treated in Chapter 5.

CONTEXTS

A contemporary understanding of television must take account of its inherently and increasingly global nature. The global or international contexts which frame much of Australian television can be grasped from a variety of perspectives. There are the international models of television by which this country's system has been influenced, and the possibility that this derivativeness can be seen as a form of 'positive unoriginality', in Meaghan Morris's (1988) terms. There is the degree, nature and process of inbound international capital and image flows, how and why they are regulated and balanced by home image production and screening. Then there is the outbound side: the international career of Australian television programming in other places.

O'Regan (1993) accounts comprehensively for the mixed, 'double faced' nature of Australian television, and for the distinctive derivativeness of the system—its 'positive unoriginality'. In contrast to the 'pure' models of public service and commercial television represented by British and American respectively (and their unparallelled scale of in-country production, limited imports, export dominance in the world and their enjoyment of the pre-eminence of their programming language, English):

> [t]he less famous Australian, Canadian, [or] Dutch television services are not at the centre of definitions of television, in that these nations import program concepts and programs . . . they do not have extensive . . . export markets; their local product is not so much critically valued with reference to itself as with reference—often negatively—to 'imports' (O'Regan 1993: 11).

However, the 'ideal' British and American systems against which these middle-order systems are compared are unrepresentative of television in general, and changes brought about in the recent decades do point to some long-term structural strengths of the Australian order—in particular, its mix of national and commercial television. In Australia, the commercial sector has always been dominant, but the leavening ethos and personnel transfer from the national sector has nevertheless been significant, not negligible as the public sector is in the United States. There has been healthy interaction between national and commercial sectors, without a dominant public service elitism or 'worthiness' that was subject to attack in Britain, Canada and New Zealand during the 1990s. The timely introduction of innovative multicultural and multilingual television (SBS) into the system in 1980 and its gradual occupation of an important niche in the overall structure has strengthened it further. As its service reach has expanded, the SBS has begun to operate as a second national network. Thus the national sector has begun to enjoy synergies, like the complementarity of the two BBC channels, without the uniformity of a one-organisation structure. Rather uniquely, there is significant programming competition between the two non-commercial networks in Australia. SBS has been compared in some ways to Britain's Channel Four (although each is dedicated to pushing beyond the normal boundaries of broadcast television, both accept advertising). SBS's recent expansion of sponsorship financing bears comparison to the American Public Broadcasting System (PBS), yet its robust innovation puts it markedly ahead of the PBS system.

The model of a broadcasting 'mixed economy', like that practised in Australia, has become the industry policy paradigm in several regions and countries during the 1990s. The restructuring of broadcasting in other nations and regions has often been governed by the perceived need to free up systems dominated by the public sector. Public sector dominance (in France, New Zealand or many East Asian countries, for instance), or its parity with the commercial sector (in Britain, for instance), has been interrogated in the light of economic rationalist public sector resource management strategies, small government ideologies, an explosion of new media, including foreign media incursions, that has seen the lowering of barriers to market entry, and a perception that popular taste should pre-eminently guide reform. Compared with other Western countries, the public sector in Australian television is comparatively better placed to respond to these emerging changes, because it has always been in a structurally subordinate position. Although many would doubt, with good reason, the wisdom of these dominant views in broadcasting policy, political and economic forces in many countries are pushing the public sector into the position it already occupies in Australia.

Second, what is the ecology of foreign versus local production and infrastructure? It is clear that programming in general on Australian television is predominantly local, although prestigious prime-time drama is dominated by US product. The most recent figures at time of writing (for 1998) indicate that the Australian Content Standard is being largely complied with, with almost all commercial stations meeting the 55 per cent 'transmission' quota (the percentage of Australian production between 6.00 a.m. and midnight), while 'evening' viewing (between 5.00 p.m. and midnight) also averages around 55 per cent. Most of this prime-time local production is composed of news and current affairs (averaging around 20 per cent), with US drama topping prime time with most stations registering in the 30 per cent range. Compliance with the content standard in prime time requires on average about 10 per cent Australian drama and documentary.

However, underlying the content is an industry that is very highly integrated into global media and communications. Significant changes to the Australian content regulations for commercial television in 1999 now allow broadcasters to count New Zealand programs as Australian for purposes of quota. This was a result of a 1998 High Court decision pursuant to the Closer Economic Relations (CER) trade agreement between the two countries and confirmed that policy objectives designed to foster an Australian cultural identity can be overridden by trade objectives, also drawing attention to the fact that most legislation is drafted to include provisions that 'domestic' law cannot contradict international treaties and agreements. This is of growing significance because the push toward trade liberalisation worldwide through the World Trade Organisation (WTO) and regional trade blocs is strongly supported by this country, as the net benefits from low trade barriers politically outweigh diminished cultural sovereignty.

Overseas companies, among them many world players, have upgraded investment in Australian audiovisual production and infrastructure. This is to some extent a function of government policy, as domestic investment guidelines of the FFC and state bodies typically require a foreign pre-sale or distribution guarantee. The official figures for 1997/98 show foreign investment was clearly the most important source of funds for Australian feature film and independent TV drama at 44 per cent, with domestic private sources at 34 per cent and government sources at 22 per cent. Foreign infrastructure investment is a major driver of growth in production activity, with Warner Roadshow Movieworld Studios on the Gold Coast, Fox Studios in Sydney and Viacom/Paramount at Melbourne's Docklands. In addition, Australian production companies have been acquired by large multinationals, including the Grundy Organisation by the British-based Pearsons; Artist Services by British broadcaster and producer Granada; and a 50 per cent stake in the major animation company Yoram Gross by the German

EM TV group. The successful regional pay TV company AUSTAR is UScontrolled; News Limited has a 25 per cent stake in leading pay TV company Foxtel; and UK Cable & Wireless has a controlling stake in the other pay provider, Optus Vision.

A final significant perspective on internationalisation is that the television production industry has become increasingly global in its sales and investment orientation. While many programs had sold into international markets before (*Skippy the Bush Kangaroo* pre-eminent amongst them), from the mid-1980s the pattern changed, with financing for much high-budget television coming from a mix of local and foreign sources, and some production companies expanding their base of operations beyond Australia (most successfully the makers of serial drama and games and quiz shows, the Grundy organisation, which eventually became a foreign company and then a subsidiary of the large British media company Pearsons). Australian serial drama (or 'soap opera') like *Neighbours*, *A Country Practice* and *Home and Away*, series like *The Flying Doctors*, *Water Rats* or *Blue Heelers*, children's programming such as *Bananas in Pyjamas* and the Australian Children's Television Foundation output, the popular science and technology format *Beyond 2000*, as well as many mini-series, tele-movies and documentaries have performed very solidly in many markets, although Britain has provided the highest profile for Australian exports. A taste for Australian television has been established internationally, and producers of any form of expensive television are having to build international sales potential into their financing and production strategies. The history, impact and cross-cultural implications for Australian television exports are traced in detail in Cunningham and Jacka (1996).

POLITICS AND POLICY

Studying television is important because it is a vastly pervasive popular enter-tainment medium as well as being perceived as a key to influence and commercial success in the information age. In their systematic study of ownership strategies of the biggest players in the ECI (entertainment–communications–information) industries in the 1990s, Herman and McChesney (1997) show how virtually all have moved to acquire or consolidate holdings in television. Strategically, tele-vision bridges, partakes in or provides a major platform for significant elements across the continuum of entertainment (cinema, music, computer gaming), information (journalism, news) and communications (carriage of signals, satel-lites, broadband cable, Internet) and thus stands at the centre of the convergent ECI complex, the most dynamic growth sector of the information age. It will always be at, or close to, the centre of powerful players' corporate and political strategies.

This is certainly the case in Australia. I shall conclude this chapter with an outline of the politics of television and media more generally and then, in case study mode, look at how the closely related concept of 'influence'—always a key notion in media policy—might be thought about.

Politics and power

Australia has a recurrent and problematic tradition in the politics of the media. There has been popular opposition to media barons such as Murdoch and Packer and their forebears, a cultural nationalist counter-tendency to the influence of American popular culture, and suspicion of the depth of links between Australia's political leaders and their 'media mates' (e.g. Pilger 1989; Chadwick 1989). However, there are limits to outright attacks on power as it is exercised by the Australian media and their moguls. The country's peripheral and subordinate position within the global system means that strategies for promoting alternatives to globalised and commodified capitalist circuits frequently involve the strengthening of nationally based institutions, in spite of the limits of such institutions, and the nation-state more generally, as a vehicle for realising progressive and egalitarian political goals.

Public broadcasting is a case in point. Like many other such institutions, the ABC can be criticised for its integrationist approach to a broadly shared official culture, its association of 'quality' with non-commercialism, and its lumbering bureaucratic nature. Nonetheless, the ABC remains a fundamental strut of the Australian information and cultural ecology, with a commitment to national news which simultaneously incorporates a range of local and regional perspectives, and a distinctively Australian perspective on international issues. Its commitment to local content in all of its TV and radio services, and to the promotion of diversity and producer autonomy in its slate of local programming, marks it out sharply from commercial services whose programming strategies frequently involve the 'rebranding' of imported material and a perpetual circulation of network 'stars' rather than providing windows to new talent and new ideas. The wars of attrition and outright attack by powerful political opponents of different political persuasions for many years of its history—and consistently during the 1990s—are evidence of its strategic and progressive place in the polity. Arguably, it is even more crucial that the ABC survives and thrives as media are remorselessly corporatised and commercialised.

Taking the issue more broadly, how should media and power be considered? This opens up questions, which have been put with particular strength in cultural studies (e.g. Hall 1986; Hartley 1996), of whether it is adequate to understand power in 'top down' terms, or whether power needs to be thought of as more diffuse and, in cultural theorist Michel Foucault's terms, 'capillary' in its operations at multiple levels of social relations. After two decades of attention to the provenance of the audience in media and cultural studies, and the potential polysemy of media texts, if we are to think afresh about the media and power, it is worth at least considering relations of power between controlling interests, media producers and audiences/consumers, with none of these three categories being homogeneous and predetermined in its forms of agency.

The power of the audience for Australian television outside the population hubs of Sydney and Melbourne (which account for approximately 45 per cent of the Australian population) to influence programming or production has certainly shrunk over the last decade, with greater centralisation of programming buttressed by more insistent rhetorics of regional sensitivity which mask the loss of actual programming responsive in the non-metropolitan areas of the country. On the other hand, the clear tendency for younger demographic segments (particularly teenagers and the 18–24-year-old group) to watch less television and engage more widely in interactive computer-based entertainment—and what this may signify for the future of broadcast television, particularly when viewing patterns during the 1990s show significant declines in share for early evening information programming—signifies a shift of power to which media owners and producers must respond over time.

Of course, none of this has modified significantly the established sources of power at the ownership end of the media power continuum. Consistent with the experience of many countries of the world, established owners have positioned themselves in the new media markets in order to spread risk and take 'first mover' advantage of breakthroughs in commercialisation potentials of the Internet. Rupert Murdoch's News has built on its dominant position in print with strategic shareholdings in the second most popular commercial television network (Network 7), and is one of two dominant shareholders in pay television company Foxtel (which is well positioned to emerge from the inevitable shake out of the new pay television industry as the dominant if not the only player in subscription television). News has moved into highly strategic partnerships with the dominant telecommunications carrier, Telstra, for both subscription television and online services, while Packer's Nine Network has joined with Microsoft for delivery of Australian online services (for a discussion of ninemsn, the Packer–Microsoft Website, see Chapter 12).

Ironically, dominant players like News have not been slow in appropriating for their own purposes the rhetorics of the active audience and of consumer sovereignty. For example, News's submission to the 1997 Review of Media Ownership Regulation and Law in Australia contained a study which purported to show that News was low on a list of media companies when measured in terms of the amount of time consumers spent with the products of those companies. (This form of measurement is, of course, highly tendentious as it conveniently skirts the influence which elite media, the metropolitan and national quality dailies such as News's *The Australian*, are able to exert on the national political agenda without commanding a large readership.) This is where media studies' championship of the active audience converges ominously with economic rationalism's championship of consumer sovereignty, which then becomes vulnerable to a takeover by corporate interests.

Australian governments have shown themselves particularly partial to not earning the ire of powerful media owners, and this has taken on a thoroughly bipartisan political colour. Lobbying by commercial interests saw government endorse a dominant commercial TV system in the late 1940s, after intense debate about the importance of keeping such an influential medium in public hands (Curthoys 1986). Murdoch was advantaged by a conservative government in the early 1980s when he was allowed to 'grandfather' his control of the Ten television network to avoid being required to sell down to new ownership reach limits. The Hawke Labor government's changes to media ownership laws in 1987 cemented the power of network control and its inevitable centralisation in Sydney and Melbourne. And it was arguably only the inability to be able to potentially assist both of Australia's dominant media moguls, Packer and Murdoch—with their irreconcilable sets of expansionary strategies—which led the Howard Coalition government in 1997 not to change the media ownership rules. Gala receptions of media moguls (such as Murdoch and Bill Gates) by prime ministers and Cabinets of both major political persuasions indicate an ongoing perception that a small power placed on the geographical and political margins of the world needs 'powerful friends' (a phrase used to describe Australia's foreign policy posture towards first Britain and then the United States during this century), not just and perhaps even more in the emerging informa- tion- and knowledge-based industries of the future.

Influence

Governments have traditionally been partial to the notion that the media are very influential. What, other than this notion, was behind the creation of public broadcasters—both radio and TV—throughout this century? In many cases, it was a case of a clear determination that commercial interests were to be kept at bay in the running of what were perceived early on to be key informational resources and education disseminators.

Governments, it should be remembered, formed these views against the background of centuries of newspaper proprietors often using their publications as personal loudspeakers for their and their cronies' points of view. There was sufficient concern about this untoward degree of partiality, as newspapers became truly 'mass' media, that the idea of the newspaper as personal megaphone was replaced by the equally problematic notion of neutrality or objectivity, wonder- fully summed up by Richard S. Salant, President of CBS News in the 1970s, who opined that: 'Our reporters do not cover stories from their point of view. They are presenting them from nobody's point of view.' (quoted in Cunningham and Miller 1994: 35)

It is also clear that the notion of influence is firmly embedded in legislation and regulation. The *Broadcasting Services Act* 1992 applies 'different levels of regulatory control to the range of categories according to the degree of influence that different categories of service are able to exert in shaping community views in Australia'. The Objects of the Act include 'to encourage diversity in control of the more influential broadcasting services' and 'to ensure that Australians have effective control of the more influential broadcasting services'.

'Influence', then, is an historically central and necessary term in media law and policy, but is rarely interrogated and there is increasing pressure to justify its relevance. Political opinion, voiced from Prime Minister Howard down, has it that the existing broadcasting law which seeks to limit foreign and cross-media ownership—a law whose legitimacy is based on curbing untoward media influence falling into too few hands—is rendered superfluous by the plethora of new media outlets. An important Productivity Commission inquiry in 1999–2000 was particularly interested in whether the BSA's enshrinement of influence at the heart of the broadcasting legislation could be sustained into the new millennium.

There are obviously certain unequivocal elements to television's influence which we can dub its pervasiveness, popularity and the platform it provides for public life. Television is a standard feature of virtually every Australian home—this phenomenon came about with considerable rapidity in the 1950s and 1960s, and there is now at least one television set in over 99 per cent of Australian homes. A very significant percentage of households possess more than one television set and a video recorder. Homes with more than one set run at about 60 per cent. Video penetration is reaching a plateau, or 'saturation'. By the late 1990s, it had reached 85 per cent of television households, but the number of video households possessing more than one VCR is growing towards a quarter of all households. Australia has one of the highest rates of video ownership in the world.

The sheer popularity of television as 'overwhelmingly the most pervasive contemporary mass medium' undergirds its social-psychological impact. Television occupies more concentrated leisure time than any other single activity in contemporary Australia. Obviously, measurements of the sheer scale of activity do not necessarily grasp the widely different types of involvement with television and its varying uses by audiences—everything from child minding through to membership of fan clubs which proclaim deep pleasure in and close identification with particular programs and personalities. And although there has been some decline in the overall hours of viewing, and today's young people are growing up with the least hours watched and the most competition for what used to be—somewhat outdatedly (given the blurred boundaries occasioned by computer use)—called 'leisure' time, it is still the case that TV massively outweighs any other leisure pursuit.

Television provides a prime platform for public life and has largely displaced the newspaper as the prime and most trusted source of news for the majority of the population. Another indicator is the extent to which television has influenced political and other public processes in our society. Whatever variety of perspectives are held about 'image politics', it is undoubted that television image management is now a central fact of the political process. Although this kind of role carries with it significant problems, it remains the case that television (albeit supported by radio and the press) is the 'glue' that holds together much of our sense of ourselves as a society; it is the main platform on which whatever passes as public debate and collective sense-making in today's society takes place.

Along with this degree of influence, however, goes the flip side: the degree to which television contributes to declining levels of social cohesion, increasing perceptions of the so-called 'mean world syndrome' and loss of faith on public institutions. *Contributes to*, not *causes*: the myriad economic and social factors in the mix defy easy scapegoating of television alone. However, there are penetrating social science studies that suggest that the two main correlates underlying declining confidence in public institutions are changing social values ('the myriad economic and social factors in the mix') and the influence of the media (Nye et al. 1997). Recent studies also confirm Gerbner's 1970s findings that there are direct correlations between heavy, indiscriminate television viewing and extreme views exhibiting fear and perceptions of imminent or present social decay (see Putnam 1995).

These ways of understanding and measuring influence are being challenged in a variety of ways, and will continue to be. The first is the argument that the plethora of new media, the Internet, and other sources of information and enter-tainment render the notion of a single medium being highly influential outdated. This is a position voiced from politicians through industry figures to theorists embracing the democratic potential for communication to circumvent the present controlling oligopolies. Despite there being almost no conclusive trends that support such assertions—indeed, as we have seen, most of the evidence points to powerful media players moving effectively to tie up new media—this argument continues to hold sway in decision-making circles and public debate, fuelled by the contemporary knockdown belief in technoboosterism.

A second challenge is thrown up by reassessments of the relative influence exercised by different traditional media—print, radio, television. The regulatory architecture has traditionally assumed that broadcast media should attract higher levels of regulation because they use scarce public property—the airwaves—and because they are relatively more influential than print and other media of 'choice'. However, these assumptions need to be unpacked, as they conflate different notions of influence. The two main notions that 'influence' the idea of media influence are a social-psychological model based on pervasiveness and emotional and sensory impact, and a cognitive model based on a political theory of elites (see Cunningham 1997: 31–34). Television's influence can basically be sheeted home to the first, while it is print—and most particularly the broadsheet metropolitan daily press—that exercised influence out of all proportion to its readership base by forming the political agenda: one elite, the media, interacting with other power elites.

As we have seen, implicit in the *Broadcasting Services Act* 1992 is the assumption that television is more influential than radio and print and thus that it attracts greater levels of regulation. This was the basis on which radio was effectively deregulated in the early 1990s. However, this might need to be rethought in terms of radio having very significant power and influence. In 1999, the ABA's 'cash-for-comment' inquiry into whether commercial radio talkback high flyers like John Laws, Howard Sattler and Alan Jones had modified their editorial opinions in exchange for financial inducements from major lobbies such as the banks brought radio's strategic importance into a very public light.

The controversy confirmed that radio opinion leaders enjoy great longevity and they radically blur the distinction between journalism and entertainment, information and persuasion. They reach a key electoral demographic—the broadly based middle-to-lower class with a stake in opinion formation—arguably far more effectively than TV with its dominant entertainment modalities and its middle-of-the-road sensibility that cannot afford to alienate any significant segment of the community. Liberal Party power broker Michael Kroger claimed that Alan Jones had had a crucial influence on the outcome of the 1998 federal election after analysing the correlations between Jones' listener demographics and outcomes in seats held or won in Sydney by the Howard government.

A third challenge to the terms in which these debates are couched is a theoretical one about the contemporary nature of the 'public sphere'. The concept of the public sphere has been regularly used within the disciplinary fields of media, cultural and communications studies to theorise the media's articulation between the state/government and civil society. Most debate about influence—and the foregoing is no exception—is conducted in modernist terms. These terms are challenged by a postmodernist argument positing that the media and society do not stand over against each other as separable categories but that one indeed exists within the other.

There are those—the high modernists—for whom the contemporary Western public sphere has been tarnished or even fatally compromised by the encroachment of media, particularly commercial media and communications (Schiller 1989), while there are others for whom the media have become the main—if not the only—vehicle for whatever can be held to exist of the public sphere in such societies. Such 'media-centric' postmodern theorists within these fields can hold that the media envelop the public sphere:

> The 'mediasphere' is the whole universe of media . . . in all languages in all countries. It therefore completely encloses and contains as a differentiated part of itself the (Habermasian) public sphere (or the many public spheres), and it is itself contained by the much larger semiosphere . . . which is the whole universe of sense-making by whatever means, including speech . . . it is clear that television is a crucial site of the mediasphere and a crucial mediator between general cultural sense-making systems (the semiosphere) and specialist components of social sense-making like the public sphere. Hence the public sphere can be rethought not as a category binarily contrasted with its implied opposite, the private sphere, but as a 'Russian doll' enclosed within a larger mediasphere, itself enclosed within the semiosphere. And within 'the' public sphere, there may equally be found, Russian-doll style, further counter-cultural, oppositional or minoritarian public spheres. (Hartley 1999: 217–18)

The media, in this account, don't influence separable parts of the social world in ways that can be isolated and researched, but rather are the main frame within which the social world is known and experienced. The proponents of such postmodern positions will often eschew the media having a direct influence in the way assumed by social scientists like Gerbner, Putnam or Nye. However, it is hard to both embrace the essential 'mediatisation' of the social world and downplay its specific effects.

In this scenario, most of us share a common culture of sophisticated media literacy. Traditional concepts of influence came from a time when 'old media were new' and people were trying to get a grasp on what they might mean for society. Now there is widespread media literacy and the time-worn anecdotes—about the only people who can tune a TV or VCR, time shift a program, or get on line or make a DIY Webpage being kids—should be extended to acknowledge that media content is simply part and parcel of the landscape and that it matters less for what it can do *to* people than for what people can do *with* it (get jobs, find self-expression and community and cultural expression, communicate globally and more equally, etc.). This view radically flattens the topography of the haves and have-nots and renders issues of ownership and control of marginal significance.

This needn't, however, lead to a monolithic and probably celebratory media-centrism that dissolves all manner of inequities, injustices and power plays into a totalising 'mediascape'. McKenzie Wark, arguably the most public postmodernist theorist of the media in Australia, regularly recouples political economy to postmodernism with his insistence that postbroadcast media comprise a highly differentiated sphere, the key feature of which is the absence of centralising control and mainstreaming vectors, that break through the controlled information flows of broadcast media (Wark 1999: 331).

Whether this is the more productive way to think about the relations between broadcast and postbroadcast media, and between media and the social and public world, will need to wait the judgment of our future history.

The sectors

Three Jock Given

Commercial networks:
Still the ones?

In mid-1999, newspaper headlines screamed one of their periodic crises for Australia's commercial television networks: 'Advertisers switch off TV networks', 'The knives are out', 'Packer axes "up to 200 jobs"', 'Julian Mounter's tough test', 'Strangled by cable'. It was enough to make you listen to the radio.

Analysts warned that the Nine Network's audiences were too old, Ten had run out of decent programs and Seven was spending too much money to earn not enough profits. Pay TV was stealing viewers from all of them, especially young people, the audiences of the future. The Internet was changing the nature of the media business before their eyes. The buoyant economy would turn down at some point, taking advertising expenditure—the main source of revenue for commercial TV—with it. The big man of Australian television, Kerry Packer, was not getting any younger.

The last time something like this happened was in the second half of the 1980s, after the federal government announced changes to the country's media ownership laws. Most metropolitan television stations changed hands twice within four years, the industry made its first losses since its first years in the mid-1950s and one analyst judged that the true value of commercial television licences was zero (Cox 1989: 5.31).

But that time, it had been suicide. Of the people who bought into commercial TV in the late 1980s, the Lowys (at Ten) decided it had all been a terrible mistake and returned to concentrate on their Westfield shopping centres, Alan Bond (at Nine) went to gaol and Christopher Skase (owner of the Seven Network) headed for an island in the Mediterranean where his efforts to stay out of the Australian courts became a staple of television news bulletins and an enduring reminder of the small screen and the 1980s.

Now, a decade on, with more experienced players back in charge of the networks, things were supposed to be under control. If there were crises, they must be a product of events beyond the control of commercial television itself. This time, it might be serious.

THE BUSINESS

Commercial television is an unusual business because of the indirect relationship between the people consuming the product and those paying the bills. The audiences for Australia's commercial TV stations do not pay the broadcasters for the programs they watch. Rather, advertisers pay the broadcasters for the right to insert advertisements for their goods and services between those pro- grams: 'programs are scheduled interruptions of marketing bulletins', writes entertainment industry analyst Harold Vogel (1998). Audiences who tune in primarily to watch the programs see the advertisements as well and change their spending behaviour as a result. The business of commercial television is the sale of advertising time, but what is really being sold is 'access to the thoughts and emotions of people in the audiences' (Vogel 1998: 155).

There are other ways of financing the television services. The government provides funding to the ABC and the SBS (see Chapter 4) which, together with the advertiser-supported commercial broadcasters and a community channel in some major centres, makes up the 'free-to-air' television sector. A direct relation- ship between consumers and service providers exists with pay or subscription TV services (see Chapter 5). Broadcasters of all kinds sell programs to other broadcasters in Australia or overseas. In Australia, this occurs through network affiliations and through the sale of individual programs for second and sub- sequent runs to pay TV and sometimes other free-to-air broadcasters. Broadcasters sometimes sell their whole channel for simultaneous retransmission on cable or satellite services—in Australia, the federal government has made an in-principle decision to amend relevant legislation to achieve this result (DoCITA 1999).

Technology

Television broadcasters in Australia and around the world use frequencies in the Very High Frequency (VHF) and Ultra High Frequency (UHF) bands of the radiofrequency spectrum to deliver services to their audiences. They do this by encoding information into the electromagnetic signals sent from terrestrial (land-based) transmitters in the frequency ranges their licences entitle them to use. This information is received through aerials mounted on people's homes or TV sets and decoded inside their TV sets to produce the images and associated sounds we call 'television'.

Most television services in Australia were delivered this way until the mid-1990s. Some people received services through small 'self-help' cable retransmission facilities installed because the local geography prevented an adequate VHF or UHF signal being received. From 1980, services were transmitted by satellite to audiences in remote areas beyond the reach of terrestrial transmissions. In 1995, pay TV services were introduced which use cable, satellite and terrestrial microwave transmission facilities. The cable services also carry the free-to-air 'broadcast' commercial and national channels.

From 2001 in metropolitan areas and 2004 in regional areas, the commercial and national broadcasters will introduce 'digital' broadcasting. This will involve a different way of encoding the signals sent from terrestrial transmitters in the same VHF and UHF frequency bands currently used for 'analogue' television broadcasting. The free-to-air broadcasters are being given access to a new frequency, generally adjacent to the one they currently use (so Channel 9 in metropolitan areas is expected to get Channel 8 and Channel 7 to get Channel 6), to simulcast their services in digital and analogue formats for several years. Audiences will require a new digital television set or a digital decoder to receive the digital transmissions. At some stage in the future, once most people are able to receive the digital transmissions, it is intended that analogue transmission will be shut down and the frequencies used for it returned to the government for reallocation.

Television broadcasters use other technologies to receive programs from suppliers and to distribute programs to network affiliates. They receive programs such as news and live sport from overseas, generally by satellite, and distribute programs to their affiliates by cable, satellite and microwave bearers.

Audiences

Since audiences are the product television advertisers buy, a great deal of expense and effort goes into measuring them. The free-to-air networks and pay operators use a research company to collect and analyse information about who is watching television programs. This information is collected from 'people-meters' installed in a number of television homes in each market (2500 in metropolitan centres, increasing to 3000 in the year 2000). These meters, which replaced individual viewing diaries in 1991, allow each member of the household and visitors to indicate their viewing patterns by pressing a button on the meter whenever they start and stop viewing. The people-meter registers the channel (or VCR) they are watching. This information is transmitted by telephone line each night to the research company which analyses it and sends a daily report to its subscribers. Television executives receive the ratings report on their desk-tops each morning at 9.00 a.m. More complex and longer-term analysis of trends is also undertaken by the research company and analysts in the television, advertising and finance industries. AGB Australia, a subsidiary of the Swiss-based AGB Group, took over from AC Nielsen as the research company handling free-to-air TV ratings from 1 January 2001.

Advertisers and networks are interested in a number of measures of audiences. Increasingly, they are emphasising numbers of viewers for particular programs, especially the numbers of viewers in particular demographics (e.g. women aged 18–39, children 5–12, men 18+), rather than ratings (the percentage of TV homes tuned to a program) or share (the percentage of homes using TV at the time, or HUTS, which are tuned to a program). Ratings and share are still important as measures of success across different networks—winning the timeslot, the night, the survey period and the year remain critical to competition in the industry. For example, Publishing and Broadcasting Ltd's media release announcing its financial results for the year to 30 June 1999 boasted that the Nine Network, in which it is the major shareholder, 'won 40 and 39 weeks respectively of the 40 ratings weeks [in the Sydney and Melbourne markets]' (PBL 1999: 1). But advertisers, armed with the mountains of data facilitated by people-meters, have become more sophisticated in their analysis of their audiences. They are more interested in reaching particular viewers whose thoughts and emotions predispose them to buying the products the advertisers sell than simply in reaching large numbers of TV homes.

Television viewing levels, and hence the revenue-earning potential of television stations, vary widely over the day, week and year. The largest audiences each day are between 6.00 p.m. and 10.30 p.m.: prime time. Around 75 per cent of a station's income is earned during this 20 per cent of the day's schedule (Peters and Leigh 1993: 27). Over 60 per cent of Australian homes had at least one TV set turned on between 7.00 p.m. and 9.00 p.m. on an average night during 1997, with Sunday and Monday nights the biggest viewing nights. Although the concept of evening prime time is shared across major television markets, the particular hours of prime-time vary in different countries. In the United States, for example, prime time is generally regarded as between 8.00 and 11.00 p.m. Through the year, Australian viewing levels are higher in winter than summer, with a significant trough during the December–January holiday period. Christmas Day is always the lowest viewing day of the year, which contrasts sharply with the United Kingdom, where it is always the highest. Australians spend around three hours each day watching television (ABS 1998). Much of this activity occurs while people are also undertaking other activities.

The importance of viewing levels at particular times marks a significant distinction between the economics of free-to-air and pay TV. Advertiser-supported television earns its money ad-break by ad-break, hour by hour, and needs viewers tuned in as often as possible. Pay TV, by contrast, earns its money when people pay their monthly subscriptions. In theory, it doesn't need viewers tuned in at all, as long as they believe there is going to be something on during the next month which is worth the fee.

Advertising

Advertisers buy time from broadcasters directly or, more commonly, through advertising agencies and media buyers. Agencies may be involved in overall sales strategy and the planning and implementation of particular campaigns, including the production of advertisements and the buying of media time or space. The role of advertising agencies varies considerably for different advertisers. Some companies appoint an agency exclusively to handle all their advertising, or all their advertising in a particular medium, for a period of time. Others request tenders for an agency to handle a particular campaign. Media buyers provide a further tier of specialisation in the industry. They deal between advertising agencies and broadcasters, aggregating the business of advertisers and their agencies to improve their bargaining position and secure better deals with the networks (see BTCE 1995: Ch 4).

About $2.6 billion was earned from advertisements by commercial television stations in 1997/98 (ABA 1999a). Television advertising represents about a third of the total expenditure on 'main media' advertising in Australia each year. Television's share of main media advertising increased steadily after the commencement of television in 1956. It is currently the second largest category after newspaper advertising, which took around 43 per cent of main media advertising in 1998 (CEASA 1999: 17). Newspaper advertising has declined since the 1960s, but has been fairly stable in recent years. Magazine advertising has increased its share of main media advertising in recent years to over 7 per cent in 1997 (CEASA 1999: 17). This reflects the growing importance of 'niche' advertising, also demonstrated by the huge increase in 'below the line' direct marketing expenditure by companies in recent years. In 1998, a little over $7 billion was spent in Australia on main media advertising but nearly $12 billion was spent on 'below-the-line' direct marketing, including direct mail, telemarketing, Internet, exhibitions and catalogues (Burbury 1999: 41). The ability of media other than advertiser-supported television to effectively target the specialist audiences increasingly sought by advertisers represents a significant long-term challenge to the free-to-air networks.

Because television has been so effective at reaching large audiences, it dominates 'national advertising' in Australia—the campaigns run by major companies selling goods and services throughout Australia. In 1998, television stations took 53 per cent of national advertising expenditure (CEASA 1999: 18). In turn, national advertising is the major source of television advertising revenue. Advertisers spend more money advertising on stations in wealthier parts of Australia. On average, $122 was spent on television advertising for each Australian in 1996/97, but this average incorporates a range from $165 per capita in Sydney to $68 per capita in the smallest country markets (Curtis and Gray 1998: 162).

The top-rating Nine Network has generally earned a larger share of advertising revenue than it has gained of the television audience. In the two calendar years 1997–98, it scored an average of 39.3 per cent of the prime-time commercial TV audience in the five major metropolitan markets but earned around 40.9 per cent of commercial television advertising revenue in 1997/98, according to the ABA. By contrast, Seven scored around 35.0 per cent of the audience but 34.4 per cent of the revenue and Ten scored around 25.7 per cent of the prime-time audience but 24.7 per cent of the advertising revenue. This reflects the 'premium' which generally attaches to advertising with the market leader—what Americans call the 'power ratio' (ABA 1999a).

There are a number of laws which directly affect television advertising. Some of the most important are the *Trade Practices Act*, which outlaws 'misleading and deceptive conduct', and standards and codes of practice made under the *Broadcasting Services Act*, which restrict the amount of broadcast time which can be used for advertising, require most advertisements screened to be Australian- or New Zealand-produced and limit sexual and violent content in programs and advertising, especially when screened at times of the day when children are most likely to be viewing. Other program regulation is described in more detail below under 'Government'.

Programs

Television stations make programs 'in-house' and also buy them, either before or after they are produced. Of the programs bought pre-production, some are individually 'pre-sold' as part of their financing while others are acquired as part of ongoing 'output deals' between television stations and production companies, particularly the major Hollywood studios. Individual program pre-sales are common for drama and documentary programming. Australia's free-to-air broadcasters are understood to have output deals with US companies including Warner Brothers, Hallmark Entertainment, New Regency, Dreamworks, ABC and CBS (Nine); Disney, MGM/United Artists, Polygram, 20th Century Fox, NBC and, after 2001, MCA Universal (Seven); and Columbia Tristar, MCA Universal (until 2001) and WorldVision (Ten). Nine and Seven share Paramount product.

These output deals with most of the largest producers of English-language programming in the world ensure a predictable flow of programs to fill substantial parts of Australia's commercial television schedules, and prevent overheated bidding amongst the Australian networks for individual US shows. However, output deals leave the Australian networks vulnerable to the peaks and troughs of their US partners' performance, over which they have no direct influence—the shows are made solely with the American market in mind, despite their importance for the commercial performance of TV networks in overseas markets.

Heavy reliance on programs from one source can also make an Australian network vulnerable if the program supplier shifts its output to one of its competitors. This occurred in Australia with the switching of 20th Century Fox and MCA Universal output from Ten to Seven, although those switches did not take place immediately and did not require a transfer to the new network of shows, like *Seinfeld*, *The X-Files*, *The Simpsons*, *Beverly Hills 90210* and *Melrose Place*, already screening on Ten. (A further complicating factor is that the network/studio which produces/broadcasts a show in the United States and has an output deal with an Australian network does not always have sole rights to sell the show internationally—this may rest with an independent producer.) The most important new programs screening on Seven under the new arrangements during 1999 were *Ally McBeal* and *The Practice*.

Although most of the top-rating programs on Australian television are Australian, overseas programs—particularly movies, telemovies, drama series and sitcoms—are also very important to commercial TV schedules. In 1999, the Nine Network's success with its Monday night American comedy line-up (including *Friends*, *Jesse*, *Veronica's Closet* and *Suddenly Susan*), Thursday night *ER* and the persistence of 8.30 p.m. movies across all three networks on most Sunday nights are examples.

The mix of 'in-house' and independently-commissioned programming varies across genres and networks. Most news, current affairs and sport programs are still produced in-house, although an increasing amount of sports programming involves joint production with pay TV channel providers Fox Sports and C7, or the transmission of program feeds supplied by or for the pay TV channels. Most drama programs are commissioned from independent producers: recent or current examples include *Water Rats, Murder Call* and *Blue Heelers* from Southern Star, *Good Guys Bad Guys* and *Halifax fp* from Beyond International and *Neighbours* from Grundy Television. The Seven Network produces two of its dramas, the long-running *Home and Away* and *All Saints*, in-house.

Of the $2.3 billion spent by the commercial networks in 1997/98, around $900 million was spent on programs. Of this, around 70 per cent was spent on Australian programs and 30 per cent was spent on foreign programs (after removing the impact of affiliation fees paid to the metropolitan stations by regional licensees). Of the expenditure on Australian programs, 29 per cent went on news and current affairs, 27 per cent on sport, 22 per cent on light entertainment, 14 per cent on drama and 4 per cent on children's programs. Almost all the overseas program expenditure went on drama programs (movies, series, serials and sit-coms) (ABA 1999a).

THE INDUSTRY

Structure and ownership

Australia's commercial television industry comprises three dominant 'networks': Nine, Seven and Ten, whose names refer to the VHF frequencies they use for their main transmitters in the capital cities. These networks consist of a core of commonly owned capital city stations linked by affiliation with groups of commonly owned regional stations.

Table 3.1 Commercial television controllers, February 1999

Stations	Nine	Seven	Ten
Metropolitan stations	Nine Network (Packer) 3 metro, 1 regional	Seven Network (Stokes) 5 metro, 1 regional	Ten Network (TNQ Television, CanWest Global Communications) 5 metro
Regional stations	TWT Holdings (Gordon) 7 regional	Prime (Ramsay) 8 regional	Southern Cross Broadcasting 1 metro, 4 regional Telecasters Australia 5 regional

Source: Communications Update, Annual Media Ownership Update, Communications Law Centre, Melbourne and Sydney, No. 151, February 1999.

This structure means that most people living in Australia can receive three commercial television channels offering very similar program line-ups across the country. The major differences in the programming on different stations in the same network are in the areas of news and sport. The different football codes followed around the country and arrangements with sporting bodies restricting live free-to-air television coverage of some sporting events produce some changes to afternoon and prime-time scheduling in different markets, and regional stations generally program a local early evening news bulletin in addition to the networked national news service, which necessitates some shifting of other early evening programs.

Viewers living in Tasmania, Darwin and outside the major mainland regional centres receive only two commercial services. Those in remote areas receive their services by satellite.

The three-network structure has existed in some form since the early 1960s, when the Ten Network stations were introduced into the Sydney and Melbourne markets, around five years after television commenced in Australia in September 1956 in time for the Melbourne Olympics. Perth did not get its third commercial station until 1988. The main regional centres in the east coast states had only a single commercial TV service until the late 1980s, when adjacent monopoly markets were 'aggregated' to form four larger regional markets covering Queensland, northern New South Wales, southern New South Wales and Victoria. Viewers in remote areas got a 'remote commercial television service' (RCTS) delivered by satellite from the mid-1980s, with a choice of two services coming with the extension of the service areas of North East and Central Zone licensees and the allocation of a second licence for the Western Zone.

Australia's three-network commercial TV industry mirrors the historical structure of the US industry, where the business was pioneered by stations comprising the ABC, CBS and NBC networks. There are now three further networks, Fox, Warner Brothers and UPN, which were started by the major Hollywood studios. They attract between 3 per cent (UPN) and 11 per cent

(Fox) of prime-time viewing (i.e. share), compared with between 13 per cent (ABC) and 15 per cent (CBS and NBC) for the original networks (Broadcasting & Cable, 12 July 1999: 39). Most Australian television viewing has historically been of commercial stations. This contrasts with the position in the United Kingdom, where the early decades of television (which commenced before World War II but was withdrawn during the war) were dominated by the public broadcaster, the BBC. British viewers waited until 1980 to receive their second commercial station, the special-interest Channel 4 in 1982 (the BBC got a second channel in the 1960s), and until 1997 for their third (Channel 5). Multichannel pay TV came to the United Kingdom in the late 1980s in what was, by the standards of other English-speaking countries, a very underdeveloped commercial TV marketplace.

The structure and financial arrangements within commercial TV networks in Australia differ from those in the United States and United Kingdom. In Australia, the regional affiliates pay the capital city stations a fee for the right to their program feed. This fee is calculated as a percentage of regional stations' revenue. The regional stations keep all the revenue earned from advertising on their stations, although a considerable amount of the advertising is sold as national advertising carried across the whole network. The capital city stations acquire from program suppliers the rights to screen their programs in both the capital city and regional markets.

In the United States, the 'networks' own and operate some stations themselves, but the majority of the stations which carry a network's programming are 'affiliates'. Networks pay the affiliates 'compensation' to carry the network's programs, but acquire the right to sell a certain amount of advertising within affiliates' schedules. Because there are more network feeds to choose from, affiliates have the ability to switch networks in a way which is currently commercially impossible in Australia, with three networks and only three stations in most markets. In the United Kingdom, the main commercial free-to-air channel, Channel 3, was originally a loose affiliation of regional commercial television monopolies. Liberalisation of ownership rules has allowed rationalisation of ownership of these regional entities in the 1990s and the development of a more tightly structured, nationally scheduled, US-style 'network'.

The owners

The owners of Australia's major commercial television stations are, by definition, some of the biggest media companies in the country.

Publishing and Broadcasting Limited (PBL, owned by Packer), which controls the Nine Network, is also the country's major magazine publisher. The Packers' broadcasting (Nine Network) and publishing (Australian Consolidated Press) interests were amalgamated into a single listed company, PBL, in 1994. The company more recently acquired a third major 100 per cent-owned business, Melbourne's Crown Casino. It publishes the two largest-circulation magazines in the country—*Women's Weekly* and *Woman's Day*—and seven other magazines in the top twenty by circulation (*AdNews* 1999). PBL also controls 20 per cent of mobile telephone and Internet access company One-Tel (a similar shareholding to News Limited) and 80 per cent of the shares in ecorp, formerly PBL Online. Twenty per cent of ecorp was floated in June 1999. It is involved in the ninemsn consumer Internet services joint venture with Microsoft and a joint venture with the United States-based eBay inc to operate Australian and New Zealand versions of eBay's person-to-person Internet trading site. It also owns the computerised network ticketing business, Ticketek (PBL 1999). Overseas, PBL controls magazines in New Zealand and Southeast Asia and owns a 20 per cent stake in US production company New Regency. The Packer private company, Consolidated Press Holdings, which holds around 40 per cent of PBL's shares, took over Australian-based cinema exhibitor Hoyts Cinemas in mid-1999 and has substantial interests in Australian ski resorts and the FXF Trust, which holds around 15 per cent of the shares in the country's second-largest newspaper publisher, John Fairfax.

The Seven Network was floated in August 1993. Its largest shareholder is Kerry Stokes, who has been chairman of the company since 1995 and was appointed executive chairman when CEO Julian Mounter left in mid-1999. The company bought in 1996 and sold in 1998 a major stake in US studio Metro Goldwyn Mayer. Seven continues to receive programming from MGM. It is involved in a joint venture with the Australian Football League and News Limited to design and manage the official AFL Website and jointly developed a Website with John Fairfax to cover the 1998 federal election. Seven is providing around $100 million to participate in the Docklands consortium in Melbourne. The project involves the construction of a 52 000-seat stadium at the western end of the Melbourne CBD. Seven will also build a new digital broadcast facility on the site (Seven Network 1999).

The largest shareholder in The Ten Group (which owns Network Ten Pty Ltd, which in turn owns directly, or indirectly, the companies which hold the Ten Network licences) is TNQ Television Ltd. However, a complex structure enables most of the 'economic interest' in the network, and hence the profits which flow from it, to be held by the Canadian television broadcaster CanWest Global Communications. CanWest, which acquired its stake in Ten in 1992 after the network had been in receivership, controls television stations in Canada, New Zealand and Ireland. Ten Network Holdings Ltd, the second largest shareholder (direct and indirect) in The Ten Group, was listed in 1998.

The involvement of the major commercial networks in pay TV in the 1990s has been significant. Nine is a major investor in one of the pay TV platforms and Nine and Seven are both investors in pay TV channel suppliers. This level of involvement in the emerging subscription television business from its earliest stages contrasts with the situation in other countries, notably the United States and United Kingdom, where free-to-air networks were prevented from participating in pay TV.

PBL is now a 25 per cent shareholder in the largest pay TV operator, Foxtel, and has an option to acquire from News Limited 50 per cent of Fox Sports, the company which provides two sports channels to Foxtel and regional pay TV operator, AUSTAR. The Seven Network wholly owns the C7 sports channel (which carries Australia's most valuable television sports asset outside the Olympics, the AFL, to Optus Vision and AUSTAR customers). Seven and Nine had previously held stakes in Sports Vision, a company which provided sports programming to Optus Vision. PBL and Seven are one-third joint venture partners in the Australian-packaged news service Sky News, alongside News Corporation's UK pay TV operation, BSkyB. Seven is also a 50/50 shareholder with American cable company US West in the company which produces the Odyssey documentary channel for Optus Vision. Nine and Seven have both sold out of their shareholdings in Australia's second telecommunications carrier, Cable & Wireless Optus. PBL also sold its stake in one of Australia's first subscription television channels, the racing-oriented 'pubs-and-clubs' service, Sky Channel, to the New South Wales TAB.

GOVERNMENT

Commercial television is a highly regulated industry. Companies can only participate in it if they are licensed to do so. Only three services are permitted in an area and only one new licence has been issued in a mainland capital city since the early 1960s. Under the legislation providing for the introduction of digital television by existing networks, no further new commercial TV licences can be granted until at least 2006, although News Limited has established a company, News Broadcasting, whose stated aim is to launch a fourth commercial television network (Blomfield 1999), despite current cross-media and foreign ownership rules which would prevent this, even if the three-to-a-market limit was lifted.

The commercial television licences granted by the Australian Broadcasting Authority authorise services with three dimensions:

- programs of wide appeal: programs must be 'intended to appeal to the general public' and be capable of reception by 'commonly available equipment';
- free-to-air: services are usually funded by advertising; and
- profit-making licensee companies. (*Broadcasting Services Act* 1992, section 14)

The breadth of appeal of commercial television broadcast services contrasts with the limited or specialised audiences of 'narrowcast' services. Their free provision contrasts with the payments made by audiences for 'subscription' services. The profit-making nature of commercial television enterprises contrasts with non-profit 'community' broadcasting licensees (see *Broadcasting Services Act* 1992, Part 2).

Ownership and control rules

In addition to laws limiting the number of commercial television licences allocated to serve an area, there are further laws which restrict the ownership and control of companies holding licences. There are three kinds of restrictions in place.

The first is limits on ownership and control of services in a local area, the most specific of which are contained in the *Broadcasting Services Act*. These include a one-to-a-market limit for commercial television services (see Division 2 of Part V) and cross-media rules which prevent the same person controlling a commercial television licence and a commercial radio licence or a major daily newspaper in the same area (see Division 5 of Part V). These cross-media rules were introduced in 1987, as part of a liberalisation of the number of television and radio stations which could be controlled by one person. The intention was to allow common ownership of more television and radio stations, while ensuring that these bigger television networks were run by different people from those who ran radio networks and major newspapers. At present, they prevent Rupert Murdoch's News Limited, with its substantial newspaper interests, from having a major stake in a television network, and the Packers' PBL, with its television stations in Sydney and Melbourne, from acquiring a controlling interest in John Fairfax, which publishes *The Age* and *The Sydney Morning Herald*. They have not, however, prevented a former senior PBL executive from taking up the position of chairman of the board of John Fairfax, because the ABA found that the chairman is not necessarily in a position to exercise control of the company (see ABA 1999(b)).

General competition law, contained in the Commonwealth *Trade Practices Act* 1974, may also limit ownership of media in an area. The law prohibits mergers and acquisitions which would result in a 'substantial lessening of competition in a market' (section 50). Assessment of whether this test has been breached requires different markets to be defined. A recent example involved the Australian Competition and Consumer Commission, which administers the legislation, examining whether free-to-air television and pay television comprised a single market or two distinct markets (ACCC 1997). The more broadly a market is defined, the less likely it is that a particular transaction will result in a substantial lessening of competition in it. General competition law might become more important for the ownership of commercial television services if proposals to remove the cross-media rules—such as those of the Productivity Commission in its 1999–2000 inquiry—are adopted.

The second kind of ownership limit is on foreign ownership and control (see Division 4 of Part 5, *Broadcasting Services Act* 1992). The Act prohibits a foreign person holding more than 15 per cent, and foreign persons holding more than 20 per cent in total, of the shares in a company controlling a commercial television licence. It also prohibits foreign control of a commercial television licence. This is the law which CanWest Global Communications has had to negotiate to retain its substantial economic interest in the Ten Network. In 1997, the ABA ruled that the network was foreign controlled, which resulted in a restructuring of interests in the companies controlling the Ten Network licences (ABA 1997).

The general law on foreign acquisitions and takeovers (Commonwealth *Foreign Acquisitions and Takeovers Act* 1975) may also be relevant to the ownership of television stations. It requires notification of proposals for significant foreign investment in Australian companies, and gives the Treasurer the power to reject those he believes are contrary to the national interest. This may occur even though the specific laws in the *Broadcasting Services Act* have not been breached.

The third kind of restriction is on the total population reach of commonly owned television stations (see Division 2 of Part 5, *Broadcasting Services Act* 1992). The limit is currently set at 75 per cent of the Australian population. The Seven Network, with five metropolitan stations and one regional station owned by the same company in February 1999, currently reaches 72 per cent of the national population *(Communications Update*, February 1999).

Program regulation

A number of aspects of commercial television programming are regulated under the *Broadcasting Services Act*.

The Act prohibits tobacco advertising and restricts the advertising of medicines. It also prohibits the broadcast of X- and R-rated programs (they may be cut to bring them within lower classification categories) and the acquisition by pay TV broadcasters of exclusive rights to live broadcasts of major sporting events included on a list of events determined by the minister. This long list has provided significant protection for commercial broadcasters, by comparison with the more liberal arrangements in other countries like New Zealand, which have resulted in the 'siphoning' of major sporting events away from free-to-air television. The Act also requires the identification of certain political broadcasts and the maintenance of records of certain broadcasts, and prevents the broadcast of election advertisements within three days of elections.

Program standards specify minimum levels of Australian programs, adult drama, children's programs, documentaries and advertisements which must be screened by each commercial television licensee. Breaches of these standards can result in fines or, in extreme cases, revocation of licences. Codes of practice developed by the commercial television industry cover a number of subjects, including the content of news and current affairs programs, the classification and censorship of sexual and violent content and the amount of 'non-program matter' (a very narrow definition of 'advertising') which can be broadcast. Breaches of these codes do not attract significant sanctions in the first instance, but continuing or flagrant breaches may result in similar regulatory responses to breaches of program standards.

In addition to the requirements in the *Broadcasting Services Act*, general laws may affect the content transmitted by television broadcasters. These include the

Table 3.2 Brisbane commercial TV stations: Program categories: 5.00 p.m. to midnight, 1998 (per cent of total hours broadcast)

	Aust.	Foreign	Aust.	Foreign	Aust.	Foreign
Program	BTQ 7		QTQ 9		TVQ 10	
Documentary	1.4	2.9	1.7	1.7	1.0	0.4
Drama	9.9	37.0	6.2	28.8	9.2	22.9
Infotainment	3.5	0.2	6.7	0.2	3.0	0.2
Light entertainment	11.2	2.4	15.0	1.0	6.5	23.3
News/current affairs	20.0	0.1	24.4	0.1	20.2	0.0
Sports events	8.6	0.1	9.8	0.7	0.2	0.1
Sports other	2.4	0.0	2.1	0.0	7.1	0.2
Other	0.1	0.0	1.3	0.1	0.8	4.5
Subtotal	**57.1**	**42.7**	**67.2**	**32.6**	**48.1**	**51.6**
ACTPF* programs	0.2		0.2		0.3	
Total	**100.0**		**100.0**		**100.0**	

Source: Australian Broadcasting Authority 1999 *Trends & Issues* No 6, ABA, Sydney, August.
* Australian Commercial Television Production Fund, a $20 million-a-year program funded by the federal government, which operated from 1995/96 to 1997/98.

prohibition on misleading and deceptive conduct contained in the *Trade Practices Act*, which applies to broadcasters' advertising (see 'Advertising', above).

STILL THE ONE

The market leader in Australian commercial television since the mid-1980s has been the Nine Network. It has built that leadership primarily on its performance in local news, current affairs and sport, but has developed strengths in info-tainment and local drama in the second half of the 1990s.

In 1998, Nine was the most Australian of the Australian commercial net-works, screening 64–67 per cent Australian programs across the schedules of its Sydney, Melbourne and Brisbane stations. By contrast, Seven ranged from 56 per cent Australian programs in Sydney to 62 per cent in Adelaide, and the more tightly networked Ten stations were all almost identical on 56 per cent (ABA 1999(c)). Nine's model for the television business is a high-cost/high-revenue model, where Ten matches lower costs to lower revenues. Both networks have been highly profitable during the 1990s. Seven's share-price pressures at the end of the 1990s came from a perception that it had not drawn the kind of revenue growth which would justify its level of program expenditure, especially on the Olympics and overseas output deals.

The prime-time schedules of the networks differ significantly, as shown in Table 3.2. Nearly half the Ten Network's schedule (46 per cent) is foreign drama and light entertainment. These categories make up less than 40 per cent of Seven's schedule and less than 30 per cent of Nine's schedule. When Australian shows are added, 62 per cent of Ten's schedule is drama and light entertainment. By contrast, 24 per cent of Nine's schedule is local news and current affairs, a category which occupies 20 per cent of the Seven and Ten schedules. Thirteen per cent of Nine's schedule and 11 per cent of Seven's are filled by sport. Ten screens almost no sport, having decided to avoid expensive bidding wars for major domestic sports rights. Nine screens less Australian drama than its two rivals but much more light entertainment, with shows like the recently-axed *Hey Hey It's Saturday* and the various *Footy Shows*. Nine also screens around twice as much local infotainment as its rivals, occupying around 7 per cent of its prime-time schedule.

There have been a number of significant strategic program shifts in recent years. Perhaps the most dramatic has been the decline of movies on commercial television. It was predicted that this would be an impact of pay TV, with its commercial-free movie runs and greater choice of titles and scheduling. As the last window in the exploitation chain, after cinema, airlines, home video rental and sell-through and pay TV (the pay TV window was created by the US studios withholding new movies from Australian free-to-air television for about a year from 1995), Nine CEO and Managing Director David Leckie says movies 'have almost disappeared as a genre on Australian television. Outside the Sunday night movie none of them rate, doesn't matter how good they are.' (Woodley 1999: 4) This has driven a desire to get exclusive Australian first-run access to made-for-TV movies from companies like Hallmark.

The major new program genre developed over this period has been infotainment. Nine had early success with *Burke's Backyard*, and has subsequently developed shows like *Getaway*, *Our House*, *Money* and *Good Medicine*. Seven has shows like *Better Homes and Gardens* (linked to the magazine of the same name) and *The Great Outdoors*. These information/entertainment programs are well suited to the converging television/Internet environment, with the opportunities they provide for deeper engagement with online information, dialogue, sales and cross-promotion with linked publications (see Chapter 12 for more on Nine's Website strategies).

Tony Branigan, from the Federation of Australian Commercial Television Stations (FACTS), stresses that 'infotainment' in Australia is not a single 'it'—there are reality shows, documentaries, docu-dramas, *Australia's Funniest Home Videos* and others in what is only a 'loosely-connected range of genres'. '*Changing Rooms*, for example, is part-documentary, part-game show, part-drama,' he says. He notes the difference compared with the United States, where the focus has been on '*Most Amazing . . .*' reality shows:

> In Australia, the programs are more home-based and there's a wider range than in the US or the UK . . . They can be made cheaply, through sponsorships, and can carry a distinctive badge for the network . . . And the links to web-sites are working. On-air promotion is proving to be the most powerful driver of Internet usage. (Branigan 1999)

Through the 1990s, news and current affairs programming has increased, with the introduction of late-night news programs on all networks, although audiences for the early evening news bulletins, which have been important anchors for the network's schedules, have declined.

Nine has finally had success with local drama, particularly *Water Rats* ('strong in the right demographic,' says the network's Director of Drama, Kris Noble), *Stingers*, *Good Guys Bad Guys* and *Halifax fp*. These successes followed a string of failures through the 1980s and early 1990s. The long-running rural medical show *A Country Practice* has effectively been replaced in Seven's schedule by the rural cop show *Blue Heelers*. Seven continues to screen the most Australian drama of the three networks, although the margin is less pronounced than a decade ago. Nine still concentrates on the higher production values drama formats (one-hour series and one-offs), leaving soaps and series shot on video to Ten and Seven. Noble says he'd like to try daytime soap, if the networks could convince the Australian Broadcasting Authority to let it qualify for Australian drama points under the Australian Content Standard (adult drama only scores towards the drama quota if it is shown in prime time).

Nine has cut a number of program stalwarts—notably *The Midday Show* and its weekend afternoon sports shows. Pay TV is cited as a strong influence on the audiences for these shows, with live sport on pay TV providing tough competition for sports magazine shows and pay TV drawing strong daytime audiences. The anti-siphoning rules are critical to commercial television's continuing central place in live coverage of major sport. Branigan says this is 'incredibly politically important—viewers blame the government, more than the networks, if they can't get their sport' but PBL's involvement in Foxtel and likely involvement in Fox Sports may see some new emphases in the sporting rights strategies of Australia's commercial TV heavyweight.

Another critical audience shift has been the success of pay TV with young audiences. Alongside the decline of the once-staple diet of Australian prime-time American movies, this is perhaps the most worrying trend for Australia's commercial networks. It is not just that young people are not watching the programs their parents watch, it's that they're watching television in different ways—less loyal and more prepared to sacrifice it to the many more options available for their time.

The economic model of free-to-air television depends on large numbers of people tuning in over and over again to a regular schedule. It is a television that gets inside audience's lives, and makes itself indispensable to them. It gets them to stay in at night. Says Kris Noble: 'We've got to work out who are the people who will make you smile, who will make you want to come back each week.'

The Nine Network is used to winning: 'We like not just to win but to win by a mile,' says Kris Noble. As society and the economy create new pressures on people's time, and pay TV and other new media services provide new ways to fill the spaces in it, the challenge for the market leader is, as always, a circular one—to draw enough viewers to justify advertising rates which enable broadcasters to make and buy programs compelling enough to keep the audiences tuned in.

Thanks to Therese Iverach and Michelle Lam at the Communications Law Centre and Rosemary Curtis and Annette Carruthers at the Australian Film Commission for assistance with data and research.

Public service TV: An endangered species?

A key assumption behind public service broadcasting, only rarely made explicit, is that broadcasting entails important moral and intellectual questions and ambitions which are separate from any technological or financial considerations. Take away those questions and ambitions and one prepares the ground for that famous 'vast wasteland'. (Tracey 1997: 16)

In the last ten years, the institutions of public service broadcasting (PSB) around the world have undergone quite profound transformations to the point where their very essence or existence seems to be in danger. In countries like Germany, France, Australia, Canada and New Zealand, PSB has been in apparent decline, suffering from shrinking audiences and a rapidly diminishing revenue base. Even in the United Kingdom, where the traditional dominance of the BBC appears to have assured it a successful passage through the present period of broadcasting history, the BBC has had to undergo a quite large reconceptualisation of its mission and to reorient itself in a number of ways. This has caused great internal upheaval, and in the minds of some commentators has undermined its traditional public service mission (Barnett and Curry 1994).

The beginning of this phase of PSB's decline began in the late 1980s and was caused by the twin forces of technological change, providing for a vast multiplication of TV channels, and the wave of deregulation which swept the Western world. Since then, the debate about the future of public service broadcasting has intensified with those who wish to defend its existence apparently more and more on the defensive.

THE PSB 'IDEA'

The idea of PSB had its origins in the 1920s in the BBC, whose founding Director-General, John Reith, shaped its philosophy in terms like the following:

> It should be the endeavour of the Broadcasting Authority to bring to the greatest number of people as much as possible of contentment, of beauty and of wisdom . . . and this over every range of worthy human endeavour and achievement. Or the responsibility may be defined as we have often defined it, in terms of the mental and moral state of the community. No authority, charged with such a task, should be timid of giving idealism a place, and a high place in its policy. The long view may not be coincident with the popular view, but principle will be vindicated in the end. (Bolton 1967: 97)

This 'Reithian' philosophy has been outmoded, deconstructed and reconstructed over the years since 1924, and yet the institutions that are dubbed 'public service broadcasters' now are continuous with those that were founded on the model of the BBC between the 1920s and 1940s (see Tracey 1997). What, then, links the idea of PSB then and now?

In the early 1980s, the Broadcasting Review Unit in London articulated a series of 'principles' of public service broadcasting which have been influential— for example, they were picked up in an Australian government review of the ABC and the Special Broadcasting Service (SBS) in 1988 (DOTAC 1988). They are:

1 universality of availability;
2 universality of appeal;
3 provision for minorities;
4 a commitment to the education of the public;
5 distance from vested interests;
6 that broadcasting be structured to encourage competition in programming standards, not for audiences;
7 freedom for the program maker; and
8 fostering of a public sphere.

Although these are clothed in language of the current period, they are principles that also informed John Reith's conception of PSB. Let's examine each in turn (see also Tracey 1997, 1992).

Universality of availability

This principle means that PSB ought to be available to all members of a society— to all 'citizens'. No one should be excluded from the broadcasting 'family' because of geographic or socio-economic circumstances. This is a particular challenge in a country as vast and sparsely populated as Australia, but the ABC succeeded in reaching all but a handful of remote dwellers with its terrestrial service until the 1980s when they also were brought into the fold through the use of satellite. The service should also be free (except for the cost of the receiving equipment). Traditionally the ABC has been funded first by licence fees, then later by direct government appropriation, but again it has also been the case that commercial broadcasting is free to the consumer, funded as it is by advertising.

Universality of appeal

This means that PSB should not confine itself to only a few genres or categories of programs; it should embrace as wide a spectrum of the possibilities as the commercial sector. John Reith justified this by suggesting that, in order to bring the audience in for the more 'serious' types of programs (talks, news, concerts and plays), the broadcaster should also program more 'popular' forms like popular music, variety, quiz shows, sport, etc. In latter years in Australia, this principle has been articulated in terms of 'comprehensive' versus 'complementary', with the commercial sector happy enough to see the ABC as a complementary service, confined to the more 'serious' end of the programming spectrum, and thus as no competition.

Provision for minorities

If the second principle deals with the public broadcaster's obligation to offer programming that appeals to a wide section of the society, this one envisages that at the same time it will provide for minority audiences in a way that commercial broadcasters—those obliged by commercial imperatives to maximise audiences in every possible timeslot—cannot. The traditional minority audiences were the regions, women and children, so both Reith's BBC and Australia's ABC had special programs aimed specifically at these sectors. In Australia the 'regions' meant not only rural audiences as opposed to the city, but also regional cities as opposed to the dominant centres of Sydney and Melbourne. In more recent years, the notion of minority has shifted in alignment with shifts to 'identity politics' to embrace differences defined along lines also of race and ethnicity, sexuality and youth (as opposed just to 'children') (Hawkins 1997). As outlined below, it was in response to the ABC's perceived failures in these areas—particularly, of course, race and ethnicity—that the SBS was founded in 1978.

A commitment to the education of the public

This was a particularly important tenet of the Reithian vision for PSB as seen in the above quotation. It has remained a central plank in PSB philosophy, albeit clothed in less authoritarian and improving language. In the early days, it was manifested both in the emphasis the PSB placed upon explicitly educational programming—for example, broadcasts to schools—but it was seen too in early practices like the broadcast of lectures, talks and panel discussions on the 'serious' issues of the day. It is also seen in the emphasis given to high-quality news and current affairs programs, and to the education and cultivation of taste that is the purpose of the broadcast of various high cultural forms like drama, concerts, opera and ballet.

Distance from vested interests

Historically, public service broadcasters around the world were founded on the principle of a separation between them and the government on the one hand, and commercial interests on the other. The first is guaranteed by the legislative requirement that, while the PSB reports to parliament (and is accountable to the citizenry through parliament), it is independent of the government of the day and cannot be directed by the government or its ministers except in very particular circumstances (such as matters of national security). Independence from commercial pressures is made possible by the fact that its funding is derived either from the licence fee (as in Britain all through the BBC's history and in Australia up to 1974) or from direct parliamentary appropriation.

That broadcasting be structured to encourage competition in programming standards, not for audiences

Unlike the commercial sector, which is funded by advertising, or the pay sector, which is funded by viewers' subscriptions, PSBs are funded through licence fee or government appropriation. This means that there is no direct relationship between the size of the audience and the capacity of the broadcaster to earn revenue, which means in turn that the PSB broadcaster does not have to appeal directly to people's immediate tastes and desires. It can program not what people want, but what they need. In recent times, this principle of PSB has been couched in terms of quality. The PSB will be comprehensive—that is, it will cover as wide a range of programming as the commercial broadcasters but it will do so at a higher level of 'quality'; in the old PSB aphorism, it will make the popular good and the good popular (quoted in Birt 1998 and Tracey 1997).

   The debate about quality is an extremely vexed one because of the apparently subjective nature of the judgment (Mulgan 1990). Many commentators have argued that the term 'quality' is code for the privileging of certain genres of program over others (drama good, game show bad for example), and conceals a system of value which has a class nature and a particular history (see Hawkins 1997). In Australia, the term 'quality' can to some extent be used to establish another dualism by ABC supporters—British good, American bad—since the characteristic that most obviously demarcates the ABC from the commercial television sector is the British origin of its imports, compared with American programming on the commercials.

Freedom for the program maker

If the PSB is independent of the pressure both of immediate audience desires and government pressure to deliver particular messages, where does control in the broadcasting enterprise lie? John Reith's answer was that it lay in the program maker or broadcaster whose ethical and aesthetic ideals should represent the highest values of the society. The professional ideology of the PSB program maker and broadcaster is consequently a very powerful one and had led to a long history of intense contestation between them and their managers. This has intensified in recent years as funding for PSBs gets squeezed and the freedom of the program makers is curtailed.

This principle also serves as the basis for the notion that it is a duty of the PSB to develop and foster expert knowledge. The PSB organisation has traditionally been founded on the notion of specialist departments—science, natural history, religion, arts and so on—staffed by broadcasters who combined an in-depth knowledge of the field in question with wide experience of how to communicate it to audiences. Such units are, of course, expensive to maintain because the work done to maintain the expertise takes time to develop and does not translate immediately into high ratings and high revenue streams. Such specialist units are under pressure as the comparative funding to PSBs falls and specialist or theme channels on subscription television grow in popularity and expertise.

Fostering a public sphere

One could really say here 'fostering a national public sphere'. This is really the cardinal principle from which all others flow. Richard Hoggart's classic formulation is that the PSB allows 'the nation to speak to itself' (quoted in Tracey 1997: 29). Broadcasting as a modernist institution was established in all its manifestations as an enterprise of national governments, although in many cases the actual broadcasting stations had only local reach and addressed local audiences (based on cities, towns and regions). However, the PSB had the obligation to address the nation as a nation, and to have the capability to reach the whole nation simultaneously, something hardly possible before the advent of broadcasting technology.

So PSBs have played a role in the formation of nations in the sense of being able to reach populations across the whole territory and foster the sense of being one collective, one polity. This is also tied in with the mission of citizen formation, with the educative role the PSB would play in training citizens to be informed about matters of national political importance and to play their part in the political process as informed voters and interest groups (Burns 1997: 58).

In the context of globalisation where, arguably, various forms of cross-border communities have as much legitimacy or relevance as the national one, the role of the PSB as fostering a national public sphere needs to be rethought. In Australia, the idea of a national role for the PSB has the extra dimension of helping to ensure Australian (as opposed to imported) content in the television mix. Such a role is less urgent in a rich, populous and central broadcasting culture like Britain where British content has traditionally been as high as 90 per cent. The provision of national (Australian) content is currently also a regulatory obligation on the commercial sector, but the legitimacy and effectiveness of the basis for this regulatory imposition are being whittled away by competition and free trade philosophies which are now on the ascendancy.

SBS AND THE IDEA OF PUBLIC SERVICE BROADCASTING

What has been said so far applies more to the ABC than to the SBS. The latter does not conform to all of these principles so the question arises as to what extent it is a PSB. Its status is in some ways rather like that of Channel 4 in Britain—a channel founded to complement the PSB role of the BBC but not expected to conform in all particulars to the central model. The SBS was founded to fill a gap that the ABC would not or could not fill—namely catering to audiences from non-English speaking backgrounds. Beginning, as we will see, as a radio service in 1978, its original mission was to be a multilingual service, broadcasting in the languages of the various groups which comprise the Australian multicultural community. When television was added in 1980, it was established as 'multicultural' rather than 'multilingual', with a brief to appeal to all Australians and to provide for them a multicultural perspective that was not available on the more solidly Anglo-Celtic services of the ABC. However, it was never envisaged that the SBS would be a comprehensive service; rather, it would provide a menu of alternatives that audiences could dip into at various times of the viewing week. Unlike commercial television, its imperative was not to pull in a loyal audience and then hold them for as long as possible.

Accordingly, of the eight principles outlined above, the most central to the SBS is the appeal to minorities—in the beginning mainly members of the Australian community of NESB, later 'communities of taste' (Hawkins 1996). The SBS has never been universally available. In its early days it was only available to Sydney and Melbourne, cities with high concentrations of migrants. Later its service was extended to some regional cities. Its appeal is to a series of minority taste groups rather than to a mass audience; it has not had a specifically educational brief, although it might be said that its multicultural mission has a pedagogical aspect to it. It originally had the same kind of independence from both government and commercial interests as the ABC, as it too was funded entirely from government appropriation. Since the early 1990s, its income has been supplemented by advertising revenue which currently accounts for 20 per cent of its budget for television.

The SBS, with only a fraction of the ABC's budget, has not had the luxury of specialist departments—and indeed most of its programs (as befits its mission, perhaps) are imported. However, SBS places a high priority on quality news and

current affairs; its *World News* program, which has been broadcast for a number
of years in different guises and timeslots, is considered by many television critics
to offer the best and most comprehensive coverage of overseas news, and its
current affairs and discussion programs like *Dateline* and *Insight* are generally well
researched and penetrating, and tend to offer a range of views and perspectives
not available elsewhere on television. Since the mid-1990s, the SBS has been
rebroadcasting news services from countries like Germany, Russia, Italy, France,
Indonesia, Hong Kong and China between 6.00 a.m. and midday in a slot called
WorldWatch.

So it could be argued that, while the SBS does not have the national public
sphere mission of the ABC, it enhances the public sphere in at least two ways.
The first is that, by providing a different news and current affairs perspective,
it adds to the views that are available in the process of public debate. The second
is that it must be seen as part of a governmental apparatus for the establishment
of a consciously multicultural society in Australia. It addresses Australians as
citizens of a multicultural society and in a muted way exhorts them to tolerance
and understanding of difference.

THE ABC: A BRIEF HISTORY

In spite of the ABC living in what appears to be a state of perpetual crisis—it
has suffered constant funding cuts since the late 1970s (Inglis 1997; Craig
2000)—the community and the government appear to believe that there is a
need to preserve Australia's dual or mixed system of broadcasting. When
television was first introduced, there was a spirited debate about whether such
a powerful medium should be put in the hands of commercial interests, but in
the end consideration of a successful mixed system in radio (and the effective
lobbying of the newspaper interests who wished to be given a 'licence to print
money') led to the mixed system also being applied to television (Curthoys
1986: 129).

The ABC continued to be based on the BBC model. Early program schedules
reveal a mix of typical PSB programming—plays, concerts, news and current
affairs, children's programming, religion (Inglis 1983: 203ff). Once tape was
widely used, there was a high level of imports from the BBC with whom the
ABC had a standing contract (Inglis 1983: 197) (but also later from the ITV
system), mostly in the area of drama. However, from the very earliest days of
ABC television, locally produced drama had an important place (Jacka 1991:
13–17).

In its first twenty-five years the ABC placed high importance on broadcasting
Australian sport, especially cricket and Rugby Union but also tennis and AFL
football (Inglis 1983: 203). The ABC was also the national broadcaster for the
Olympics, beginning of course with the Melbourne Games in 1956 (Inglis

1983: 198). In the mid-1960s, the ABC broadcast more sport than the commercial channels (Inglis 1983: 203). This was to change with the commercial networks' discovery of the pulling power of sport and the increasingly close relationship between sporting bodies and the media, together with the huge investment in sports broadcasting as spectacle that was a feature of the 1980s and has accelerated in the 1990s (Cunningham and Miller 1994: 63–89).

It is probably fair to say that the 'golden age' of public service television, both here and in comparable overseas countries like the United Kingdom and Canada, was the decade that stretched from the mid-1960s to the mid-1970s. These were the years of pioneering and definitive current affairs programs like *Four Corners* and *This Day Tonight* (Inglis 1983: 215ff, 266ff), and of innovative documentaries—or 'features', as they were called—like *Chequerboard* (Inglis 1983: 287). ABC television also introduced to the screen new forms of drama—for example, the television equivalent of the radio soap opera with *Bellbird*, and a new form of gritty television realism with the feminist soap *Certain Women* (Jacka 1991: 17–18).

The ABC met its charter obligations to the child segment of the audience through extensive educational programs including broadcasts to schools (Inglis 1983: 209) and also pioneered programs for younger children like *Playschool* and *Mr Squiggle* (Inglis 1983: 209ff). The rural constituency was catered for by various specialist programs, the most enduring of which was *A Big Country*, which gained a large mainstream audience (Inglis 1983: 290). The regional obligations of the ABC were met by having state-based news and current affairs, a situation which continued until the early 1990s when there was a retreat from state-based current affairs due to funding constraints, a situation bitterly resented by Melbourne and the so-called BAPH states (BAPH stands for Brisbane, Adelaide, Perth, Hobart). ABC Television also broadcast both imported programs and those produced by its specialist departments in the categories of science, religion, arts and natural history.

By the second half of the 1960s, a slow decline—at least in budget terms—began, initiated by the Fraser government. Between 1976 and 1981, government funding to the ABC fell by approximately $50 million from just over $200 million to just over $150 million (DOTAC 1988: Paper 2, 11). This was a result of the combination of general belt tightening following the so-called extravagances of the Whitlam years and the fact that governments of all colours are apparently always eager to hobble the ABC. By the end of the 1970s, the ABC appeared to be an organisation that had lost its way and it was not until the appointment of David Hill as managing director in 1986 that the ABC really began to change direction. By this time, broadcasting had begun its inexorable shift to a multi-channel environment in which, with the multiplication of channels, the ABC's position was to become even less secure. Under Hill there were various attempts to become players in the new broadcasting game—for example, the ill-fated foray into pay television and an equally doomed attempt at an international television service, Australia Television (Cunningham and Jacka

1996: 205–13). Even though, in the long run, these initiatives did not work, they were reasonable strategies for an ABC both strapped for funds and concerned about being left behind in the march towards new delivery technologies (Burns 1997). More dubious was the strategy of producing sponsored programs—for example, *The Home Show*—in association with various companies, where the line between disinterested reportage and advertorial became blurred, leading to a huge furore about implications for the ABC's independence (Senate Select Committee 1995).

During the late 1980s and early 1990s, the ABC exhibited a slightly more commercial turn in its programming style, particularly in the area of television drama where, assisted by the bounty of various production support mechanisms (first 10BA then the Film Finance Corporation) and the possibility of international coproduction, the ABC produced a number of lavish and successful mini-series and series (Jacka 1991; Cunningham and Jacka 1996: 76–80).

The new Coalition government that came to power in March 1996 applied yet more pressure to the ABC, announcing its intention to impose a $55 million funding cut (that is, around 10 per cent) in 1997–98. At the same time, the government announced a new inquiry into the ABC to be chaired by former Optus CEO, Bob Mansfield. This inquiry, which was nowhere as thorough as the Dix Inquiry—obliged as it was to be concluded in six months—attracted a huge amount of interest from ABC viewers and listeners. It received a total of 10 615 written submissions, the vast majority from ordinary citizens. Mansfield reports being overwhelmed by the level of community support for the ABC and his report is a succinct and cogent case for retaining a national public broadcaster in the 1990s. He recommended a revised charter that would give the ABC more precise guidance on its core obligations (Steel 1997); controversially, however, Mansfield accepted that the cut in funding was inevitable, and proposed means by which the ABC could manage it, notably selling off real estate including the Gore Hill television studios in Sydney and outsourcing a higher proportion of program production to the independent sector. This was, unsurprisingly, a suggestion warmly welcomed by that sector, but deplored by others who saw it as the last nail in the coffin for independence (Davis 1997: 85).

The ABC began to implement a number of the Mansfield recommendations, including selling off Gore Hill (not yet finalised in 1999), and increasing levels of outsourcing. However, to date the charter has not been modified. By the late 1990s, the ABC was facing the serious challenges of the arrival of the Internet as a third delivery mode for audiovisual material (alongside radio and television) and of the move to digital television. As I outline in the next section, the ABC has proved to be a leader in Internet service, but the move to digital has created huge issues for it because of lack of sufficient funds to make the transition readily.

The savage cuts in funding that occurred in 1997–98 and the need to find capital investment for new technologies have placed the ABC under almost unbearable strain and this is reflected in its television schedule, where the level of new Australian production has fallen considerably and the incidence of repeat material has soared. Surprisingly, in 1999 it was still retaining the same level of audience as it has had since the mid-1970s, perhaps because it has found a way against the odds of preserving the quality of its news and current affairs. However, it must be admitted that, beside the news, in the late 1990s the highest rating programs on ABC Television were the most conservative forms of British drama like *The Bill, Heartbeat, Hamish Macbeth* and *Ballykissangel.* In August 1999, history was made when for the first time an ABC program—the weekly drama, *SeaChange*—was the most popular program in Australia.

SBS TELEVISION: A BRIEF HISTORY

By the late 1970s, a number of changes had occurred in Australian society that placed the need for a multicultural broadcaster firmly on the government's policy agenda. These included a new sense of Australia as a culturally diverse society, official recognition of the contribution immigrant Australians—especially those from non-English speaking backgrounds (NESB)—had made to the development of Australia, and the growing political influence of 'ethic communities'. This created an environment in which an official multiculturalism, a governmental technology for the 'management of cultural diversity' (Long 1995: 18), developed. The concept of multiculturalism is a complex and contested one (Bottomley 1994; O'Regan 1994).

SBS Television was established in 1980 following the advent of SBS radio, which developed from two ethnic stations set up by the Whitlam government in 1975: 2EA in Sydney and 3EA in Melbourne. Whereas the principal purpose of SBS radio was to be multilingual—thus providing support for new migrants to settle in their new country as well as to maintain links with the homeland and with the homeland cultural heritage—the mission of SBS Television was to be a 'multicultural service'. That meant, in the words of the report of the Ethnic Television Review Panel (ETRP), established in 1979 to make recommendations about SBS Television, that the service should:

- seek to provide a service to complement and supplement the cultural and linguistic perspectives of other broadcasting sectors;
- give particular emphasis to meeting the specific needs of the ethnic communities; and
- be accessible to the community at large. (Patterson 1992: 46)

As Patterson (1992) comments:

the most striking feature of the ETRP policy framework [was] that it advocated a *multicultural* approach to television programming designed to reach the wider Australian community through the use of English language subtitles, as opposed to an *exclusively ethnic* approach, which is 'ethnic radio with pictures' directed to specific linguistic groups. (1992: 46)

The ERTP recommended that 75 per cent of programs be originated overseas and 25 per cent locally produced and that they consist of both entertainment programs (variety, drama, comedy, movies) and information programs (news and current affairs, documentaries, education).

The establishment phase of SBS Television was extremely difficult. For one thing, it was such an innovative concept that normal television protocols were inadequate to deal with it; for another, there were technical difficulties which continued until the late 1980s (Jakubowicz 1987: 27). Lastly, it was the victim both of policy confusion and reversals and also of various forms of tension within and across ethnic groups. The 1980s saw some ferocious battles over what its true mission should be, with critics upbraiding it for lack of attention to employment policies that would present a more culturally diverse face to viewers (Seneviratne 1992: 54) There were also attempts to have the SBS play a more active role in social intervention and to take the lead, for example, in implementing explicit anti-racism strategies but this direction for the SBS was not pursued (Jakubowicz 1987: 25–26).

Inter-ethnic tensions in the SBS were brought to the fore during the late 1980s as old regimes in Europe began to disintegrate and new strident ethnic nationalisms began to emerge. This affected *Vox Populi*, one of SBS's most successful and high-rating programs directed specifically to an ethnic audience. It was a multilingual current affairs program, founded in 1986, which provided a regular forum for ethnic voices (O'Regan 1993: 156). Its founding presenter, Vladimir Lusic, was Croatian. Once the Yugoslav conflict broke out, this became a problem for non-Croation viewers, and he was replaced in 1991 with an Aboriginal presenter, Rhoda Roberts (O'Regan 1993: 164–65). Later, during the tension over Greek and Yugoslav Macedonia, the newsreader Mary Kostakidis was seen to represent too closely Greek interests against those of the republic of Macedonia (O'Regan 1993: 164–65).

On several occasions during the 1980s, the government came close to merging the ABC and the SBS, as had been discussed in a number of government inquiries including Dix. In 1986 the Labor government announced that the merger would go ahead from 1 January 1987, but the howls of protest from the ethnic communities were sufficient to ensure that the necessary legislation did not pass through the Senate (Jakubowicz 1987: 30).

In 1988, as part of a yet another review into national broadcasting, the Department of Transport and Communications recommended that, in the new broadcasting environment that was emerging, it was necessary to strengthen the focus of both the public broadcasters (DOTAC 1988). In June 1989, the government launched an ambitious new multiculturalism strategy—the National Agenda for a Multicultural Australia—which included provision for broadcasting, and the future of the SBS as a separate entity seemed assured (Patterson 1992:

48). In 1991, SBS was for the first time given its own Act of Parliament and was established as a corporation with a new charter. At the same time, the new legislation it permitted SBS to accept sponsorship as a way of supplementing its meagre income from government.

While the charter did not change dramatically, the way it was interpreted by the organisation did. Whereas in its first phase the programming strategy had tended to highlight the 'colourful exoticness' of ethnic communities, now the emphasis became a focus on 'Australian society as a whole, rather than as a collection of diverse ethnic groups examined in isolation from each other' (Patterson 1992: 49).

This change of emphasis reflected the way in which the SBS audience was constituted. It was less the stereotype of the working-class migrant with poor English and more the urban cosmopolitan of varying ethnicities. From 1991 onwards, SBS Television pursued this audience actively (Lawe Davies 1998) with its 'the world is an amazing place' campaign. Chris Lawe Davies shows how the need to pursue an AB demographic (senior managers, professionals) to secure advertisers led to the SBS constructing its advertising around the image of the urban cosmopolitan even though the audience demographics were rather different. Extensive audience research conducted in 1993 showed that the SBS TV audience was more skewed towards overseas born than the trend in the general population and, more significantly, the representation of the AB group (senior managers and professionals) was less than the average in the population (Lawe Davies 1998: 98).

PSB AND THE AUSTRALIAN TELEVISION LANDSCAPE

There are currently five television networks in Australia, with varying degrees of national coverage. The three commercial networks between them command more than 80 per cent of the audience measured in ratings. Audience shares are reasonably stable in Australia, with the Nine and Seven networks having about 30 per cent each (Nine usually slightly more), Ten about 20–23 per cent, the ABC between 13 and 16 per cent and SBS between 2.5 and 3.5 per cent. However, ratings figures are an average of total audience in each quarter hour; they do not measure how much turnover of audience there is. Other kinds of audience research reveals that if reach (the number of viewers who switch to a station at least once in a given period) is measured rather than ratings, both the ABC and the SBS reach a large proportion of the Australian audience.

ABC television has a consistent reach of 70 per cent, which means the proportion of Australians that tune in for more than five minutes in any week. The SBS claims to reach 4.6 million Australians each week—roughly one quarter of the population. But research shows that, at least for the ABC, the demographic is woefully skewed towards the 55-plus age group and to the AB (senior managers and professionals) and C1 (clerks, teachers, salespersons, service industry workers) occupational groups. Gay Hawkins argues that, in spite of the extremely clever and appealing set of ABC promotions that appeared on the ABC from 1996 onwards (diverse members of Australian society draw the ABC logo in smoke on the screen), which show no limit to the cultural diversity of the ABC audience, the schedule itself 'seems less and less able to offer a real diversity of programs' (Hawkins 1997: 17).

Thus opinions about what ABC television contributes to the diversity of the Australian television landscape vary. One view sees it as a stodgy old channel catering for an AB Anglo-Celtic liberal-voting demographic with endless reruns of *Yes Minister* and *Hetty Wainthrop Investigates*. For example, in his Australian column of 26 May 1999, cultural commentator McKenzie Wark, who speaks for the 30-something audience, laid into ABC television's programming strategy in the following terms:

> ABC television seems terminally brain dead. Like those 99 per cent fat free desserts, ABC television is 99 per cent brain-free. The remaining one per cent is often to be found on the religious affairs show, *Compass*. As the reading public has become progressively better educated, ABC TV gets dumber and dumber. Its idea of literature is one of those endless BBC frock-and-carriage soap operas, based on some safe novel or other by someone safely dead. (Wark 1999)

Defenders of the ABC see it as the guardian of diversity, quality, the public sphere and an Australian voice in a television landscape dominated by the imported pap diet on the commercial channels. The truth is more complex than both of these. Let us examine ABC programming strategies since the mid-1980s to see where the ABC sits.

The ABC has always been—and remains so even in these days of serious funding constraints—a space of experimentation and innovation in the television form. It has acted almost as a research and development unit for television as a whole. It has also served as a training ground for television presenters. This is especially true in the field of comedy and satire. Programs which have broken new ground in the last ten years, some of which have migrated to commercial television, include *The Gillies Report*, the *D Generation*, the Andrew Denton programs like *Live and Sweaty*, *Elle McFeast*, *Frontline*, *Roy and HG* and *Race Around the World*.

The ABC is also known for authoritative news and current affairs programs which have the expertise, personnel and resources to explore issues in depth and to present an Australian perspective—for example, *Four Corners*, the *7.30 Report*, *Lateline*, *Mediawatch*, *Foreign Correspondent*. Its strength was illustrated during the Kosovo war when ABC television coverage, including documentaries directed by Chris Masters, provided extensive background to the conflict. Even though, for a viewer with cable, constant coverage was available through CNN and the BBC, these latter sources did not give audiences the perspective which the ABC was able to provide.

ABC Television has provided specialist programming unavailable on commercial television in the areas of science *(Quantum)*, consumer affairs *(The Investigators)*, natural history *(Wildscreen)*, religion *(Compass)* and the arts (including magazine programs like *Express*) and broadcasts of opera, dance, concerts and theatre. It also caters for the rural audience with programs like *Landline* and, in the past, *Countrywide*. Such programming is very unlikely to be found anywhere on commercial television. In the late 1980s and early 1990s, the ABC endeavoured to cater for Indigenous Australians and Australians from other countries with an Aboriginal Program Unit and a Multicultural Program Unit. The former was responsible for a number of programs about Aboriginal issues, while the latter did not make much impact, but due to funding constraints neither unit has survived, leaving this ground almost entirely to SBS.

From the late 1980s to the early 1990s, ABC Television's Australian drama output was respectable and included titles like *GP*, *Police Rescue*, *Brides of Christ*, *Embassy*, *Heartland* and the sitcom *Mother and Son*. Some of this programming was not very different in character from what can be found on commercial television, but some—for example, *Phoenix* and *Janus*—broke new ground for Australian drama. Production fell in the latter half of the 1990s, but there were some notable successes—for example, *Wildside* and *SeaChange*. Documentary is stronger and makes a distinctive contribution, notably the Tuesday and Thursday prime-time slots, *Inside Story* and *The Big Picture* and the successful documentary/interview program *Australian Story*.

In the same way as we posed two different visions of ABC Television above, and then discovered that the real story lay somewhere in between, there are also contradictory views about where the SBS sits in the television landscape. One view sees it as a boutique channel for sophisticated urban cosmopolitans enabling them to consume difference at a safe distance (Hage 1995: 76); another would see is as the voice of multicultural Australia, to be defended at all costs. Again, the truth is probably a mixture of these. The SBS certainly provides a cornucopia of programs from all around the world, with broadcasts in 60 languages. Half the programming on SBS is in languages other than English, all of which is subtitled. SBS programming is paradise for the elite cosmopolite—there are any number of arts documentaries, stylish history and archival documentaries, foreign movies, experimental video *(Eat Carpet)*, cooking shows, travel shows, movie shows, and so on.

There are now many audiences for SBS Television. As Gay Hawkins so aptly puts it: 'SBS has several logics of narrowcasting at work in the one channel' (Hawkins 1996: 47). By contrast, on cable services, the narrowcasting strategy requires one channel per interest group. In 1999 it was possible to discern at least four different audiences for SBS Television (and then within each one there would be subdivisions). There is a urban cosmopolite as described above; there is the soccer fan, presumably of all ethnicities and demographic groups (but woe betide SBS if they lose the rights to soccer to Rupert Murdoch); there is the segmented ethnic audience than tunes into *WorldWatch*, which broadcasts home country news services from 6.00 a.m. to midday every day; and there are the other others—gays (the *OUT Show*), Indigenous Australians *(ICAM)*, the disabled—whom at various points SBS Television has explicitly addressed.

For both the ABC and SBS, the 1990s have already proved challenging as the media environment has changed and television outlets have increased. For both, their original mission and place in the media landscape have changed. In the case of the ABC, the problem is how to remain relevant in a situation in which revenues will inevitable continue to decline; for the SBS, it is how to find a role as a 'secondary public service broadcaster' and 'serial narrowcaster' in a situation which promises to be dominated by narrowcasting. In the next section we examine the dilemmas which face both broadcasters in the digital age.

PSB IN THE DIGITAL AGE

In retrospect, in spite of various perturbations, controversies and struggles, it now appears that the Australian television environment has been extraordinarily stable for a very long time. From 1962 onwards, the commercial scene was dominated by three networks, alongside which stood only the ABC until 1980, and then both the ABC and the SBS. In that time, audience shares have also been remarkably stable. At the end of the 1990s it seems inevitable that this will change. The factor of change is the advent of the multi-channel environment—that combination of technological and regulatory transformation which means that instead of spectrum scarcity and a handful of channels, the spectrum plenitude brought about by the digital revolution will provide many more.

There are currently two technological developments occurring that will transform the television landscape. The first is the growth of the Internet and the second is the introduction of digital television. In fact, these concurrent developments blur the boundaries between television and other communications technologies such as the computer and telecommunications, because with video and audio streaming the computer will become like a TV set, and with interactive digital television the TV set will become like a computer (Given 1998: 22–23). This convergence of technologies leads to an increasing difficulty in the traditional separation between media and media sectors, and we are seeing tussles developing in the communications business as companies try to manipulate business and regulatory environments, to maximise their chances in the digital world (Given 1998: 39).

In this much tougher environment where the prizes go to the players with the really deep pockets, how will our two national broadcasters fare? As discussed above, the ABC has already put a toe into the water of the multi-channel environment with a failed attempt to get into pay TV. But in the 1990s, in common with other public service broadcasters around the world, it has made a quiet but very successful entry into online services. So far these have built on ABC radio rather than television, with audio streaming of several ABC radio networks and various opportunities for interactive online discussions with ABC presenters (for example, the Jazz On Line segment with Classic FM jazz announcer Jim McLeod), as well as constant news updates on the Website. The ABC Website is currently one of the most visited in Australia and the possibilities for further synergies with both radio and television seem obvious.

The difficulty is that originating programming—or providing content, as it is now called—is expensive even in these days of relatively cheap low-band cameras and digital editing equipment. With initiatives like *Race Around the World*, the ABC has already shown a propensity for what is almost 'guerilla television' which interacts very nicely with online delivery, and this is clearly a direction in which it should continue to move.

At the same time as Internet broadcasting begins to emerge, a second technological development—digital television—promises to be more problematic, both because of the high costs of introducing it, and because of the problem of filling the channels that are made available, although some of the extra channel space will be filled with 'data-casting' rather than full picture video. The ABC has expended considerable energy in developing a digital strategy and petitioning a less than sympathetic government for special one-off funding for digital conversion. It has been granted some such funding but is enjoined to provide the rest by selling off property assets.

The ABC's digital strategy reiterates the fundamental principles of public service broadcasting which I outlined at the beginning of this chapter, and they are as relevant to the digital age as they were to the analogue one. In fact, the increase in channels at last solves a problem ABC television has long suffered: having only one channel (in contrast, say, to the BBC which has long had two), which makes delivering on the complex PSB remit extremely difficult, because of the pressure to be comprehensive and specialised at the same time. The digital strategy identifies the ABC's strengths and intended directions in the digital age as a strong information provision record (news and current affairs); lifelong learning (education, children's programs and specialised information); regional and local responsiveness including both geographic communities and communities of interest; and the arts, including drama, music and cultural innovation.

The SBS has been more successful with its venture into pay television: the World Movies channel which is available on all three pay services is a welcome source of extra revenue. The SBS has also developed a digital strategy and believes, as the ABC does of itself, that the niche in the television landscape currently being filled by the SBS will translate into the multi-channel environment. In a submission to a government inquiry into multi-channelling in 1999, the SBS said:

> SBS is recognised by viewers as the chief source of foreign news, movies and documentaries, and they look to SBS for foreign 'art house' material and information on world events that is not available on other networks. SBS is also the place where viewers expect to find a reflection of Australia's social diversity, and vigorous discussion of issues facing Australia's multicultural society. (SBS 1999)

The SBS intends to explore the use of the extra channels to expand its foreign language news services, to provide coverage of multicultural arts and community activities, to provide existing SBS programming streams in varying time slots and for data-casting. Like the ABC, the SBS has to convince government it should be supported to provide these extra services because there is a demand for them, but at the same time convince the commercial free-to-air and pay sector that such services will not constitute a threat to their revenue streams—a very delicate juggling act.

As this book goes to press, Australia is just on the edge of this new age, and it is difficult to predict what will happen in the next ten years. Just as this new age blurs the boundaries between television, computing and telecommunications, so too does it threaten to blur the divisions between public service broadcasting and the rest. It can now be argued, if not convincingly, that the diversity and difference that at bottom justified public support of these services will be delivered by the multiplicity of narrowcasting channels now available. Public broadcasters will need to argue that, even in this era of plenty, there are some essential communities which will never be catered for, and that is where such services will continue to be needed.

Five

Terry Flew and Christina Spurgeon

Television after broadcasting

After a long period of relative stability in Australian television, where there had only been the introduction of one new commercial TV network and one new public broadcaster (the Ten Network and the SBS) since the early 1960s, it was widely anticipated that the 1990s would be a decade of fundamental change in the structure of Australian television. The *Broadcasting Services Act*, introduced to federal parliament in 1992, was designed to enhance the diversity of broadcasting services available to Australians. It would do this by reducing regulatory barriers to the development of new service types, by enabling new entrants to harness the potential of new delivery technologies such as satellite, cable and microwave delivery systems (MDS), and by addressing the limits of broadcasting spectrum scarcity. These arrangements were intended to facilitate the development of a television system that was more competitive and more directly responsive to consumer choice (see Davies and Spurgeon 1992; Flew 1994 for accounts of the legislation). Developments in North America and Europe suggested that, as monopolistic and oligopolistic market structures withered, new providers would identify significant niche audiences. Consumers would 'vote with their wallets' and bypass 'broad appeal' free-to-air television in favour of the specialised fare offered by services such as CNN, MTV, HBO, ESPN, Discovery or Rupert Murdoch's Sky TV. This seemed likely to be replicated in the Australian context, at least to the promoters of regulatory change. Moreover, there was the possibility that minority groups such as those involved with community TV, who had struggled for funding and access under the existing regime, may be able to piggyback these services on to the new technologies, to develop genuinely local and community-based TV programs.

Looking at how new and alternative television services developed in Australia in the 1990s, many of these prophecies were not borne out. The significance of pay TV into the future, however, needs to be considered from a number of angles, including trends in subscriber numbers, actual audiences for particular services and programs, share of advertising revenue and competition for program supplies and audiences between free-to-air (FTA) and pay TV. In the United States, the prime-time audience share of the 'Big Three' free-to-air (FTA) networks (ABC, CBS and NBC) has fallen from 92 per cent in 1977 to 56 per cent in 1997, and the total share of the cable networks is now 36.9 per cent. But the FTA networks still account for over 80 per cent of advertising revenue, a reflection in part of there being only one cable network (TNT) which attracts an audience share of over 2 per cent (Peters, 1999).

The development of pay TV and other new TV services in Australia contrasts to the other major development in media in the 1990s: the popularisation of the Internet and World Wide Web. Australians have taken to the Internet with great enthusiasm. The Australian Bureau of Statistics estimated that, in December 1999, 1.6 million households (23 per cent) had access to the Internet from home, and 5.6 million adults (41 per cent of Australia's adult population) had accessed the Internet from work, home or a place of study in the twelve months to February 1999. The rate of growth of Internet access has been rapid: there were 1.5 million users in February 1996 (262 000 with home Internet access), 3 million users in February 1998 (1 million with home Internet access), and 5 million users in February 1999 (1.3 million with home Internet access) (ABS, 1999). Developments such as electronic commerce, online education and teleworking (working from home through networked personal computing) are likely to make Net access a necessity into the future while the costs of access decline and the capacity of networks continues to grow. As Nicholas Negroponte colourfully puts it: 'Computing is not about computers any more. It is about living.' (Negroponte 1995: 6) The major development to be considered in the early twenty-first century is the convergence of the Internet with television services through the digitisation of all media. This will support increased access to audiovisual materials through networked personal computers, or 'Web TV', and the addition of Internet-type services through television with the development of digital TV. Developments in the corporate sector such as the US$350 billion merger of Time-Warner and America Online (AOL) proposed in January 2000 clearly point in this direction.

PAY TV

Pay TV is a relatively recent but important development in the diversification of Australian television. Unlike other sectors of broadcasting, which are principally government, advertiser or community funded, the principal source of funds for the pay TV sector is subscription revenue, with the viability of pay TV services being dependent upon their ability to attract subscribers to their multichannel services. Under the *Broadcasting Services Act* 1992, these services—which include Foxtel, Optus Vision and AUSTAR—are termed 'subscription broadcasting services'. By, 1999 pay TV services had about one million subscribers, or 15 per cent of total TV households. Pay TV dramatically increases the number of TV services available in many parts of Australia. In 1998, a household which subscribed to both Foxtel and Optus Vision services had the choice of 52 channels, in addition to the five free-to-air networks, while in rural and regional Australia take-up rates have been high, as pay TV has significantly extended entertainment choices for these communities.

In contrast to Europe and North America, where pay TV had been in operation for between ten and thirty years, pay TV services did not commence in Australia until 1995, after thirteen years of public inquiries and political delays. Although a 1982 Australian Broadcasting Tribunal (ABT) inquiry recommended the immediate development of cable and subscription TV services (ABT 1982), the Fraser Coalition government, and subsequent Labor governments, did not adopt the recommendations. It was not until the 1992 reforms of broadcasting and communications laws that adequate legislative provision was made for the development of residential markets for pay TV services. The development of pay TV in Australia was strongly resisted by commercial TV licensees (Flew 1995; Hawke 1995; Appleton 1997). O'Regan has argued that, in contrast to the United States, regulators in Australia 'have gone out of their way to protect the interests of free-to-air broadcasters at the expense of pay TV and other new television services in advance of their operations' (O'Regan 1996: 70; on Australian pay TV policy history, see Dwyer 1995). For example, pay TV operators were prohibited by legislation from earning advertising income until 1997. By 1999, pay TV advertising revenues were $18 million, or less than 1 per cent of those of the commercial FTA sector of $2.3 billion (Peters 1999). These figures also reflected the ongoing preference of most major advertisers for the mass audiences provided by FTA broadcast television.

Resistance to the direct user-pays model of pay TV extended well beyond commercial TV interests into activist, community and academic communities, and was part of a more general rejection of 'economic rationalist' policy discourse which positioned TV as a commodity (e.g. *Communications Update* 1992). In the context of communications policy, including that relating to pay TV, this rejection was informed by an expectation that the social and economic benefits of media and communications services would be distributed in a 'roughly equitable' manner across Australia (CLC 1999: 5.1).

Pay TV services represented an important departure from the 'rough equity' approach to developing Australian communications in terms of how decisions would be made about where to provide services. They marked a new era in which investment decisions in electronic media and communications infrastructure would be explicitly tied to market considerations and, arguably, would be less responsive to social needs in an increasingly convergent media environment. For example, aggressive competition between Australia's two telecommunications licensees, Optus and Telstra, saw very costly cable infrastructure duplicated in many parts of Sydney and Melbourne in the first few years of rollout. This wasteful duplication contrasted with many other parts of the country that would never have access to this infrastructure, or to the social and economic benefits that it was perceived to deliver. International trends to private communications network development, facilitated by digital technology and deregulation of market entry, also influenced the decline of rough equity Australian media and communications policy from the mid-1980s onwards.

Thus pay TV developed alongside the introduction of competition to Australian telecommunications. The investment strategies of Telstra and Optus, Australia's two principal telecommunications carriers, linked development of cable infrastructure for pay TV services to their market strategies in telephone call markets. For example, it was observed that Telstra's move into broadband cable was primarily motivated by a desire to protect its local telephone call market from competition (e.g. Budde 1999).

A series of rather extraordinary policy and political developments contributed to further post-1992 delays in the start-up of pay TV services, including a flawed allocation process for satellite-delivered pay TV services through public auction which was exploited by speculative bidders. Satellite delivery was also mandated as the first delivery platform for pay TV. This had the effect of guaranteeing much-needed revenue streams for the financially troubled national satellite system (AUSSAT), which had been sold to Optus in 1991 to form the basis of the first competitor to the government-owned Telstra in the newly created domestic telecommunications market. A legislative requirement that a digital transmission standard be used for satellite delivery of pay TV also contributed to delays in the development of services. These last two developments also violated the principle of 'technological neutrality' that the *Broadcasting Services Act* 1992 had sought to enshrine. Pay TV services are now delivered into residential markets on a mix of satellite, cable and microwave (MDS) delivery platforms.

Ownership and control of pay TV licences is less restricted than for free-to-air TV, and both foreign ownership and cross-media ownership have been characteristic of pay TV in Australia. Rupert Murdoch's News Corporation is a major joint-venture partner with Telstra in Foxtel, and was joined in 1998 by the Packer family's Publishing and Broadcasting Limited (PBL), which had previously been a major shareholder in Optus Vision. In 1997, the British cable communications company Cable & Wireless bought out US telecommunications giant Bell South's interest in Australia's second carrier, Optus (now the sole owner of Optus Vision), which then underwent a name change to become Cable & Wireless Optus. AUSTAR's parent is the United States-based media investment company United International Holdings Inc (UIH), which has investments in pay TV and

Table 5.1 Pay TV in Australia, March 1999

	Foxtel	Optus Vision	Austar
Ownership	Telstra 50% News Corp 25%	Cable & Wireless Optus	United International Holdings (UIH) Inc.
Area of operation	Sydney, Melbourne, Brisbane, Gold Coast, Adelaide, Perth	Sydney, Melbourne, Brisbane	Regional NSW, NT, Qld, SA, Vic, Tas
Delivery platforms	Cable, satellite	Cable, satellite	Cable, satellite, MDS
Number of channels	36	31	27
Potential market	2.5 million homes passed by Telstra cable	2.1 million homes passed by Optus cable	2.2 million homes
Subscribers	500 000	210 000 cable	325 000 satellite and MDS
Total penetration	15.2 per cent (1 035 000 subscribers from 6.8 million households)		

Sources: AFC (1998). Get The Picture (5th edn); Communications Update, February 1999; AdNews (1999); Richards (1999).

telephony businesses in twenty-two countries around the world. The only restrictions on market entry that now remain are those connected to spectrum and channel access and the costs of starting up a pay TV service. Despite these apparently liberal entry conditions, the number of pay TV operators in the Australian market has actually declined from six to three since 1997. A snapshot of current pay TV service providers is provided in Table 5.1, and discussed in further detail below.

It has always been doubtful that an Australian pay TV market could support more than one or two national operators, and therefore be genuinely competitive. High service delivery infrastructure costs combined with high recurrent program costs have meant that pay TV operators have faced huge losses in the early years of service, estimated to have exceeded $2 billion in the first three years (Bulbeck 1998). In 1998, the pay TV sector went through a painful period of rationalisation. Australis, the first pay TV operator to move into Australian residential markets, went into receivership while two other regional operators, Northgate and East Coast Television, had also ceased providing pay TV services by the end of 1998. At the end of the 1990s, the Australian pay TV market was divided between AUSTAR, serving non-metropolitan and regional areas, and Optus and Foxtel which competed head-to-head in metropolitan markets. Optus Vision differentiated itself from Foxtel by positioning itself as a platform provider for a range of new media and communications services, not just pay TV. Foxtel was the largest pay TV provider, with a subscription base of about 500 000. With strong programming drawn from the global media resources of Rupert Murdoch's Fox network—including the high-profile Fox Sports—and with significant cross-media promotion through News Corporation's Australian newspapers as well as through Telstra outlets, Foxtel was expected to begin turning a profit in 2002 (Bulbeck 1999a). AUSTAR had a distinctive focus on developing pay TV markets in non-metropolitan and rural areas and was the first pay TV provider to move into the black. This was due to a range of factors including lower programming and infrastructure costs and the willingness of people in rural and regional Australia to subscribe to pay TV as an alternative to enduring long distances to local video stores, poor reception for free-to-air TV, and limited access to cinemas.

In a multichannel environment, programming—not spectrum—becomes the scarce resource (Fist 1996). Pay TV operators rely on channel providers to deliver program streams that will attract and retain subscribers. Minimising programming costs is a key ingredient in the recipe for profitability of pay TV services in the medium to long term. Fierce competition to secure Australian rights to TV programs supplies contributed to the high start-up and ongoing operational costs of pay TV. For example, Optus Vision and Foxtel initially entered into exclusive program supply arrangements for movie channels that were amongst the most expensive in the world (Fist 1996).

In relation to certain programs—most notably high-profile sports—the interests of free-to-air broadcasters in programming are privileged in broadcasting law over those of pay TV operators. The ABA maintains an inventory of programs for which pay TV operators cannot secure rights unless they are also held by a free-to-air broadcaster. The 'anti-siphoning' list contains sporting events that must be broadcast free to air. The aim of the anti-siphoning regime is to prevent these major events from being siphoned off to pay TV to the detriment of free-to-air viewers. Arguably this is another example of the principle of 'rough equity' at work in Australian media law and policy. As the business interests of pay TV and free-to-air service providers become more enmeshed, it is also likely that the hostility of commercial TV licensees to pay TV—especially around program rights—will soften. For example, Kerry Packer's Publishing and Broadcasting Limited has a program supply arrangement with Fox Sports and Seven is now the pay TV sports service provider to Optus Vision.

Like free-to-air TV, program content is co-regulated by pay TV licensees under the ABA code registration system. The code which applies to pay TV operators was developed by a new industry association representing a range of new media service providers, called the Australian Subscription Television and Radio Association (ASTRA). The pay TV code covers the classification of program material, the presentation of news and current affairs, advertising placement and complaints procedures. It also covers matters that are particular to pay TV, such as dispute resolution processes for billing and repairs on equipment rented to consumers. Australia has no 'must carry' rules for public broadcasting and community television services, which places it at odds with twenty of the 27 OECD countries with cable television systems (OECD 1999).

The approach taken to regulating Australian content on pay TV is quite different from that applied to free-to-air commercial TV. The free-to-air requirements support Australian content in a variety of program formats. Pay TV Australian content requirements have focused on, and are likely to continue to emphasise, support for Australian drama and feature films. Section 102 of the *Broadcasting Services Act* 1992 requires 10 per cent of total program expenditure on predominantly drama pay TV channels to be spent on Australian drama. There is also provision for increasing the proportion of expenditure on drama over time.

Australian content has not been a dominant feature of pay TV services, although pockets of local production have developed. The ABA's investigation into Australian content levels on pay TV found that, in June 1996, total spending on new Australian drama among the eleven drama channels made up 7 per cent of total expenditure ($1.74 million). At the time, this was considered to be a necessary consequence of the start-up phase for services whose revenue growth over time would enable them to commission more local production (ABA, 1997a). A 1998 ABA survey found, however, that only four out of sixteen drama channels had complied with the legislative requirement to spend 10 per cent of annual program expenditure on new Australian drama. A further seven spent between 0.4 per cent and 5.5 per cent of annual program expenditure on new Australian drama, and four spent nothing (ABA May 1998). In the twelve months to June 1998, the predominantly drama channels on pay TV had spent $8.17 million of their $100.8 million budgets on new Australian drama—or about 8 per cent. In light of the notable lack of improvement on the part of the pay TV services, legislation to enforce the 10 per cent minimum requirement was passed through federal parliament in late 1999.

With 15 per cent of Australian TV households subscribing to pay TV after five years of operation, and an overall audience share of 7.3 per cent (Meade and McKenzie 1999), pay TV industry spokespeople point out that take-up rates in Australia have exceeded those of Britain and New Zealand at comparable periods of development (Richards 1999). It is also projected that the take-up rate for pay TV will be 30 per cent by 2004. This is at the slow end of development according to projections of subscriber numbers made by the Bureau of Transport and Communications Economics (BTCE 1995). This was an important contributing factor to the enormous losses of pay TV operators in the establishment years as, amongst other things, prices paid for programs supplied were based on optimistic projections for service adoption. Estimates are affected by what is known in the industry as 'churn'—the rate at which new subscribers replace cancellations. The early years of pay TV in Australia were marked by high churn rates, as revealed in October 1998 when C&W Optus released its prospectus in anticipation of a public float. The prospectus showed that in 1996, 1997 and 1998 the churn rates for Optus had been 40 per cent, 116 per cent and 50 per cent respectively (Bulbeck 1998a).

All of the pay TV services offer a mix of movie, news, entertainment, sports, children's, music, documentary, home shopping and weather channels. Optus Vision has been unique in its emphasis upon providing a series of foreign-language channels, ranging from those which source locally, such as Greek, Lebanese and Arabic channels, to being a carrier for Japan's NHK, China's CCTV, Italy's RAI (also carried on Foxtel) and the Hong Kong-based TVBI. Optus Vision also operated a local access channel, LocalVision, until 1997. All carry the SBS

World Movies channel as a premium service (i.e. one which is available at additional cost to the basic service).

The impact of pay TV on programming on free-to-air TV is difficult to discern at this stage. While the free-to-air networks see the impact as having been minimal in an overall sense, it has been significant in particular areas, including children's TV where channels such as Nickelodeon have had a major impact. It is estimated that pay TV had taken up to 21 per cent of audience share among children aged five to twelve from free-to-air TV by 1999 (*AdNews* 1999: 30–31). Households with children were also twice as likely to have pay TV as those without children (20 per cent penetration rate compared with 10 per cent in March 1999).

The other areas where pay TV has had a major impact are movies and sport. It was always anticipated that sports and movies would be major drivers of demand for pay TV. Pay TV has first option on most major Hollywood films compared with free-to-air where screening is now two to three years after cinematic release. Live coverage of Rugby League, Rugby Union, Australian Rules football and popular international sports such as soccer and boxing is far more extensive on pay TV than free-to-air. The so-called 'Rugby League wars' of 1996–97, where News Corporation set up a rival 'Super League' competition to compete directly with the traditional Australian Rugby League competition, was a battle fought partly over pay TV rights to a popular winter sport. Further migration of the sports audience to pay TV could lead to FTA networks such as Seven and Nine seeking to renegotiate television rights for major sports such as Australian Rules football and cricket, or even following Ten and ceasing to broadcast high-cost sporting events altogether.

There is continuing uncertainty about the number of pay TV operators that can be viable in the Australian market. There is also the likelihood that, under the Coalition government, Telstra will be fully privatised, which will have implications for its 50 per cent stake in Foxtel. Another important issue around the future development of pay TV which has yet to be resolved is the question of whether the technical interfaces for new broadband media services should be 'interoperable'. In the simplest terms, an open technical standard would allow consumers to move between services and delivery platforms, or subscribe to new services, without having to rent a different set-top box or interface from each new service provider. It would also facilitate the delivery of convergent digital media and communications services to homes. Another important issue for pay TV concerns the matter of whether or not, under Australian competition law, pay TV services should make their delivery infrastructure open to anyone who would like to use this capacity to offer services into residential markets. Under current arrangements, it is highly unlikely that a new pay TV service provider could enter the Australian market unless they could also develop their own delivery infrastructure. The Australian Competition and Consumer Commission is inquiring in 1999 into whether there should be such a structural separation of pay TV content and carriage services. Pay TV has clearly diversified Australian television in a number of important ways. However, the extent to which it has led to a diversification of electronic media ownership and control is open to question.

COMMUNITY TV

Since the mid-1970s, community-based electronic media have been developed in Australia and elsewhere as a strategy for diversifying media ownership and content, and for democratising media access for groups, individuals and interests not adequately addressed by commercial or national broadcasters. In both North America and the United Kingdom, community TV initiatives were associated with the development of cable delivery systems in the 1970s (Bibby et al. 1979). By the time that cable delivery platforms began to be rolled out in Australia in the mid-1990s, community TV in Australia had taken a different turn. This sector had laid claim to 'sixth channel' free-to-air spectrum, so called because major metropolitan centres had three commercial and two national services, which meant that community TV would be the sixth service in these markets. The idea of a space for a sixth free-to-air TV channel was based on a notional spectrum reservation for educational television services first proposed in the early 1960s, and tentatively incorporated into broadcast spectrum planning assumptions (ABT 1985: 54). Although educational institutions had been major supporters in the development of community radio, and do currently participate in community TV, they did not rush in to take up this opportunity to develop TV services. Rather, the lead had been taken by video access groups from the 1970s onwards. A key driver here was a strong interest in increasing exhibition opportunities for independent audiovisual producers.

As community-based video production centres evolved, against a background of declining localism in national and commercial services, the idea of educational TV was broadened and transformed into community TV. Various options for developing community-based content within existing national services, such as program 'windows' within the ABC or SBS schedules, were explored in the early 1980s (White et al. 1982), but when these options were exhausted, community TV groups began to campaign for access to the 'sixth channel' spectrum. A very important demonstration of the needs-based case for community TV was also made by remote Aboriginal settlements. Communities in the remote settlements of Ernabella and Yuendumu started their own low-powered services in anticipation of satellite-delivered TV services that were likely to exacerbate conditions of cultural genocide (Michaels 1986; Spurgeon 1989). Throughout the 1980s and 1990s, successive federal governments and agencies such as the Australian Film Commission repeatedly stated that community television would not receive direct government financial assistance. In lieu of funds, community TV groups attempted to secure guaranteed spectrum access. By the late 1980s, they had been successful in their campaign, and the then Labor Minister for Transport and Communications, Ralph Willis, opened up sixth channel spectrum to community TV groups for test broadcasting. Numerous test transmissions in most state capitals and some regional centres began in earnest from this time. Organisational structures for the ongoing operation of community TV also began to be developed.

In 1992, a parliamentary inquiry into the future development of sixth channel spectrum recommended that community TV be allowed to continue experimenting with sixth channel spectrum until final decisions had been made on how this spectrum should be used. By this time a variety of competing demands for this spectrum had been identified, including an educational channel, another commercial service, an arts channel and a so-called 'family' channel (briefly favoured by former Prime Minister Paul Keating). A follow-up inquiry by the Australian Broadcasting Authority recommended that, if it was to be used at all, the sixth channel 'should be used for community access television, as most socio-economic benefits presently appear likely to flow from this use' (ABA 1997b: xii). The report also outlined various schemes of staged development for community TV that would eventually lead to the full licensing of services as the sixth channel of Australian free-to-air TV.

Despite the long and difficult struggle for spectrum access, and ongoing financial difficulties, by 1999 community TV stations were providing fulltime services in Brisbane, Sydney, Melbourne, Adelaide and Perth. Two regional centres (Bendigo in Victoria and Lismore in Northern New South Wales) also had licences to broadcast in these locations but were off air. This represents a remarkable achievement in the circumstances, but there is still a great deal of uncertainty about the future of community TV. Community TV services have frequently struggled to remain financially viable and on air, which has in no small way militated against developing diverse and innovative programming. The most successful community TV services (Briz 31 in Brisbane and, until a financial crisis in 1999, Channel 31 in Melbourne) have effectively combined programs aimed at a diverse range of specific interest groups with more 'broad appeal', or so-called 'catchment' programs, that bring audiences over to have a look at the service. They have also established sustainable programming arrangements with their sponsors. Channel 31 in Melbourne underpinned its highly diverse mix of programs, including alternative news to local variety and comedy, 22 locally based ethnic programs, Arab TV drama, university lectures and local music shows, with significant sponsorship arrangements with the Victorian Harness Racing Board and the Victorian Racing Commission to broadcast trotting and horse racing. When these sponsors were lured to pay TV, the service ran into serious financial difficulties, and problems were exacerbated by legal action from disgruntled program producers (Dodd 1999). Briz 31 is perhaps less diverse than the Melbourne service, but has proved to be sustainable on the basis of charging all program makers for the air time, as well as strong 'catchment' programming ranging from harness racing and old movies to more eclectic fare as diverse as American evangelical preachers on Sunday nights and *Tamara Tonite*, a Saturday night comedy chat show hosted by a local drag artist. By contrast, community TV in Sydney has consistently struggled to develop, especially since a disastrous and highly publicised power struggle within the organisation in 1994 and financial problems that resulted in the service being administered by creditors.

Some of the groups traditionally attracted to community TV include: those wishing to produce alternative or critical forms of news, current affairs and documentary programming; ethnic community groups; Indigenous community groups; young people seeking a start in 'the industry', or simply the opportunity for creative self-expression; gay and lesbian groups; people with disabilities; independent film and television producers; religious organisations; and educational organisations.[1] Some of the issues involved in producing community TV programs which address a particular community are discussed by McKee (1996). In discussing the thirteen-part documentary series *BentORama*, for Bent TV, a gay and lesbian television community production group working with Melbourne Community TV on Channel 31, McKee notes that one of the challenges of working in community TV lies in recognising the diversity of groups held to be within a single 'community' such as lesbians and gay men. At the same time, one of the possibilities of television in achieving a more diverse form of address is that its domestic context of consumption enables those who do not identify with a particular urban and commercial 'scene' to be viewers and participants. The need to address diversity, and to produce programs that not only provide platforms for alternative viewpoints and access for community groups, without appearing to be 'aesthetically impoverished vanity video' (Cunningham and Miller 1994: 24), is an issue for the management and participatory structures of community broadcasting services, as well as those who put programs to air.

It is not at all certain that community TV will survive the digital transformation of broadcasting in Australia. While supporting community TV's use of the sixth channel spectrum in the analogue mode, the ABA's *Sixth Channel* report (ABA 1997b) also recommended that this spectrum should be taken into account in any future decisions about the introduction of digital terrestrial TV transmission systems. Powerful interests, especially Rupert Murdoch's News Corporation, were lobbying hard for the development of new services that would preclude the further development of community TV. Legislative arrangements for the introduction of digital television did not envisage an allocation of digital transmission spectrum to community TV. Rather, they provided for the possibility of an obligation upon a new category of commercial datacasters to carry community TV.

If the datacasting access arrangement is to develop, then Australian community TV groups could benefit from the experiences of North American and British groups who have relied on various types of 'access' rules from their inception. The main advantage of this approach is that community groups are freed from the burden of financing and maintaining complex and costly TV broadcasting and distribution systems and can concentrate resources on program making, by 'piggybacking' their services on to infrastructure developed by commercial providers. In the Australian context, however, political control of a broadcasting resource ultimately resides with the communications infrastructure provider, not program makers or suppliers. The goals and interests of not-for-profit community groups will inevitably be vulnerable in any conflict that might arise with a commercial carrier, and the track record of successive Australian governments in ensuring this type of access to broadcasting resources by not-for-profit community-based groups is not encouraging.

WEB TV OR WEBCASTING

Web TV, also known as Webcasting or Netcasting, involves the transmission of audio-visual or audio content over the Internet, received through the user's networked personal computer. While the possibility of streaming media content over the Internet has existed for as long as the capacity to combine text, sound, picture and moving image in common digital formats, services have been relatively slow to develop compared with text-based media such as online newspapers. This is because of the need for high-bandwidth cable networks, powerful computers with high capacity and memory, and powerful cable modems to support Webcasting and make it a worthwhile exercise for users. 'Web-TV' set-top boxes have been available in the United States since 1997, and Internet content has been adapted to be more icon or graphic-based rather than text-based, which will better suit use through television receivers.

There is considerable scepticism about the likelihood of Web TV developing into a significant media form, in part because of the limitations presented by available means of carriage and reception, and the costs associated with time spent accessing such services. Even if TV-type content is delivered relatively efficiently over the Internet, consumers may use the medium for different purposes due to the different association of the personal computer with active engagement as a user in work-related tasks, and of television with leisure, entertainment and 'immersion' in the medium as a consumer rather than a communicator. The speed at which these communicative forms are converging, particularly with the development of digital TV, suggests that attempts to differentiate broadcasting from Webcasting or datacasting may be overtaken by events, although the federal government has put forward legislation to prevent datacasters from developing broadcast-type services. Nonetheless, a continuum of digital services is likely to be available in the near future, accessible from personal computers, televisions with set-top boxes, and new hybrid reception technologies.

A number of Webcasting services had developed by the late 1990s, including digital sound and image libraries with content downloadable on demand; live Webcasts of major sporting and public events, such as the AFL Grand Final or the Sydney Gay and Lesbian Mardi Gras; 'push technology' services such as Pointcast, which automatically send new content to subscribers' personal computers based upon their identified interests; and bundles of services derived from multiple sources (OECD 1997). Broadcast.com was a significant innovator in the latter area, enabling users to access multiple broadcast television and radio services over the Internet. In the United States, this was particularly popular with followers of sports events with insufficient appeal for national broadcast, such as college football and basketball. Webcasting refers not only to the delivery of audio-visual material over the Internet, which can include one-to-one or small group Internet video-conferencing as well as material broadly accessible through the World Wide Web, but also the delivery of audio services. Web radio has in fact developed far more quickly than Web TV, with over 2000 stations being accessible in 1999 (BRS Media 1998). Public broadcasters such as the Australian Broadcasting Corporation have been early adopters of Webcasting, as have providers of specialist and foreign-language services catering to diasporic communities. This suggests that Web TV is more likely to develop as a series of multiple niche or community interest services catering to audience needs not met by broadcast and pay TV services rather than as a direct competitor to them. The adult entertainment, or 'Web porn', industry, which has made by far the most profitable use of Webcasting, has clearly built its success upon the capacity to provide content and services to the home PC which will never be provided through mainstream broadcast channels. It was estimated that online adult services transactions were worth between US$750 million and US$1 billion in 1999, and constituted about 4 per cent of total online transactions (May 1998; Pringle 2000).

The case of Webcasting points to the limits of arguments which predict the demise of mass-appeal broadcast media in the face of development of the Internet. For technological utopians such as George Gilder and Nicholas Negroponte, the demise of a passive, mass cultural, one-way communications medium such as television is an obvious corollary of the emergence of an interactive, decentralised and networked system such as the Internet. Negroponte (1995: 58) predicted that: 'The media barons of today will be grasping to hold on to their centralised empires tomorrow', while Gilder (1994: 46) proposed that what he called the 'teleputer' 'would reverse the effects of the television age . . . Rather than cultivating passivity, the teleputer will promote creativity.' Such prognoses ignore a number of important points. First, there are significant social and cultural, as well as technological, reasons why television is consumed in domestic contexts, and the uses and pleasures which are derived by audiences from television are not the same as those associated with personal computing and the Internet. In other words, many would prefer to access the same content from a TV than a PC. Second, there is the technological determinist fallacy of assuming that one medium replaces another, rather than recognising the processes of coexistence and mutual adjustment which occur between media. The introduction of TV did not lead to the demise of radio, although it did change radio, as audiences accessed the 'old' medium in different places—and for different reasons—after the advent of TV than they did before its existence. Finally, television broadcasters are powerful, profitable and politically well connected, as well as having considerable experience in producing content tailored to audience desires and expectations, and it was never likely that they would simply resign themselves to obsolescence in light of the challenge presented by digitisation and convergence to traditional media forms and practices. The way in which decisions about digital television have been made, in Australia and elsewhere, provides a powerful indicator of the continuing significance of 'the dense politics which surrounds decisions about technological change' (Given 1998a: 71).

DIGITAL TV

The introduction of digital television will involve two dramatic transformations. First, it will mark the most significant transformation in the technological form of television since it was first broadcast in analogue formats. Television is ubiquitous in Australian homes. Yet, since its introduction in 1956, the only significant change in the form of signal received has been the introduction of colour television in 1975. In contrast to other home-based activities, such as cooking or listening to music, the stability of the technological form through which broadcast television signals have been received has, until the introduction of digital TV, been largely stable for the second half of the twentieth century. This points to the second major implication of digital TV's introduction: it will gradually expose virtually all Australians to the types of services accessible by digital means, as analogue television gradually will be phased out between 2001 and 2008. In this sense, pundits such as Negroponte and Gilder will be right: the televisions of the future will be computers, just as microwave ovens and CD players are computing machines designed not to look like desktop computers. Where they are wrong, at least so far, is in believing that this transformation will mean the demise of the television industry or the sorts of consumption habits that have been based upon the uses of television.

Compared with analogue television, digital TV offers the scope for more diversity of content, through both greater capacity to carry signals and greater efficiency in spectrum use, and better technical quality of content, through both the improved quality of sound and images and the dynamic flexibility of the medium. For example, each service could take the form of single high-definition television (HDTV) services or multiple channels of standard broadcast sound and image quality. It makes TV more complex and brings to it the benefits identified with digital media generally. These include the capacity of digital information to be manipulated and navigated by users, networked, carried in large quantities and compressed in order to reduce storage requirements, regardless of form (sound, text, image) at the point of origination (Feldman 1997). It also potentially provides the 'return link' absent in the analogue 'broadcasting panopticon' (Robins and Webster 1988: 57ff) and thereby raises issues of data mining, privacy and surveillance. While the emphasis has so far been upon the capacity of digital TV to deliver 'cinema-like experiences' to the home (e.g. DoCA 1998), the real significance of digital TV will lie in the extent to which it makes television the conduit for a diverse range of services, with the spectrum being able to facilitate new levels of access to residential markets for Internet service providers, data-casting networks, educational institutions, community groups, and myriad other groups for any number of means—much as the Internet is currently being utilised—in addition to television programs (Kilmurray 1998).

This tension between 'broad' and 'narrow' understandings of digital TV's impact, and the important corollary of who will be the principal players in the television of the future, has been played out in the public policy domain. In Australia, policy-makers have thus far opted for 'narrow' understandings of digital TV as primarily an extension of existing TV services. The Howard federal government's framework for managing the transition to digital television, developed by Senator Richard Alston, the Minister for Communications, the Information Economy and the Arts, has given the existing commercial and national free-to-air television broadcasters 7 mega-hertz (Mhz) of spectrum at no cost, in exchange for a commitment to offer high-definition TV (HDTV) and standard-definition TV (SDTV) broadcasts from 2001, and to simulcast existing services in analogue and digital formats until 2008. The existing free-to-air broadcasters have also benefited from the decision to continue prohibition of new free-to-air broadcasters until 2007, and to restrict the development of datacasting services in order to prevent them from providing most genres of traditional television programming. Public broadcasters such as the ABC and the SBS have been provided with free access to spectrum, and are hoping for legislative and financial support from government to upgrade to digital broadcasting and develop innovative multichannel and datacasting services.

Jock Given has observed that this policy approach, which is similar to that developed in the United States, provides existing commercial broadcasters with 'a "rails run" into digital transmission . . . [as] the carrot with which to ensure free-to-air broadcasters' commitment to providing television "in the public interest" into the future' (Given 1998: 48). It also marks a continuation of what has been termed the *quid pro quo* approach to broadcasting policy, where local content quotas and other public policy goals are underpinned by industry protection for existing broadcasters, and a political culture prevails which political scientist Hugh Emy has termed 'protection all round', where 'each major interest or producer group acquiesced in policies designed to accommodate the others in return for a special *quid pro quo* for itself' (Emy 1993: 60). This approach has been attacked by those who have the most to gain from a 'broad' understanding of digital TV that stresses its capacity to blur existing lines of distinction between media, and who see restrictive legislation as the last gasp of the 'old guard' of media proprietors (e.g. Stutchbury 1999). Critics have included subscription television providers, telecommunications companies such as Telstra and Optus, Internet service providers and media interests dominant in areas other than broadcasting, such as News Corporation and Fairfax. The issue of concern is not just restrictions upon new services, but the way in which HDTV is something of a spectrum 'hog', and mandatory requirements for HDTV broadcasting work against the freeing-up of available spectrum that the transition from analogue to digital otherwise enables. Given has indicted that the distinctions being proposed between digital TV and datacasting services 'are going to prove unsustainable—legally, technically, commercially and politically' (Given 1999) as television changes from being a limited-channel 'dumb box' to the carrier of multichannel and interactive services.

The digital TV decision has also been heavily criticised by the Productivity Commission, an independent Commonwealth agency within the Department of Treasury concerned with microeconomic policy, regulation and national competition policy, which conducted a review of broadcasting legislation in 1999. In a withering critique of the *quid pro quo* approach, the Productivity Commission believed that current policy on the transition to digital TV would generate policy outcomes that reduced the efficiency of spectrum management; created complex, artificial and arbitrary restrictions upon the development of new services; restricted the diversity of services available to consumers; limited the likelihood of developing new and innovative media services in Australia; and maintained an anti-competitive arrangement which unduly benefited incumbent broadcasters in ways not commensurate with other social and cultural policy benefits from local content regulations (Productivity Commission 1999: 131, 134, 136). The Productivity Commission instead recommended a liberalised conversion regime, a broad definition of data-casting, a lifting of the laws preventing the entry of new free-to-air broadcasters, and the establishment of greater tradeability of access to spectrum rights in order to promote the introduction of new services and new players by establishing a more contestable market in broadcasting.

CONCLUSION: TELEVISION AFTER BROADCASTING?

At the beginning of the 1990s, the promise of greater competition, diversity and consumer choice in television was widely expected to arise from the introduction of new services such as pay TV and community TV, and the convergence of telecommunications and broadcasting, which would challenge the existing free-to-air sector and transform the logic of Australian television broadcasting. From the vantage point of the twenty-first century, it is apparent that this did not happen to any significant degree. It is now being promised that convergence of the Internet with broadcasting, through Web TV, digital TV and data-casting, will lead us to what George Gilder called 'life after television', and what Nicholas Negroponte described as a 'post-information age', where 'we often have an audience of one [as] information is extremely personalised' (Negroponte 1995: 164).

Yet, as we have seen, any such predictions about the impact of new technologies have to account for four factors. First, there is the nature of the audience. While television may look like a one-way 'dumb box' to many of its critics, it is still the pre-eminent entertainment medium for the vast majority of Australians in their domestic environment. It is therefore likely that changes to television arising from the development of Internet-like capacities, such as accessing text and other data related to programs, will constitute evolutionary, rather than revolutionary, changes for the majority of its users. Second, the giants of existing media are very likely to be major players in the development of digital television, so their current strategies will provide important insights into how this new medium will develop in the near future. Third, the demographic and economic limits to achieving perfect market conditions in Australia remain in spite of the rapid shifts towards this goal that occurred in the closing decades of the twentieth century. Finally, the overview of public policy undertaken in this chapter shows that there is no simple alignment of the development of new media technologies to any particular policy outcome: the parameters of policy influence remain broad, unpredictable and, above all else, continue to be political as well as purely technical or bureaucratic.

NOTE

1 The focus of this chapter is on community TV groups who access the sixth channel. It is not discussing those Aboriginal and Torres Strait Islander community groups which provide community television in regional and remote areas under the Broadcasting for Remote Aboriginal Communities Scheme (BRACS). Television and Indigenous Australians is discussed elsewhere in this book (see Chapter 14), but it is important to note that Indigenous broadcasters have been highly critical of classification of their services as 'community broadcasting' under the *Broadcasting Services Act*, and have sought to have Indigenous broadcasting recognised as a distinct sector in Australian broadcasting, as is the case in New Zealand and Canada. See Meadows (1999).

Part

III

The program formats

Six

Graeme Turner

Television news and current affairs: 'Welcome to Frontline'

THE STUDY OF TELEVISION NEWS AND CURRENT AFFAIRS

Unlike film or literary studies, where academic interest has focused on texts which are studied in their own right, academic analyses of television have largely concentrated on the medium's participation within what John Hartley (1996) calls 'popular reality': the cultural production of a mass mediated account of what constitutes the real world. Television news and current affairs address and inform, perhaps more directly than any other programming format, the viewer's understanding of 'popular reality'. It is not surprising, therefore, that the majority of academic research into television has focused on these formats. In particular, researchers have investigated the relationship between what is represented on the television screen and some version of objective 'truth' about the world. The products of these investigations can include detailed content analyses of bias, distortion and misrepresentation or ideological critiques which see news and current affairs programming as structurally aligned with conservative views of the world (Glasgow Media Group 1976; Hall et al. 1978).

Since television news relays its pictures of the world for us to see for ourselves, it can be regarded as a particularly transparent or 'unmediated' vehicle of reportage—more so than, say, print, where the ordinary reader has no means of evaluating the accuracy of the reporter's rendition of what he or she has seen. The common promotional tactic of depicting television news as an 'eye upon the world' (the naming of *EyeWitness News*, for example) builds upon this assumption. On the other hand, precisely because television news does use images in what appears to be a relatively unmediated manner, any misrepresentation of the world which *might* be accomplished through those pictures would be especially convincing. Consequently, there has been great interest in investigating precisely how the television message is mediated or constructed. Among the subjects of these investigations has been the medium's propensity, through selection and transformation, to manipulate the image and therefore the meanings it generates—the ideologically or politically aligned character of the perspective from which the television 'eye' surveys the world, and the information-rich and thus slightly uncontrollable nature of the readings which can be generated from moving pictures (the notion of semiotic excess) (Hartley 1992).

News and current affairs on television share much the same ethical standards and professional ideologies as other forms of journalism: a commitment to balance and impartiality and a clear differentiation between news and comment. Like other news media, too, television's treatment of news material—both in reporting and in comment—is not only aimed at passing on information, but also at doing so in a way which reinforces the audience's sense of the medium's importance. Television's provision of visual access to the real world is the competitive advantage it has over other news media. This is vividly apparent when, for instance, it is covering live or 'breaking' events. Consequently, as television news has developed its conventions of representation and performance, it has also learnt to mask the processes of its production—that is, to minimise the noticeable traces of mediation. Stuart Hall and his colleagues (Hall et al. 1978) talk of the 'reality effect' produced by our direct consumption of images on the news. Because pictures are in a sense self-evidently true, we recognise what we see as 'real'. This effect dramatically enhances the television message's credibility, it helps to naturalise the explanations it carries (another function of the 'reality effect'), and is a crucial component of the communication compact between the news and its audiences. So it is not to be given up.

Television news has developed conventions of representation which work not only to systematise and naturalise the re-presentation of content but which also serve to authorise and legitimate the genre itself. The importance of the newsreader or presenter, for instance, is related to their embodiment of the trustworthiness of the news service; the selection of the right personality for this task is a critical decision in both the production and the promotion of the news. Further, while the reality effect Hall describes is dramatically enhanced by such strategies as live crosses, frequent 'updates' (often, of course, pre-recorded hours before they are screened) and foreign correspondents doing pieces to camera on location, so is the specific program's signification of immediacy. To enhance their realism, television news and current affairs programs have developed a repertoire of specific techniques which have become so familiar and routine we barely register them as formal representational techniques anymore. Among them I would include the use of close-ups for high drama (we may notice some of the more obvious variations of this, such as the close-up on the interviewee's hands during moments of stress); the use of shaky camerawork to signify urgency and immediacy (even in the age of the steadicam, this is still a frequent tactic and is often used in carpark confrontations); the gratuitous use of the live cross (to a courthouse, say, and a reporter who can tell us that there is nothing to report at this time) which displays the power of the technology itself; and the use of the 'noddy' (the re-recording of interviewers' questions or responses after the conclusion of the interview) to simulate the conventions of a 'real' conversation rather than the more formally structured interview process which has actually occurred.

Other legitimising strategies include the employment of a discourse of consensus and democratic discovery whereby the interviewer willingly accepts their implicit surrogacy for the average viewer by routinely referring to issues which might concern 'the average person in the street'—asking 'what about the viewer at home?' and so on. Speaking for the viewer in a kind of 'ventriloquism' (cf. Hall et al. 1978), the skilled news and current affairs presenter works away at removing the traces of mediation between the program, the content and its viewers, while simultaneously building familiarity and trust in their capacity to perform a social service for the audience.

Given the potential power of this relationship, it is not surprising that a great deal of the existing analysis of television news and current affairs is devoted to outlining the precise cultural and political assumptions embedded in the industrial processes of story selection, transformation and representation. Some of this work, such as that of the Glasgow Media Group (1976), has been profoundly useful in explaining how simple and routine production practices can have significant political effects. In the coverage of industrial disputes, for instance, the choice to interview the employer in his office and the unionist on the picket line might seem perfectly reasonable and practical but, in terms of how each is likely to be read by an audience, not at all impartial. Understanding such factors has encouraged the subjects of media attention to take a little more interest in how they are represented—even on the supposedly objective terrain of the evening news. The limitation of this kind of research, however, is that it can be appropriated to support an overly simple, conspiratorial account of television news producers and their personal political objectives that would be vigorously and justifiably denied by those concerned.

Such accounts also overlook another factor which may be far more important to these producers. Much of the work of news and current affairs programming is devoted to shoring up the appeal and authority of the specific program in comparison with competing programs. This is the commercial reality. Television news and current affairs are flagship formats within a highly competitive industry which has downsized newsrooms as a means of cutting costs, and which is continually trying to find ways of providing a service that will interest viewers more but cost proprietors less. The credibility of a news service is a bankable commodity, but it is easier, quicker and sometimes even cheaper to build credibility through, for instance, the promotion of a key personality or the occasional live cross rather than through the quality of story selection, innovative story-telling or the allocation of more resources into investigative reporting.

Most of us recognise that the relationship promoted between the audience and the news or current affairs presenter is constructed. However, as long as they present their material without producing a clear disjunction between our view of the world and theirs, most of us are prepared to play along and allow them to operate as our representatives. Maintaining the 'fit' between the apparent world view of the presenter and that of the individual audience member has become a special skill; it involves both a stylised and deliberate mode of address (a way of speaking to the audience that may be program- or format-specific, or tied up with the identity of that presenter), and the presenter's specific ability to routinely enact a 'special relationship' between the presenter and the projected audience. An example of this, embodied at its most economical, would be former *A Current Affair* host Ray Martin's wry twinkle and slight turn of the head at the end of a story, cruelly but accurately lampooned in the influential ABC satire *Frontline*, in host Mike Moore's habit of uttering an emphatically thoughtful 'Mmmm' at the end of every story. Performed well, such moments can turn the provisional relationship between the individual presenter and their audience into a contract of committed identification that encourages networks to invest heavily in the promotion of that presenter as a means of winning and maintaining their audiences.

Television news and current affairs are formats which, though highly constructed, have to mask the processes of construction if they are to be trusted and believed—little wonder that academic and community discussion of television news and current affairs circulates around the key political, cultural and social contradictions seen to underpin its contemporary practice. News and current affairs programming is caught between the competing (sometimes mutually exclusive) imperatives of providing information and entertainment; between the requirement for objectivity and the necessity of analysis; between offering high-quality journalism for their colleagues and media commentators, as against the commercial necessity of being popular with an audience of non-journalists. As a result of some of their responses to these conflicting imperatives, news and current affairs programs in recent years have been accused of excessive sensationalism, of a failure of credibility, of the blurring or hybridisation of information and entertainment genres and of a decline in ethical standards. They remain, however, the frontline in the competition between networks for Australian audiences.

TELEVISION NEWS AND CURRENT AFFAIRS IN AUSTRALIA

News has been fundamental to television in Australia from the beginning. The BBC was slow to exploit the visual capacities of television in its early newscasts (initially it just ran the radio news over a slide of the BBC logo!) and the first

American network newscasts were forced to struggle with the limited technology available to provide filmed material. However, television arrived in Australia (or, at least, in Sydney and Melbourne) at a point when the basic formats for television news had been established internationally, and when (as the 1978 feature film *Newsfront* showed us) it could capitalise on the existence of a well-developed newsreel industry to produce enough filmed footage to satisfy the audience's hunger for evidence of 'the wonders of television'. The celebrated moments when curious Australian citizens gathered in front of electrical stores (or, in my case, in a marquee in the park across the road) frequently involved watching the news. Virtually from the outset, the evening news on one commercial channel or another (predominantly those of the Nine Network in most capital cities other than Perth) has occupied a spot in the top ten rating programs. Also from the beginning, the evening news has been seen as the flagship, initially for the channel and more recently for the network. When the ABC began broadcasting, it was reluctant even to name its announcers on air; now, television news readers have become key personalities, prominent markers of the identity of the networks.

Australian current affairs programming is more recent, and slightly less securely placed. The ABC's weekly program *Four Corners* began in 1961 and set about creating the conditions within which current affairs programming could be produced. (These conditions included, for instance, some acceptance from politicians that they were obliged to defend their positions in public through, among other things, interviews with television journalists.)[1] The first attempt to run anything like the nightly current affairs programs we see today occurred in 1965. This was *Telescope*, modelled on the 1950s British program *Tonight*, produced by Channel Ten, and anchored by Bill Peach. While *Telescope* started out as a twenty-five-minute program, four nights a week, it was soon reduced to a fifteen-minute segment folded into the nightly news. The first successful venture into nightly current affairs was ABC-TV's *This Day Tonight (TDT)*, which began as a half-hour weeknight program in 1967 (again with Bill Peach as the founding anchor), and ran until 1978.

Innovative and adventurous, *TDT* is usually seen as the gold standard for Australian current affairs because of its commitment to investigative reporting, its evident relish in confronting politicians, and the fact that so many of those who worked on the program went on to become high-profile figures in Australian television (among them George Negus, Gerald Stone, Michael Willesee, Peter Luck, Stuart Littlemore, Mike Carlton, Paul Murphy, Caroline Jones, Ray Martin and Kerry O'Brien). At its peak, *TDT* routinely topped the ratings for its timeslot. On the commercial networks, similar levels of success have been enjoyed by the various formations of *A Current Affair* (the first series began in 1971, hosted by Michael Willesee), *Willesee* and *Sixty Minutes*.

Current affairs programs have played a crucial role in the commercial competition between networks. Eventually, as a result of this competition, Channel Ten was forced out of the current affairs business altogether—producing the current situation where the Seven and Nine Networks slug it out every weeknight at 6.30 p.m. in their attempts to capture the audience for prime-time viewing from 7.00 p.m. onwards. As we shall see below, however, while the battles continue to rage on with a grim ferocity, in recent years the audience available for capture has begun to shrink.

The history of these forms of programming in Australia has witnessed some dramatic changes over the years. Networking has turned local news editions into a complex amalgam of local and national style and content; the availability of live satellite feeds and access to twenty-four-hour cable channels has transformed the coverage of international events, and while the relationship between the news reporter and their subject has become much less respectful, it is also much more informative. The introduction of pay TV to Australia (see Chapter 5) has changed our potential relation to breaking international news, as well as our habitual modes of consuming news—in the latter case, for instance, challenging the centrality of the early evening news bulletin to the home viewing schedule. Consumer issues stories have dominated current affairs programs, displacing politics over the years. The continuing importance of current affairs audiences to political debate, however, is implicit in the increasingly institutionalised practice of using these programs' presenters to chair televised debates between party leaders at election time. The power of television current affairs to influence broader debates has become significant as well.

Both formats, however, have been accused of giving way to commercial pressures over the years, with a subsequent loss of responsibility to the information needs of the public. When the federal government finally sanctioned the establishment of national networks in the late 1980s, it ushered in a period of intense competition between Nine, Seven and Ten. At the forefront of this competition, as always, were the news and current affairs programs. At the time, these programs were mirror images of each other, occupying the same timeslot, employing the same format and, in the case of news, presenting very much the same repertoire of stories. So competition concentrated on such differentiating factors as the audience appeal of those in front of the camera and the promotability of the night's key stories as exclusive, entertaining and visually exciting. Competition for exclusive rights to stories encouraged the kinds of arrangements usually referred to as chequebook journalism (that is, paying subjects for their stories in return for exclusivity); the need to provide entertaining stories encouraged the sensational, the conflictual and (overwhelmingly) the visually spectacular, and the need to represent everything coming up on the screen as new and exciting, encouraged a particularly hyperbolic mode of self-presentation. Such attributes have provoked a critique of the 'tabloidisation' of news and current affairs—not only on Australian television but also in the United Kingdom and the United States (where the competition from pay TV has provided the major impetus). I will return to that issue later in this chapter.

Suffice to say at this point that in recent years the target for arguments about the 'dumbing down' of news and current affairs has been the evening commercial current affairs programs—particularly the market leader, *A Current Affair*. While *A Current Affair* has maintained its ratings and earned its former host, Ray Martin, a Gold Logie, it is widely regarded as having done so by heading downmarket. As I noted above, the battle for market leadership in this field has resulted in an increasing emphasis on promoting the specific contents of each program. *A Current Affair, Real Life* and, more recently, *Today Tonight* have had to find ways of differentiating their program from their competitors on a night-by-night basis. Given their similar view of what the audience finds inter-esting and entertaining—the stories on small business scams, bad back cures and weight loss treatments, the use of hidden cameras, and foot-in-the-door (or what has been called in America 'attack') journalism—the ground for competition has been largely that of exclusivity: of running a story which is not available to the opposition. One way of doing this is to spend more time generating promotable stories in-house; another way is by paying subjects for the exclusive rights to their stories. A consequence of these commercial strategies has been that nightly current affairs programs have moved away from what was once their primary objective: providing background to and analysis of the day's news stories. Less current affairs on commercial channels is devoted to the day's (or the week's) news agenda; more is devoted to the 'infotainment' end of the news spectrum. As a result, the once complementary relation between news and current affairs is changing, and the formats are starting to mutate.

This has affected news as well as current affairs. Competition between networks in Australia produced a distinctive group of news programs in the mid-1980s, which blurred considerably the distinction between news, information and entertainment (cf Turner 1996a). The cult success of Clive Robertson's Sydney late night news program *Newsworld* led to its being networked by the Seven network all over Australia in 1987. Robertson, a former ABC radio breakfast show host, presented a highly idiosyncratic version of news and comment in the late-night slot of 10.30 p.m. Robertson spurned the objectivity of the conventional newsreader, offering acerbic comment not only on the content of the news stories he introduced but also on the manner in which they were constructed. He exercised his own preferences, too, on what was suitable material to read—sports stories, for instance, were screwed up and thrown away on air. Robertson was the reverse of objective, his relation to his material critical and parodic, and he was frequently visibly depressed by what he did for a living. To a nation used to the objective, the reliable and the self-controlled in its newsreaders, Robertson was an unexpected breath of fresh air.

The success of Robertson's show produced a response from the Nine Net-work, luring Graham Kennedy out of retirement in 1988 to present *Graham Kennedy's News Hour* (later retitled *Coast to Coast*) in the 10.30 p.m. timeslot. Here the confusion created by Kennedy's disrespect for TV news conventions was even more radical. Kennedy was a comedian and thus made only token attempts to model his delivery on that of the conventional television newsreader. He read the news and made jokes about what he was reading, but this immediately produced irate responses from viewers who felt that some stories were simply not a laughing matter. A newsreader was introduced to read the stories in separate segments, while Kennedy provided entertaining chat with a sidekick (John Mangos or Ken Sutcliffe), and the newsreader himself became the butt of Kennedy's jokes. Still, the format was an uncomfortable one until an audience was introduced who could laugh at Kennedy's jokes while also providing a laughtrack to guide those watching at home. This finally proved to be an effective strategy, turning news-talk into comedy. Robertson and Kennedy battled head to head over the remainder of 1988, significantly increasing the sets in use for the 10.30 p.m. timeslot. By the end of 1989, Kennedy had won the battle, Robertson's show had folded and Kennedy had the timeslot to himself. Ironically—and in a twist typical of the politics of network television—Kennedy declined to return to the show in 1990, and after a brief attempt to run it with comedian Gretel Killeen as replacement host, Channel 9 hired Robertson to present *Robbo's World Tonight* instead.

In 1990, a further hybrid program, Steve Vizard's *Tonight Live*, appeared. This program was initially designed to enable Ten to compete with Seven's Robertson and Nine's Kennedy and their transgressive blend of news, current affairs and talk in the 10.30 p.m. timeslot. Although it borrowed most of its format from David Letterman's late-night talk shows in the United States, *Tonight Live* also included a pitch to Robertson's news audiences with live news updates from newsreader Jennifer Keyte. Never entirely integrated into the format, the news segments nevertheless remained as a constitutive component for the life of the program. *Tonight Live* was very successful, picking up an audience share of 42.3 per cent in its first year of production, winning Vizard a Gold Logie in 1992, and in its last year, when even the host seemed to have become bored with it, rating 30.2 per cent. Under the heat of the competition, Nine folded *Robbo's World Tonight* in 1992, gave up the genre-bending exercise and replaced it with the conventional late-night news bulletin, *Nightline*, hosted by Jim Whaley.

All of these programs were news, current affairs and talk show hybrids which to varying degrees subverted the conventions of television news and current affairs in order to exploit their potential for light entertainment. They were innovative and extremely popular. They turned what had been a graveyard timeslot into the location for a fierce ratings contest—and, often, very lively television. Ironically, while none of these three programs identified itself with conventional news programs, the ultimate consequence of this ratings contest was that by 1994 they had all been replaced by a 10.30 p.m. conventional news bulletin. At the time of writing, there are still three substantial late-night news bulletins in the timeslot, with the ABC running its high-end current affairs program, *Lateline*, there as well. Although it is customary to accuse television of dumbing down its programming in order to chase audiences, the development of the late-night news bulletins and their proven capacity to build their audiences (*Nightline*, for instance, recorded an audience growth of 18.5 per cent from its inception to 1998) provides a significant counter-narrative which suggests that innovative strategies for reaching the news audience have been—and can still be—successful.

THE AUDIENCES FOR NEWS AND CURRENT AFFAIRS IN AUSTRALIA

Nevertheless, although the various shifts in format and content outlined above all constitute attempts to differentiate network products and win a larger share of the national audience, it has to be said that in the most contested territory, prime-time programming, such attempts have not really had much impact. In the case of the prime-time news and current affairs programs, there is very little evidence that anything has been gained in terms of extending the reach of these programs into the viewing community.

The networks have known for some time, for instance, that news and current affairs programs have been attracting an ageing audience. The broad demographic addressed by these programs is skewed towards those over 39, and current audience figures suggest that they have the strongest appeal for those over 50. There have been endeavours, from time to time, to win back the youth audience by addressing their known distaste for the conventional news and current affairs formats. Youth audiences see these formats as 'visually boring, narrow and conservative in the range of points of view [they] canva[ss]'; worse, they routinely treat 'youth culture as an object of derision or prurience' (Turner 1996b; see also Sternberg 1995). Of course, this does not only affect television news; all mainstream news providers across the various media are finding that the youth demographic is using them less frequently. Newspapers, in particular, are facing a crisis as their readers are ageing as well.

The most interesting attempts to reverse the trend in television over recent years, the ABC's *Attitude* and the Seven Network's *The Times*, both recast current affairs formats in a more youth-oriented mode through, among other things, the elimination of the authoritative adult presenter and the use of relatively complex strategies of visual design lifted from computer displays and music video. As programs, they were very different—*The Times* was probably the true inheritor of the *TDT* tradition in that it was iconoclastic, opinionated and cheeky, while *Attitude* was cooler, more investigative, but ultimately so worthy and serious that it appealed more to the parents than their children. However, both programs were damaged by the failure of network nerve: they were moved around the schedule in search of the youth audience (or, in *Attitude*'s case, in response to the requirements of other, better supported, programs) until the inevitable poor ratings rendered them unsustainable (Turner 1996a: 83–86). More recently, Seven's *The Big Breakfast*, a copy of the successful British morning chat show of the same name, has pitched for this audience at a time when all other free-to-air programming is addressing the adult at home.

Less widely acknowledged until recently was the fall-off in total audiences for television news and current affairs. In an extensive survey of audience numbers for television news and current affairs in Sydney between 1991 and 1998, conducted for *The Sydney Morning Herald*'s *The Guide* (22–28 June 1998), journalist Jon Casimir found that there had been a dramatic decline in the audience numbers for both forms of programming. Even though the total television audience there had grown by 8.6 per cent, the audience for the early evening news bulletin fell by an average of 10 per cent. To some extent, this could be accounted for by such variables as a decline in the total number of viewers in the time slots of 6.00–7.00 p.m. (a drop of 6 per cent) and 7.00–8.00 p.m. (a drop of 4.14. per cent), as well as the introduction of the late evening news on all channels—where, as we have seen, audiences have in fact grown substantially.

Nevertheless, the picture to emerge from Casimir's survey is sufficiently dramatic to demand better explanations than these. The market leader, *National Nine News*, for instance, had dropped 140 000 viewers or 23.1 per cent of its audience over the period surveyed, and *Seven National News* had dropped 75 000 viewers (18.1 per cent). Interestingly, considering their relatively peripheral involvement in the intense competition between the commercial networks, *ABC News* ran against the trend by gaining 38 000 viewers—an increase of 11.1 per cent. Further, Network Ten, having broken ranks and left the 6.00–7.00 p.m. timeslot to its competitors in order to offer a one-hour, so-called 'tabloid' news at 5.00 p.m., recorded a massive 19.6 per cent increase. It is not possible to read from these figures a guide to the right mix of news values or presentational format which would guarantee retention or even development of the audience. However, the interesting and paradoxical fact is that it is the top-rating news programs which have lost the largest share of their audience over the period surveyed. While they may have still maintained their lead in the ratings because of the slight drop in the total audience for the timeslot, their aggregated audience numbers reveal their failure to grow or even maintain their existing audience.

With current affairs audiences, the decline is even more pronounced, as well as more uniform across the commercial and public sectors, affecting ratings winners and losers alike. Over the period in question, the market leader, *A Current Affair*, had lost 29.2 per cent of its audience (202 000 viewers), *Today Tonight* had dropped 22.5. per cent (95 000 viewers) and *The 7.30 Report* had fallen 27.3 per cent (93 000 viewers). Of the weekly current affairs programs, *Four Corners* was down by 29.9 per cent (78 000 viewers), *Sixty Minutes* had lost 18.3 per cent (114 000 viewers), and the soon-to-be-canned *Witness* 16.2 per cent (52 000 viewers). While there is some question as to how generally these patterns have been repeated across other capital cities and regional markets, they challenge any suggestion that the changes in formats we have seen in recent years (the move downmarket, for instance) have been successful in arresting the drift of viewers away from these programming formats. At the same time, these changes in formats have provoked criticism about the kind of service these programs provide to the community—not in terms of the entertainment they might offer, but in terms of their claims still to operate in the critical tradition of the 'fourth estate'. Indeed, as Julianne Schultz (1998) suggests, there is now serious doubt as to whether the democratic assumption that the media serve as a watchdog over the interests of the public has much substance any longer. For some, the news media have become the enemy of democracy rather than its defender (see Franklin 1998).

THE CRITIQUE OF TELEVISION NEWS AND CURRENT AFFAIRS

In recent news and current affairs programming, there has been a shift away from politics and towards crime; away from the daily news agenda and towards editorially generated items promoted days in advance; away from information-based treatments of social issues and towards entertaining stories on lifestyles or celebrities; and towards an overwhelming investment in the power of the visual in the news as an entertaining spectacle (Turner 1999: 59). It is perfectly plausible to regard such shifts in content and approach simply as part of the ongoing evolution of the function of the media and the role of journalism within it. Certainly, it is abundantly clear that the media can no longer be viewed solely in terms of their provision of information, as much of their output constitutes a vital component of the processes through which cultural identities are adopted, shaped and disseminated. Nevertheless, the developments I describe have provoked a great deal of liberal concern about what is regarded as a broadly pervasive trend towards 'tabloidisation'. The tabloid format—a format identified with the popular press, usually seen to operate most definitively in the UK print media but often extended to include a wide range of television programming (news, current affairs, talkshows, 'reality TV' and so on)—is regarded by its critics as sensational, unreflective, inaccurate and irresponsible. In its application to television, the targets of the tabloidisation critique have been such tactics as the use of hidden cameras, reconstructions, the entrapment of interview subjects, and so on. The major point of concern in such cases has been either the incompatibility between these tactics and professional ethics, or a more abstract debate which hinges on what is regarded as an abuse of media power—and the assymetrical distribution of power that makes such abuse possible, even unavoidable.

It has to be acknowledged that some expressions of this kind of concern may be motivated by considerations of taste rather than ethics. Cultural studies theorists such as John Hartley have pointed out that there is nothing new in journalism which aims at being entertaining, or which opts for the sensational rather than the reflective. In his view, the current revaluation of what counts as news has opened the media up to new, hitherto silenced, voices in productive ways. Similarly, Catharine Lumby has argued in her two books, *Bad Girls* and *Gotcha*, that what conservative media critics have attacked as the 'dumbing down' of the media is actually a long-overdue process of democratisation:

> Contrary to the common view that the global mass media [have] suppressed
> political speech and replaced it with commercially viable drivel, I argue that the
> contemporary media sphere constitutes a highly diverse and inclusive forum in
> which a host of important issues once deemed apolitical, trivial and personal are
> now being aired. These new voices often speak in a language which is foreign to
> the rational, educated discourse we associate with the traditional quality media.
> But then, rational, educated conversations between experts are not the only
> meaningful kind of speech. (Lumby 1999: xii)

It would not be the first time that attacks on the democratisation of popular
culture have expressed themselves through accusations of falling standards and
cultural decline, so Lumby's work is an important counter-argument to be placed
alongside concerns about the decline in pertinence of notions of the fourth estate.

That said, it is worth asking whether, in fact, there has been a significant
change in the content and form of news and current affairs, and if it matters.
Whether we are witnessing a dumbing down or a diversification of the forms
and content of the media generally, it is clear that there are certain claims made
from within what John Langer (1998) calls 'the lament' for the decline of
journalism which can be tested empirically. I claimed at the beginning of this
section, for instance, that the content of news and current affairs programs had
moved away from politics and towards crime or more sensational stories. In
figures which come from a survey of television news and current affairs completed
during 1996 (Turner 1996c), crime and sport accounted for more than 50 per
cent of the Channel 9 news, and peaked at 40 per cent for the ABC bulletin.
In both cases, the treatment of politics varied significantly from week to week,
but reached a peak of 29.3 per cent for the ABC and 17.9 per cent for Channel
9. In relation to the claim that a significant number of current affairs stories
are produced solely for entertainment rather than for information, the survey
counted those stories which were not tied to the news agenda, and which
appeared to have been generated primarily for the purposes of 'infotainment'.
The percentage of infotainment stories generated by *A Current Affair* according
to this measure was just under 30 per cent, but for *The 7.30 Report* it was around
3 per cent.

Given these last figures, it is probably not surprising—nor entirely inappro-
priate—that, in Australia, the accusation of tabloidisation has been levelled at
commercial current affairs in particular. This may be a little unfair inasmuch as
TV current affairs is by no means the only, or even the most obvious, location
for 'tabloid' material (the print media and ABC TV are hardly free of this), but
I think it reflects a widespread dissatisfaction with the story mix generated by
the competition between the commercial networks I referred to earlier. According
to many observers, the continual recourse to small-time consumer scam stories
and the failure to find ways to make important political stories interesting has
dogged at least the last ten years of Australian current affairs. However, it has
to be admitted that such judgments cannot be freed of their taste assumptions—
that there is a preferred, and fixed, model for what constitutes an appropriate

story mix for current affairs programs—and that they have an elite or middle-class political orientation.

I have argued elsewhere that the concept of tabloidisation has a limited usefulness (Turner 1999), partly because of its implication in a conservative critique of popular culture and partly because it has been applied so indiscriminately to so many cultural symptoms that it is often simply implausible. Unfortunately, it is also a critique which television's competitors, particularly in the print media, are keen to seize upon as a means of challenging the medium's authority. As a result, it has probably diverted us from more important critical concerns with current affairs programs in Australia which have little to do with tabloidisation, although they may well have a lot to do with the competitive environment within which these programs operate and with the consequent pressure upon their staff and resources.

The most legitimate and urgent public criticism of current affairs programs must focus on the issue of their level of responsibility. In recent years, producers and reporters on current affairs programs have repeatedly demonstrated a worrying level of assurance in their capacity to advance the interests of the program, rather than those of the public, through their lack of concern for the effects of their actions on others. The ABC satire series *Frontline* has produced a virtual anthology of stories about the hubris and insouciance of current affairs program producers: episodes of *Frontline* have included thinly fictionalised depictions of Michael Willesee's extraordinary failure of judgment in interviewing a child being held hostage by two gunmen in a New South Wales farm; the successful request by a gunman holding office workers hostage in Brisbane to speak to a current affairs presenter on air; and the theft of photos and memorabilia from bereaved relatives in order to advance a story. The ABC's *Media Watch* has focused attention on the manipulation or entrapment of subjects through their coverage of the notorious case of the Paxtons, and the tragic suicide of a subject of a hidden camera story, Benny Mendoza. In all cases, the critique has focused on the way in which the misfortunes of relatively powerless people have been turned into entertainment, and how this represents a travesty of the more noble purposes once claimed for this kind of programming.

While these instances emphasise the need for a review of the ethical practices on these programs, they also raise another question. Australia has very little in the way of protection for subjects of news and current affairs stories who feel they have been misrepresented, entrapped or subjected to an unwarranted intrusion upon their rights to privacy—but not necessarily defamed or slandered. There is no adequate, speedy process of redress (cf. Tiffen 1994) or correction in place, nor any independent administrative body charged with the responsibility of protecting the ordinary citizen against the media. Given the way in which stories are now generated in television current affairs, the establishment of such protection and such an administrative body is well overdue.

In *Gotcha*, Catharine Lumby (1999: 220–23) refers to the ambivalent way in which people talk about media practice: that while they are relatively unconcerned about how the media is regulated in general, and while they certainly exercise their right to watch the programs they prefer and shun those they don't, they do have concerns about specific instances of media behaviour which are seen to be irresponsible or callous. The content of news and current affairs programs is one of the areas where public concerns are most routinely expressed through personal complaints to the channel, on talkback radio or letters to the editor, or in submissions to publicly funded inquiries. Whether it be the representation of violence, issues of taste or political bias, there is a high degree of community concern about these programs which is consistent with an equally high level of certainty that such programs have an effect on the community which consumes them. There is no escaping the fact that news and current affairs programs perform a crucial public function in shaping our view of the world and in locating the issues and topics of concern for large sections of the population. This fact, coinciding with the clearly contrasting evidence of a decline in total audience numbers actually watching this important genre of programming, should lead us to think a little more about the cultural function of these programs and thus the regulatory structures within which they operate.

NOTE

1 Memoirs of this period, including those of Bill Peach (1992) and Robert Raymond, the first producer and presenter of *Four Corners* (1999), point out that, before the arrival of television current affairs programs, politicians could silence criticism by simply refusing to appear to defend their positions. Due to the strict requirement that balance be achieved within the one program, producers were required to seek a response from the relevant minister if criticism was to be aired. If the minister refused to appear, this effectively stopped the item from running. *Four Corners* and then *TDT* adopted the now routine strategy of announcing that the government member concerned had declined their invitation but still ran the story. Once this method was established, politicians were more readily available for interviews (see also McKnight 1998).

Seven Frances Bonner

Lifestyle programs: 'No choice but to choose'

For the week 9–15 May 1999, the top ten television programs nationally consisted of three dramas, one each of a game show, a news bulletin and a current affairs show, plus four lifestyle programs: *Getaway*, *Hot Property*, *Better Homes and Gardens* and *Good Medicine*.

Lifestyle has been the boom program type of the 1990s (as the mini-series was for the 1980s), yet prior to the arrival of the category of lifestyle programming in the late 1980s, related programs were hidden in a category called 'information', usually agglomerated with 'religious' and 'arts' into what was still the smallest program category identified. The program that is regarded as the first of the lifestyle wave, *Burke's Backyard*, started in 1987, but signs of what was to come were evident in Australian programming long before this.

As with most of the changes to Australian television, the precursors of lifestyle shows were developed on the ABC before moving to the wealthier pastures of commercial television. As well as the move to greater production budgets, the shift can be seen as sealing the move from 'information' to 'lifestyle' as product promotion became more central, but it is necessary to be cautious about this claim. Although it would be difficult for contemporary viewers to perceive the links to lifestyle shows immediately, one of the first programs that I believe showed signs of what was to come was a very popular ABC program of the 1970s, *The Inventors*. This popular prime-time program started in 1970 and continued until 1981. It was a panel show where each week a number of inventors would present their products for display and investigation. Signs of lifestyle programming characteristics could be seen in the prevalence of domestic gadgets among the inventions discussed, the insistent stress on availability and the way the program was promoted through the personalities of the panel members—especially the quirkier ones like Diana 'Bubbles' Fisher, whose regular question, 'Does it come in other colours?', rapidly became a popular catchphrase.

When *The Inventors* finished, the ABC screened a more serious and certainly more scientific look at innovation in its adaptation of the BBC program *Tomorrow's World*, renamed *Towards 2000*. This was a much more conventional information program than *The Inventors*, which had drawn more on light entertainment practices. In 1987 it moved to Channel 7 with its key production and on-air team under the slightly changed title *Beyond 2000*, then as ratings dropped, it shifted to Channel 10 in 1993 before finally disappearing from broadcast outlets. Unlike other examples, it has continued life through its international pay TV presence (established through packaging while it was still on air) as well as through its role as the foundation of the production company Beyond. The departure of the program from broadcast television, despite the financial strength of the production company, demonstrates how thoroughly information has been replaced by lifestyle.

Although information programs were an important part of the public service remit of the ABC, the network under the more populist direction of David Hill had no hesitations about screening new programs which were thorough-going examples of lifestyle shows. From 1990 to 1993, Maggie Tabberer and her then-partner Richard Zachariah presented *The Home Show*. Channel 9's version, *Our House*, started in 1993. *Everybody* (ABC, 1991–94) was a health-focused lifestyle program featuring, among others later to become fixtures of commercial lifestyle programs, Gabriel Gaté, Dr Kerryn Phelps and Trish Goddard (who moved to present a similar show on Channel 9 then Channel 10 before returning to the United Kingdom to host her own talk show, *Trisha*). The ABC's role as developer of lifestyle programming ceased in 1994 with a scandal focused around *Holiday*, itself the inspiration for Channel 9's *Getaway*.

Holiday, which ran from 1987 to 1994, was produced in cooperation with the Australian Tourism Commission and involved a team reporting on various Australian holiday destinations. An item screened on *Sixty Minutes* in 1994 exposed the extent to which it was indebted to its sponsors and the debate around this reduced the importance of lifestyle programming for the ABC, as well as contributing substantially to the resignation of David Hill as the ABC's managing director at the end of 1994. Objections were raised both to the provision of favourable treatment to sponsors of programs like *Holiday*, *Everybody* and *The Home Show*, but also to the way that this was done through programs outsourced to production companies run by former ABC staffers. The key to the complaints of critics like Errol Simper, though, was that the programs were not information and thus should not have been screened on the ABC: '[t]houghtful television viewers turned to the national broadcaster to be confronted with shallow infotainment' (Simper 1994). From this point on, lifestyle programs—having been tested on the ABC where their attractiveness to audiences and even their appeal to sponsors had been demonstrated—became, with very few exceptions, the domain of commercial broadcasters.

The disappearance of dedicated consumer watchdog programs like the ABC's long running *The Investigators* during the ascendancy of lifestyle is not incidental. Watchdog segments still exist, occasionally within lifestyle programs but more often in current affairs shows. Having a whole program predicated on the need for providers of goods and services to be monitored for sharp practice by an outside body capable of disseminating negative publicity indicates a perception of the operation of the market as one where the powerless need help to combat injustice. This has been relegated to an occasional comment while the concentration shifts instead to giving advice on product choice.

WHAT IS LIFESTYLE?

It was not only as a program category that 'lifestyle' was new; the term itself has only recently had much prominence. In popular use, until the mid-1980s it could be seen primarily in the phrase 'alternative lifestyles', referring to the living practices of hippies or ferals, or within health promotion literature where lifestyle was what needed to be changed to prevent disease and apparently consisted of nutrition, exercise and, in some cases, sexuality. Both of these instances carry the important notion of choice, but they also imply a degree of stasis: that once adopted they are resistant to change, which is certainly how lifestyles were conceived by sociologists until recently. In late-modern societies, though, Anthony Giddens (1991) emphasises the breadth of the concept and the implication of continuing change:

> we all not only follow lifestyles, but in an important sense are forced to do so—
> we have no choice but to choose. A lifestyle can be defined as a more or less
> integrated set of practices which an individual embraces, not only because such
> practices fulfil utilitarian needs, but because they give material form to a particular
> narrative of self-identity. (Giddens 1991: 81)

And Mike Featherstone (1991) notes that:

> within contemporary consumer culture it connotes individuality, self-expression and
> a stylistic self-consciousness. One's body, clothes, speech, leisure pastimes, eating
> and drinking preferences, home, car, choice of holidays etc. are to be regarded as
> indicators of the individuality of taste and sense of style of the owner/consumer.
> (Featherstone 1991: 82)

The list of sites where style or taste was able to be evident overlaps substantially with the concerns of lifestyle television, but the assertion of individuality in this statement needs more attention. Featherstone argues very emphatically against the idea of a free-for-all with no links between classes and tastes. In this he is in accord with Giddens, who warns about seeing lifestyle only in terms of advertising images and commodified consumption and thus as something available only to the more wealthy, seeing class and other forms of social inequalities in part defined by 'differential access to forms of self-actualisation' (Giddens 1991: 6). For both writers, Pierre Bourdieu's analysis of the stratifying function of lifestyles is highly important, establishing as it does the way in which tastes and consumption practices confer distinction on those operating on one rather than another set of routines (1989; see also Bennett et al. 1999).

Everyone has a lifestyle which acts in part to assert who that person is and where he or she fits in society, and in a consumer culture this is evinced by the purchase and display of goods and services. Television has an important role to play in this, through being a site where the options and the consequences of their adoption are displayed and their consumption advocated. The contradictions whereby lifestyle is held both to reveal individuality and membership of particular social groups are themselves characteristic of television, especially the dominant commercial form, which must simultaneously maximise profits by seeking large markets and addressing viewers as individuals to maximise consumption of advertised products.

WHAT IS LIFESTYLE TV?

Lifestyle television addresses an individualised viewer with advice about consumption practices ostensibly designed to improve the quality of life. Actual audience members are addressed only inasmuch as they recognise themselves and their desires within what the program is offering, but the fantasies on offer are structured to be inclusive wherever possible. In the overwhelming majority of cases, the advice given aims to bring viewing consumers up to date with recent practices and fashions so that they may maintain an appearance not too out of step with their peers. The common assumption is that the viewer has a problem which can be solved by a product or service; the problem may be of the nature of insufficient light in a room which can be solved by a new type of skylight, or it may be one more directly tied to self-identity such as worries about appearing old-fashioned, which can be solved by advice about more contemporary products.

The first type of problem is one that would be amenable to treatment within the older information program but the second, centred on fashionability and its meanings inscribed on the viewing self, needs a program form which provides provisional solutions amenable to constant updating. In the first case, once the lighting problem is solved no more is needed apart from intermittent maintenance, but if the room can be read as a sign speaking about the owner, then advice can be sought and proffered on other, more frequently occurring, bases. Its colours and appurtenances may speak of decades or interests past, once exclusive objects may have since become mass produced, and fabrics appropriate to a previous family composition may be misleading now. The primarily functional role of what previously was conceived as 'information' is relegated to the background, while the semiotic power of lifestyle moves to centre stage.

A more direct comparison of information and lifestyle programming can be seen by looking at two very different programs ostensibly dealing with the same kind of topic. *Money* is one of the great success stories of lifestyle television, produced by Tim Clucas (who had been the original producer of *Beyond 2000*, but more recently made the lifestyle hit *Sex*) and broadcast during prime time on the Nine Network since 1993. *Business Sunday* is also a Nine Network show but screens at 8.00 a.m. on Sundays and has been on air since 1986. Both programs deal with financial concerns, but *Business Sunday* targets business people and substantial investors with news about the economy and other financial information, assuming a reasonably high degree of economic literacy together with a willingness to pay attention to a television program with longish segments, lots of talking heads and few, if any, gimmicks. *Money* is the reverse, offering gimmicks galore, short segments, colour and movement and very little requirement for economic knowledgeability. The audience is provided with hints primarily about maximising returns on household expenditure, with investment given much less prominence.

After the success of *Money* had been demonstrated, most of its more business-oriented topics were hived off into a separate program, *The Small Business Show*, screened each week before *Business Sunday*. Despite the oddity of the message of financial prudence in a commercial medium based on encouraging expenditure, *Money*—targeted at wage and salary earners—advocates a lifestyle of sensible consumption aimed at contributing to the creation and display of a self at home in a deregulated market economy. Its role in the continuing process of making share ownership ordinary rather than something only engaged in by the few should not be underestimated. The Sunday morning programs look at managing, making and investing money, but have only the most distant interest in how it could be converted into lifestyle markers.

It is important to note that it is not only non-fiction programs that have been influenced by the growing centrality of lifestyle; drama programs have been shown to provide data about the habitus of emerging social segments and none more notably than the new petite bourgeoisie (see Bonner and du Gay 1991; Andersen 1995). Though both these studies centre on the late 1980s program *thirtysomething*, many of the same points can be made about the current American sitcoms so popular with viewers in their teens and twenties untargeted by lifestyle shows. Because the kind of niche market required in their home territories by dramas like *thirtysomething* or the more recent *Sex and the City* can only be delivered by larger audience fractions than Australia can provide, locally made equivalents are unavailable. The whole weight of lifestyle programming on Australian television is targeted at minimally differentiated markets by non-fiction shows.

The classic example: Burke's Backyard

As noted above, the first undisputed lifestyle program on Australian television was *Burke's Backyard*. Presented by the horticulturalist and author Don Burke, the program was a development from his radio show and newspaper column, initially as a late-night, low-budget television program but soon an hour-long Friday-night prime-time show repeated on Sunday afternoons. The program's focus on the backyard gives it a distinctive Australianness which brings together various sized plots of land from terrace gardens to hobby farms and allows the combination of gardening segments with exterior building tasks and the long-running 'road test' segment dealing with the suitability of particular pets for various situations. Occasionally the program ventures inside the house, especially when it visits the week's 'celebrity gardeners', but these latter segments are always offset by the ordinary folk Burke calls on.

The tenth anniversary program began by juxtaposing the past and the present as the Burke of 1987 introduced the first program saying it was 'created for the ordinary Australian family a bit like mine, one which lives in their backyard. We will look at gardening, but at much, much more . . .' This was followed by the 1997 Burke commenting how 'we'd sort of dreamt up the idea of doing a lifestyle television program but had no real idea of how to do it, because it hadn't been done anywhere in the world to that stage'. From the beginning, then, the keynotes of the program had been the Australian family's life and how it was embodied in the figure of the host. Only later was it possible to enunciate the focus on the 'lifestyle'.

Although the focus of the program is suburban, the touchstone is the bush—or more accurately 'the Bush', which can be evoked in conversation about the past, in reference to native plants or in the incorporation into backyard settings of bush memorabilia. Each week the tone is set by the bush band, Bullamakanka, singing the customised version of what was once just a song called 'My Backyard'. It all helps the program to maintain its place with the holiday and the fishing programs' 'mythologising of Australia, its landscape and people' simultaneously with domesticating it, as Sue Turnbull notes (1993: 19). One of the most telling of its many makeovers was its transformation of the inner Sydney terrace of a soap actress into a 'real old country backyard' complete with bits of farm implements and a simple clothesline with traditional clothes-prop. Rural detritus and the signs of poverty were transformed into markers of a kitsch distinction.

Burke is the linch-pin of the show (and indeed the owner of the production company), the man through whom the bush is articulated for the city in a thoroughly suburban way. Archetypally the ordinary bloke, a little on the short side ('nuggety' in the vernacular used by the program), able to turn his hand to most things and at ease with all types of people, Burke is one of the most skilled exponents of televisual sincerity Australia has produced. Television presenters operating in their own personae are chosen in part because of their ability to project appropriate images for their respective programs. Burke's ability to convey sincerity and trustworthiness is key to his place as the person who has been the longest lasting of those persuading us about the desirability of this week's lifestyle suggestions.

The appeal of the program so identified with the personality can be seen in another piece of tenth anniversary program information, this time from what Deborah Malor (1991: 61) calls the 'fact tag' flashed on screen at the end of a segment; in the first ten years on air, *Burke's Backyard* distributed more than two million fact sheets. After the anniversary had passed, a print magazine version of *Burke's Backyard* appeared and less than a year later its circulation was over a hundred thousand a month, putting it ahead of such long-term alternatives as *Gardening Australia* and *Australian Home Beautiful*. The magazine was published by Australian Consolidated Press, making it—like Channel Nine—a Packer property. As well as calling on the same cast of experts that the program does, the magazine provides behind-the-scenes glimpses of the making of the show and extends the range of material covered.

Problem examples: Good Medicine, fishing programs, fashion and food

While it is easy to see home improvement programs or shows investigating different types of holiday destinations as lifestyle programs, other types are less straightforward. *Good Medicine* is concerned with illness, its prevention and treatment and thus might seem not to be susceptible to 'individuality, self-expression and a stylistic self-consciousness'. Surely illness is beyond these concerns. Yet, despite the word 'medicine' in the title, the program is much more concerned with well-being. Thus it is readily able to be dominated by fashion and novelty (the latest treatment, the newest advice on nutrition) and the project of the self, nowhere more than in its recurrent focus on cosmetic surgery. While for most people, until very recently, modulations in the signs of identity stopped short of surgery, the resituating of face lifts and similar procedures from the domain of vain rich women into common topics for mass market magazines and television shows is a significant shift in the reach of the term 'lifestyle'.

Equally informative is what is revealed by a consideration of the place of fishing. Uneasily situated between sport and leisure, shows such as *Rex Hunt's Fishing Adventures*, *Hooked on Water* and *Wildfish* attest to the popularity of the subject but are more often described by the broader term 'infotainment' than as 'lifestyle'. This can indicate how, on Australian television, the category 'lifestyle' is particularly articulated to the domestic and the family—even the travel shows seem happiest when talking of family holidays or comparing being away with being at home. The inclusion of fish cooking segments or, in *Hooked on Water*, other water-based leisure pursuits moves the programs towards or away from clear membership of the lifestyle category. Soon after he started presenting fishing on television, Rex Hunt was quoted saying '[f]ishing is one of the world's great pastimes. In bringing it into people's living rooms we can also show it's not the last bastion of men. That it's also enjoyable for ladies and kids.' (Stapledon 1993: 34) Lifestyle programs are not a fully gendered genre, but as Hunt's living room and kids' comments indicate, shows aimed solely at male activities outside the home are problematic inclusions. Fishing shows with their predominantly male audiences (the two commercial ones are screened on Saturday afternoons), their narratives of contest (man versus fish) and their opposition to the domestic stake a claim to being sport or at most infotainment. Yet, even without cooking segments, the propriety of regarding them as part of the lifestyle category, contrary to Australian practice, is indicated by the role of fishing in the assertion of distinction and the frequency with which the programs advocate particular patterns of consumption.

Food and cooking programs sit unhappily in the lifestyle category. It is very rare for a program devoted solely to cooking and food to be broadcast in prime time on a commercial channel. Cooking programs are absent from the top-rating lifestyle programs of the 1990s and those which have any noticeable popularity (like the *Two Fat Ladies* series) are to be found on the public broadcasters. Yet cooking programs are among the oldest types of information show, and the place of food in the distinctions of taste and status is undeniable. Cooking segments can certainly be found within other lifestyle programs: *Healthy Wealthy and Wise* has long featured Iain Hewitson preparing food outdoors; *Better Homes and Gardens* uses food to bring its two concerns together; as we've seen, *Hooked on Water* shows fish cookery; and even *Gardening Australia* has been known to venture into the kitchen. But the only 'pure' cooking show on commercial television in 1999 was Geoff Jansz's *What's Cooking?* at 2.00 p.m. weekdays on Channel 9.

There could be some similarity in the absence of programs devoted to an even more important aspect of lifestyle—fashion itself. Again segments can be found, though much more rarely, in other lifestyle shows (though more commonly on daytime programs like *Denise*), but neither on public nor commercial channels is there an Australian clothes program. There is no local equivalent of that or of the highly popular British *The Clothes Show*. Perhaps it is that both fashion and food, unlike the other topics, reveal class and income difference too much, resisting the extent of homogenisation seen in the home and garden shows and exposing in the process some of the ideological contradictions of the possibility of individualised lifestyles as a basis for television programming in a country with a relatively small population.

CHARACTERISTICS OF LIFESTYLE TV

The development of the lifestyle category and the examples cited so far have set the stage for a closer look at what makes a lifestyle program. The majority of lifestyle programs are structured as magazines, but this is not a consequence of the rise of consumer culture or the recent development of print magazines existing in tandem with televisual ones. The magazine format, with its short, disparate segments united by some kind of general topic link and a continuing host, has been a staple of programming since the beginning of television. Sporting magazines like the *Wide World of Sports* are prime examples and so was the ABC light documentary program *Weekend Magazine* which ran from 1956 to 1985.

On-screen presenters are one of the prime characteristics of lifestyle programs, whether or not they are magazine style. Usually there are also reporters or other cast members, but they are not necessarily present each week, nor do they act as the glue holding the items together. The only recent exception is the SBS program *A Foodlover's Guide to Australia*, which usually depended on a narrating voice, presumably to offset the high costs (for an SBS production) of filming all over Australia for its thirty episodes. For some programs, especially those that are able to arrange contra deals with advertisers or sponsors, the cost of a 'name' presenter is the greatest production expenditure. The expenditure is justified not so much because of the internal cohesion produced through the presenter's continuity, but because of their role in promotion.

All on-screen personnel directly address viewers both in their speech and in their look to camera. The direct address aims to establish and maintain an intimacy between program and audience, through familiarly telling 'you at home' how to perform some task and through revealing snippets of personal information. *Better Homes and Gardens* was especially designed for this with its husband and wife presenting team and its 'studio' location supposedly within their own home. Banter between Noni Hazelhurst and John Jarratt purported to be ordinary domestic chat about collecting the children or being late for other tasks. A friendly intimacy is effectively required by any lifestyle presenter, since giving unsolicited advice to people constructed as strangers may appear officious, while giving advice to those represented as friends is a sign of caring.

One of the main modulations in the shift from information to lifestyle programming has been a devolution of the information function into extra-televisual sites. The information that once was provided during the program— even to the extent of advising viewers one week what they would need to buy to emulate instructions the next—is now routinely available through other means. The spread of domestic communications technologies during the 1990s can be traced quite straightforwardly by following how this has happened and the ways in which new media coexist with, rather than supplant, older ones is very clear.

Even before the tight links between current lifestyle programs and magazines of the same title, viewers would be directed to magazines for further details, but the fact sheet did not come into its own until lifestyle programs were fully developed. *Burke's Backyard* was the first to institutionalise them on a regular basis and may even have been the place where the term moved into common use (viewers had long been intermittently invited to 'write in for further details'). The fact sheet not only functions as immediate feedback about the popularity of individual items; over time it can serve to indicate fluctuations in numbers of devoted as opposed to casual viewers.

The most characteristic print companion to Australian lifestyle programs is the associated magazine. Far more than fact sheets, these provide the details that the program omits in its search for liveliness. Almost every one of the programs mentioned so far has a magazine, some of which pre-date the program, though more do not: *Better Homes and Gardens* was a magazine long before it spun off a television program, while *Burke's Backyard* had celebrated its tenth anniversary and *Money* its fifth before the related magazines appeared. For both *Good Medicine* and *Our House*, the magazine and program appeared more or less together. One term for television shows which share titles with magazines is 'masthead program', but this indicates particular production practices. The program is produced by the magazine publishers and made available to television channels by barter. That is, channels pay no money for the program and the magazine pays no money for advertising before, during and after the show; profit is generated for the magazine by increased sales consequent on the show and the advertising, while for the channel it comes from selling the remaining advertising space in the show. The structural similarities of the magazine format make the crossover either way easy to effect. The relationship is not totally reciprocal; print magazines do not require television programs as much as television is advantaged by a successful magazine. *Australian Good Taste* had a short run on Channel 10, but has not continued in its televisual form. Its status as the Woolworth's in-store magazine appears an adequate promotional tool; it rapidly entered the top twenty selling Australian magazines and has not required a continuing television show to stay there. Many more magazines have been rumoured to be intending to run a television show than have actually done so, and for magazines which are not directly lifestyle publications, celebratory one-offs seem sufficient: *Cleo* and *Australian Women's Weekly* both have had one or two masthead specials.

The first moves to increase the range of supplementary tools came with changes in telephony. Both the introduction of telephone-based information services (0800 and 055 numbers) and of domestic fax machines made the provision of contact information at the end of show a more complicated affair. The more recent addition of Internet addresses marks a further shift. Established lifestyle programs like *Money* have archives of fact sheets available on their Websites for those able to access them, and are able to continue to provide updated information even when they are not on air. For Channel Nine programs, the Packer Internet company ninemsn means a thoroughly integrated system with many opportunities for entry points and profitability. A slogan from the *Our House* Website indicates this: 'Not just a Website, but a TV show and a magazine. Get help navigating our new site, or meet the TV presenters here.' There is also an *Our House* club with contact details available from the site. It is no longer quite accurate to talk about these various other sites as 'supplements' to television. Instead, what is evident is that there has been a convergence between the media of television, magazines and the Internet such that while each can stand alone, any single one offers only a limited range of what is available. Substantial overlaps and references from one to another interact with material only available on one site to establish the way in which the ideal reader is one who accesses all three forms.

Even without these benefits for those that own the outlets (or those viewers who commit themselves most wholeheartedly to the show), separately delivered details have a number of advantages for the television programs. The presentation of instructions and advice which could be laboured, dull and unattractive on traditional information programs, and which could never be delivered at a pace suitable to all watching, no longer impedes the production of lively television. Demotic delivery ('add a slurp of olive oil'; 'whack on a coat of emulsion') allows personalities to flourish without alienating those who want to follow instructions but worry about what constitutes 'a slurp'. Fact sheets and telephone services can also be sources of extra revenue requiring much less outlay than books, though subsidiary marketing of this more traditional kind remains important.

A further characteristic of lifestyle programs—shared with many other kinds of non-fiction television programs—is the way in which ordinary people as well as celebrities are used on air. When Don Burke visits 'your' street or a reporter from *Money* uses a 'typical' office worker to show the advantages of using a particular financial product, the distinction between those showing and those viewing is reduced. In addition, the implicit argument of the programs—that the self is a project which requires work and the worked-on self is revealed through the lifestyle choices guided by and responsive to the program material—is strengthened.

Who watches?

Conventional wisdom asserts that lifestyle programs are targeted predominantly at women and at the middle-aged. The first of these is not because lifestyle is somehow intrinsically feminine, but because, as was seen earlier, domesticity is regarded as a key component of the programs. The gender divide can be supported. Figures for 13–19 June 1999 show five programs in the top fifteen for women: *Better Homes and Gardens* (no. 5), *Our House* (no. 7), *Good Medicine* (no. 8), *Burke's Backyard* (no. 9) and *Hot Property* (no. 13); only one rates there for men—*Burke's Backyard* at no. 14 with the others appearing between 18 and 27 (Dale 1999). The age distinction has been shown to be an even more significant marker of television program preferences. Programs rate very differently with viewers over and under 40. Age-differentiated national ratings for 2–8 August 1998 showed emphatic support for the view that lifestyle programming was an older viewers' taste: *Money* was the only program on the under-40s' top fifteen and that was at no. 15 itself. In contrast, four programs rated well with the over-40s: *Burke's Backyard* at no. 3; *Getaway* (no. 7); *Money* (no. 12) and *Our House* (no. 14).

Why the growth?

In trying to account for the growth of lifestyle programming during the late 1980s and 1990s, influences inside and outside the world of television need to be taken into account. It was during this period that the challenge to broadcast television from pay alternatives had to be acknowledged. Lifestyle programs were part of the answer for three major reasons: their localness, the comparative cheapness of production and their timeliness. In the main, lifestyle programs are locally produced rather than imported. Advice about gardening or financial planning comes most convincingly from people in the same country—indeed, preferably in the same state—and although not quite so obviously, the same applies to suggestions about home renovations.

Locally made lifestyle programs are certainly cheaper than locally made drama, but part of this cost-control requires the subsidising of costs by sponsors who will also favour local material since that is what they are likely to promote. Masthead programming is by far the most cost-efficient way for this to occur. The importance of timeliness—of the information being relevant now—to current ways of demonstrating distinction comes in here too. Importing programs generally involves a time-lag, and while this might be able to be used to accommodate the seasonal differences between the Northern and Southern Hemispheres, programs intended to provide advice about fashions in home decorating, for example, or recent treatments for health or beauty problems, could not easily sustain the appearance of talking of 'now' if known to be talking of 'then'. Some program types, though, are able to be imported (or for that matter exported). Cooking programs are the most common—arguably because of the links with tourism which characterise so many cooking shows (like *Far Flung Floyd*) and because of the importance of colourful personalities (see Bonner 1994; Strange 1998). Both personality and tourism can also be seen in one of the successes of Australian lifestyle exports: *Rex Hunt's Fishing Adventures*. It is no accident that it is these more problematic members of the lifestyle category that are the kind that are amenable to importation; they are also the kind most likely to be repeated.

Lifestyle programs can be seen to be cost-effective ways for broadcast channels to compete with pay television, precisely because—except for the premium channels—the majority of pay TV programs are repeats and the timeliness of most lifestyle shows militates against this. Yet cable channels totally devoted to lifestyle programs do exist, recycling dated local or imported programs, part of the package one gets 'free' with subscription. In larger markets, some new material is generated, but this is usually extremely low-budget, studio-based and live-to-air (at least for the first screening). In the United Kingdom, the Lifestyle Channel has a flower arranging program of this kind. Here, Foxtel's lifestyle channel constructs its schedule from Australian material that has had a past broadcast life, like *Gardening Australia* and *Healthy Wealthy and Wise*, together with imported material which has had no prior Australian screening like *The Great American Quilt* or the British *Antiques Roadshow*.

The central place of lifestyle programs in the televisual presence of consumer culture helps to solve another problem of contemporary television: technological developments that reduce the amount of time spent watching ads. To explore this, I want to call on Robert C. Allen's argument that television operates a gift economy (Allen 1992: 119–20). His focus is on free-to-air commercial channels where he explains the relationship between viewers and the compound of channel and the advertisers who make the operation possible as founded on the 'gift' of the program to the viewer who responds by attending to the ad. Ideally this response is actualised with the purchase of the product. With the wide dispersal of remotes and VCRs, and the consequent breakdown of such an economy as viewers evade their part of the implied relationship, channels can respond to maintain the economy only by synchronising their ad breaks, and indeed their general scheduling, or by incorporating products into the programs themselves. Lifestyle television is ideally placed for this latter activity and is able to return the gift economy to high-rating sections of Australian television.

NEW VERSIONS AND FORMATTING: CHANGING ROOMS AND MAKEOVERS

A standby throughout lifestyle programs has been the makeover—that most explicit of statements about the generic importance of showing change and the centrality of fashion to the concept of lifestyle. Since 1990 at least, *Burke's Backyard* has moved in on some unsatisfactory patch of land, whether untended wasteland or out-of-date patio, and transformed it into a site more fitting to the owner. For most of that time, it has included the risk that a designer will be given full rein to his whimsy, as was the case in 1995 when the actor Peter Phelps discovered his rooftop garden had been revamped with wheelie-bins as plant containers.

The most recent variation on lifestyle programming takes the makeover and adds elements of the game show. Highly popular in the United Kingdom, there is currently only one Australian example and that is formatted on one of the most popular British shows, using the same name—*Changing Rooms*. Here two couples known to each other work with a designer to transform a room in each other's houses, operating to a limited budget and time-frame. The lifestyle elements are less in the advice given, although hints on transforming interiors without spending large amounts of money are certainly provided and detailed instructions available here through the involvement of *Woman's Day*. The key lifestyle component lies rather in the way in which the room to be transformed needs attention only in terms of its no longer saying what the owners want said about them—they want something that expresses their current lifestyle, or the one they aspire to. The program goes along with this only so far; what it wants is a more entertaining, even dramatic, result. The owners are challenged by being given a more striking redesign than they had wished—indeed at times their expressed desires are disregarded. The implicit hope is that the dissonance between the lifestyle wished for and that expressed in the redesign will be so great that it is visible on the faces of the owners. For if the room does not express the owner's lifestyle, if it has been moved too far (usually, as far as the programs have gone so far, into the theatrical), it will misrepresent the owner in a way that impinges painfully on the project of the self. The British experience includes instances of owners stalking off screen, crying or screaming. They demonstrate, far more than is possible for the more normal lifestyle program, how fully the self is invested in the signs of the chosen style.

CONCLUSION

Lifestyle programs reveal much of the situation of contemporary television, dominated still by broadcast networks attempting to maintain or even extend their hegemony over other televisual systems, both cable and satellite, as well as co-opting Internet outlets and print media to their service. Most importantly, they reveal the shifts in late capitalism that act to increase consumption by tying it to identity through the ongoing project of the self and linking that project through directed development of lifestyles into a continuing fruitful sequence of programs providing advice and example. While forces of globalisation might be seen as reducing the national distinctiveness evident in this process, lifestyle programming indicates that the local (meaning here the national) is still an important intermediary, customising the details of particular lifestyles offered by televisual programming. This means that national programs, or local formats of imported programs, are the main type of lifestyle program on offer. The value of local presenters and the national meanings of particular consumption patterns seem at the moment to mean that this is one genre where the Australianness of our television remains evident, albeit mutable.

Eight

Kate Bowles

Soap opera: 'No end of story, ever'

> Dennis Potter's *The Singing Detective* wasn't soap. The story ran for many weeks. There were cliffhangers of the kind essential to soap opera. There were standard soap issues: love, betrayal, suffering. *But the show wasn't soap because it dealt with ideas.* (Kingsley 1989: 1–2, my emphasis)

As a term, 'soap' enjoys a paradoxical familiarity: despite its apparent obviousness, it refers to a genre of television which is difficult to define. Working out what is and isn't soap in the context of Australian television has sent many writers off in search of common or contrasting elements of form, style or content. This search is only made more fraught by the fact that the Australian television industry professes at many levels to recognise no genre distinction at all between soaps and other forms of drama, bracketing everything together when it comes to local content regulations or awards categories, for example. Nevertheless, there is a commonsense appreciation of the term 'soap' within the industry which enables it to be used, as it is above, as a form of protective discrimination. In a 1986 interview, the Executive Producer of *A Country Practice* claimed that 'if you look at it closely it isn't a soapie in the way that some of our continuing story sagas like *Prisoner, Sons and Daughters* and *Neighbours* are soapies . . . *It's a very romantic serial* in that it's set in a country town and it's an escape from the pressure of the big city with lots of animals' (*Encore* 1996: 9, my emphasis).

SOAP HISTORY

One of the reasons that the term 'soap' flickers in and out of industry discourse as a common name for the romantic serial is that, historically, it has functioned as a perjorative label, in ways that date back to the origins of both the form and the term. The popular account of this origin explains that US radio serials of the 1930s were sponsored by companies such as Proctor & Gamble, Colgate-Palmolive and Pepsodent, hence the term 'soap opera'. The most well-known of the early soap originators was university graduate Irna Phillips, who was acting in live radio drama for Chicago radio station WGN at the end of the 1920s (Kingsley 1989: 3). Following on from the success of a comic strip narrative advertising campaign for Ivory soap, Phillips was commissioned to write a narrative radio advertisement featuring a family called the Suddses (Nochimson 1992: 12). Although Phillips went on to devise *The Guiding Light* for radio in 1937, and remained a primary force in American soap opera writing and production until the termination of her contract by Proctor & Gamble in 1973, Allen (1985) argues that it is misleading to see her as the mother of all soap operas as there were already continuing radio serials, notably *Amos 'n' Andy*, by the time Phillips came up with *Painted Dreams* in 1930. And Nochimson (1992) points out that it is further misleading to see *Painted Dreams* as the first soap opera, given that it was itself the advertising campaign, rather than drama which delivered listeners to advertisers. However, it did convince radio stations of the format's appeal to women, and confirmed the mutual interest of radio producers and soap manufacturers in that audience (Nochimson 1992: 13–16; Allen 1985: 144). What eventually evolved as the continuing drama serial transferred to American television in the late 1940s, flourishing in the 1950s, and the longevity of many of the American daytime soaps which originated in this period is the hallmark of the genre's peculiar adaptability to changing circumstances.

The appeal of the soap opera to television programmers and producers lay in it being relatively inexpensive to produce (Allen 1985: 142), and its potential to structure a daily habit of television viewing. But its preoccupation with family affairs and emotional matters, and its early popularity with a predominantly female mass audience, brought hostile criticism from many commentators. Critics of mass culture in the 1940s and 1950s, such as Adorno and Horkheimer, made passing reference to the popularity of the daily soaps as evidence of a more general cultural decline and, as Barbara Klinger has argued, this denigration of the soap opera contributed to a 'climate of opinion' in which other cultural artefacts, such as the lavish melodramas of Douglas Sirk, were able to be similarly dismissed (Klinger 1994: 83). Along the way, the term 'soap' acquired such negative connotations that it was scarcely necessary to pay attention to the real complexity of its content, its distinctive and ingenious narrative style or its peculiarly telephilic format.

SOAP CONTENT: NATIONAL VARIATIONS

Despite the continuing and rapid evolution of the television soap, the common view remains that a soap is a conservative and conformist serial drama which demonstrates the following predictable textual features: an emphasis on family life, personal relationships, sexual dramas, emotional and moral conflicts; some coverage of topical issues; set in familiar domestic interiors with only occasional excursions into new locations; and characterised by low-cost production over-heads which may be blamed for a reputation for poor acting, unconvincing sets, excessive reliance on coincidence and over-hasty plot resolutions. This critical stereotype takes little account of the considerable variation between soaps produced in different countries, or for different language groups. Neither does it account for the range of soaps produced even by one national system—for example, the yawning gap between the hyperbolic yet strangely exhilarating boardroom/bedroom struggles of the US prime-time supersoaps such as *Dallas* and *Dynasty* in the 1970s and 1980s, and the mundane drama of perpetual suffering of the twentysomething soap *Party of Five* in the 1990s. This is partly because the stereotype itself is sourced in that sub-genre of product which even industry discourse recognises unproblematically as soap: the long-running American daytime television serials (including those which screen on Australian free-to-air television, *Days of Our Lives*, *The Young and the Restless* and *The Bold and the Beautiful*).

These American daytimers showcase a certain kind of tragic glamour which can be regarded as a house style: some characters may be extremely wealthy, but the dramas are those from which money can't buy relief. Take, for example, the CEO of a major company who suffers through several divorces and dramas of paternity. For all his wealth and power, he cannot immediately secure the release of his son from gaol; nor can he prevent his daughter's teen marriage. Meanwhile, his former wives and his children are all at various times estranged from him or simply furious with him. Only very occasionally are his private jet, elegant wardrobe and stylishly gloomy apartment assets to him as he struggles to control both his feelings and the lives of those around him (*The Young and the Restless*). What his lifestyle does furnish, however, in terms of what Bernard Timberg referred to in 1981 as the 'rhetoric of the camera' in soap opera, is the mid-shot of characters viewed through a frame of lavish floral displays, glittering crystal decanters or gleaming antique furniture. These serve to entice the viewer's gaze towards the developing art of set design and costuming, as much as towards the searching looks or expressions of admiration, secrecy, surprise, or anger rehearsed by the actors.

Given that these shows are widely regarded as typical soaps, then perhaps part of the confusion over the definition of soap arises from their having such a different rhetorical style from their British counterparts, long-running prime-time shows such as *EastEnders* and *Coronation Street*. These are naturalistic dramas, notorious for their lack of glamour, where characters turn to crime to pay the rent rather than as part of a high-powered corporate takeover strategy, for example. Set design and wardrobe display a highly self-conscious attention to social detail, particularly in terms of the producers' perception of class authenticity. Although the close-up is still common, characters are frequently given a social context in mid- or long-shot. Indeed, there is much more location shooting in the UK shows than in the entirely studio-based American daytime soaps, where the difficulty of maintaining credibility with obviously staged outdoor scenery leads to a strong preference for the domestic or corporate interior (Allen 1985: 143).

Meanwhile, Australian soaps have skirted the two extremes and colonised the lucrative middle ground, recognising the market appeal of young, attractive actors rather than the older character actors of the traditional British soaps, but avoiding the displays of excessive wealth and glamour which have drawn such critical fire on the American soaps, particularly in their domination of their foreign markets. Adult issues such as adultery and its consequences are dealt with seriously, but not at the expense of plotlines which involve young teenagers in pranks, adventures, money-making schemes and problems with lost homework assignments. Relationships between young and old are generally cordial, or at least respectful, and there is a particular emphasis on community life, with a number of sets specifically designed for all characters to meet and interact—pubs, cafes, surf clubs and schools. Storylines will take characters out on location in ways that partly capitalise on lucrative stereotypes of the Australian landscape for overseas markets: camping expeditions and fishing trips throw up their share of risks, and offer particular opportunities for heroism or the testing of relationships. A group of teenagers go camping together, and what starts as an argument about teenage sex between a young couple ends in a near drowning (*Neighbours*).

Beyond these nationally peculiar features, the demands of perpetuality mean that all soaps are permitted to stretch credulity in generically particular ways, although it is more common for the US soaps to take advantage of this. In US daytime shows, characters may be played by different actors, or the same actors may play different characters (identical twins, for example); characters disappear and return with amnesia; plot reversals can be explained by dream sequences; characters can be possessed by demons, or communicate telepathically with one another in moments of crisis (particularly between couples); all characters talk to themselves, think aloud or experience flashbacks to orient viewers to plot developments. Australian and British soaps, by contrast, attempt to meet the industrial demands of cast changes by naturalistic means, avoiding the plot device of the seance, the dream sequence and the veiled mystery figure.

Australian soaps, however, have flirted with elements of the fantastic, both in terms of dream sequences and flashbacks, and in the use of comedy: special theme Christmas episodes, for example, allowing the cast to operate momentarily outside the conventions of naturalistic drama. In terms of genre mixing, a discourse of comedic sentimentality often seems to threaten the Australian soap, with shows from *A Country Practice* to *Neighbours* allowing animals of all kinds, both native and domestic, to play a starring role. Social comedy is generated by means of affectionate cultural stereotypes, particularly among elderly characters, and many Australian casts will contain a particular comic figure (usually male) whose lively ineptitude sees him lurch through a series of comic pitfalls and relatively harmless disasters, as a comic foil to the emotional drama around him. While the British soaps will make room for some similar comic stereotypes (community gossips or grumpy old men), in the American soaps such comedy is rare.

A more obvious contrast between the US tradition and the naturalistic or at least socially utopian trends in British and Australian production lies in their narrative styles. A US daytime soap will typically cut between several simultaneous conversations, returning to each at exactly the point where it was left, and in an hour-long episode may cover as little as ten minutes' conversation time. It may take two characters more than a week to finish a single conversation. This alone counts for the most significant distinction between US daytime soaps and other forms of American television drama. Australian and British soaps, meanwhile, apply more conventional rules of narrative engagement with the audience, cutting between multiple parallel storylines but allowing significant plot time to pass off screen, with the result that the pace of the show roughly corresponds to that of other types of television drama. And where American soaps efface the connections between the lives of their characters and the social or political life of the nation in which they live, perhaps except when screening Christmas episodes, Australian and British soaps structure their timing to infuse their storylines with topicality: in a first-run drama, teenage characters sit school exams at the same time as their viewers, for example.

SOAP FORM

As this brief sketch should make clear, the generalisable traits of television soap are surprisingly few. So if soap cannot be quarantined from other forms of television drama in terms of content, is form a more reliable factor? As Hilary Kingsley (1989: 2) points out, what defines *Hamlet* as not-soap is the fact that when it's over, it's over. Even the most ardent Shakespeare fan does not imagine a life for the surviving characters beyond the confines of the play itself:

> *Hamlet* isn't soap, because Hamlet's problems are introduced, complicated and then ended by his death and the death of almost everyone else. End of story. In soap, there is no end of story, ever.

According to Albert Moran, soap opera is 'that form of television drama that works with a continuous open narrative. Each episode ends with the promise that the storyline is to be continued in another episode.' (Moran 1989: 245) Moran reiterates the commonplace distinction between the soap opera or serial, in which a set of overlapping and interweaving storylines allow for moments of plot resolution within an overall logic of endlessly deferred conclusion; and the series, in which some degree of viewer familiarity with a continuing cast or set location may extend over time, but the primary action centres on discrete events which are rounded off and effectively forgotten in one, two or three named episodes. Although this formal distinction seems relatively unproblematic, it conceals a further aspect to the critical stereotyping of soap opera, again in terms of gender, and the attraction of a particular audience to a particular televisual format.

Moran suggests that a 'noticeable feature of the series [from the mid-1960s to the mid-1970s] was that they were male, action genres' (Moran 1989: 245). Meanwhile, the larger cast of the serial created more opportunity for complex female characterisation and this coincided 'with a general feminisation of our culture' (Moran 1989: 248). Whether or not Australian culture was generally feminising, or being feminised, in the mid-1970s, we see in Moran's assertion the interconnectedness of assumptions about form and assumptions about content when it comes to defining the soap opera. It is a circular argument: because a soap/serial requires a large cast to create enough storylines for the show to keep flowing indefinitely, it depends upon the kind of content that will make connections between that cast. Stories of families, neighbourhoods and small towns are ideal, and the motivational drive behind the narrative will be generated by the creating of a web of relationships between the characters. Thus soap operas must be of particular interest to women because relationships are what women are interested in. It follows neatly that if the programming of soap opera then favours a female viewer, being scheduled at times of day when women form the bulk of the available audience, then women are likely to be in the majority among soap watchers. If the status of the action series, not to mention its appeal to commercial sponsors, is elevated by its assumed male viewership (and again, the interaction between content, form and assumed viewer is something of a chicken and egg situation), then the feminising of the relatively low-status soap opera becomes a self-fulfilling prophecy.

Is the sorting out of television into masculine and feminine (Fiske 1987) still a reasonable point of discrimination? High-status police action series such as *Water Rats*, *Stingers* or *Police Rescue* have all used the emotional lives of the primary characters, and their evolving relationships and relationship histories, as part of the meaning of each episode. Cops and their colleagues are now not only seen in the office or on the street, but at home, in bed, in restaurants, arguing with their children, their lovers and their parents. As Cunningham and Miller (1994: 14) observe:

> A set of emotional tendencies merges with action and office life to produce
> soap-operatic forms such as *Police Rescue*. Police stories, like other dramatic genres,
> increasingly work to broker the relationships between the private and public
> spheres.

Despite the somewhat hesitant neologism of this attempt to work out what a police show is doing with a set of emotional tendencies, the soap-operatic form is not a recent development. Prime time US crime series of the 1980s, such as *Cagney & Lacey* and *Hill Street Blues*, underwrote long-term viewer loyalty with continuing storylines involving the health and relationship crises of the main characters. Yet it has taken some time for critics (and academics) to acknowledge that this strategy undermines the strict formal discrimination between high-status drama series and the low-status continuing serials. But as it has become more obvious that viewers of a crime series who understand that a character is alcoholic, or has had an affair with a colleague, or has lost a child, are rewarded with a more complex appreciation of an otherwise closed episode, then it is also slowly becoming clear that simply in using a regular cast and location, even the most strictly episodic series is working to schedule viewers into habits of repeat viewing and station loyalty, which have long been considered to be the primary industrial functions of the soap opera's ongoing form.

The reverse is also true. Soaps have been brokering the relationship between the public and the private for some time, particularly in their meshing of workplace and personal relations. This may be in a US daytime soap where a dynastic family-run company enables all personal conflicts to have disastrous business consequences, or any one of the Australian or British soaps involving a local cafe, pub or small business at which most of the characters work or meet socially. In all cases, the interaction between public and private spheres becomes more compelling when characters turn to crime, whether for business or personal reasons, or find themselves in hospital. While these episodes of crisis may not be explored to the same degree as they would be in a crime or medical series, they do nonetheless bring into the supposedly domestic realm of the soap all the generic markers of those other drama categories.

THEORIES OF SOAP

Given that neither matters of content, nor even the formal distinction between the open-ended serial and the episodic series, now sustain the definition of soap, it is worth returning to the academic study of television drama in order to re-evaluate the nature of this discursive preoccupation with working out what is and isn't soap. As television studies evolved from its American and sociological origins, many writers turned their attention to the soap opera, with a range of different motives and results (Geraghty 1991; Buckingham 1987; Harrington and Bielby 1995). As a dramatic form which appeared to have a certain amount in common with the Hollywood melodrama, soap offered the same opportunity as melodrama for critical writing to meditate on the interaction between popularity and morality—just as its mass popularity, particularly among women, had led to soap acquiring a poor reputation in terms of quality. Storyline credibility was challenged by its very openness of form, which seem to predispose all marriages to failure and precipitate all successes into an immediate spiral of loss. As a result, the defence of soap opera by some feminist writers seemed torn between sympathy for their audience and a kind of indignation that this was the best that mass culture could offer women (Haskell 1973). As Tania Modleski (1984: 108–9) concluded in her study of soap operas as 'mass-produced fantasies for women':

> The fantasy of community is not only a real desire (as opposed to the 'false' ones mass culture is always accused of trumping up), it is a salutary one. As feminists, we have a responsibility to devise ways of meeting these needs that are more creative, honest, and interesting than the ones mass culture has supplied.
> Otherwise, the search for tomorrow threatens to go on, endlessly.

Modleski's analysis of American daytime soaps suggested that the open-ended fluidity of the serial form gave soaps their special relevance to women, in their mirroring of the seriality and interruptibility of housework, and that the popularity of the facial close-up was part of a learning system in which women adopted the positional 'gaze of the mother' in order to satisfy their 'desire for connectedness'. She cited approvingly Marcia Kinder's assertion that soap opera is 'open-ended, slow paced, multi-climaxed' and that this offered a structuring mimicry of female sexuality. While this analysis now seems particularly dated, and other feminist writers were later to disagree, Modleski's essay remains useful as a demonstration of the ways in which mildly psychoanalytic textual analysis evolved into a mythopoetic way of thinking about soap.

John Tulloch summarises this as the 'audience-in-the-text' approach to television studies: assuming the general features of an audience from the specific address contained within a text to its ideal (or even ideally resistant) viewer (Tulloch, in Tulloch and Turner 1989: 188). To an extent, this approach has been sidelined by proliferating studies of real soap audiences, whose energetic and committed fandom has made them peculiarly vulnerable to ethnographic curiosity. The ratings significance of these popular and long-running shows is taken to mean that these real audiences must harbour some relevant information concerning the genre's appeal. Following Tulloch, we might call this the 'text-in-the-audience' approach: what these audiences reported that they saw and liked (or disliked) in soaps became, increasingly, the means by which those shows were defined, and the study of serial television itself contributed significantly to the shepherding together of a set of textual features which were considered to be hallmarks of the genre—no matter how the results were skewed by the selection of interview subjects and by the interviewers' own preoccupations with particular content. Even when researchers began to look at audiences who did not conform so neatly to the stereotype, it was still rare to find acknowledgment that what those shows were about was only tangentially relevant to their popularity.

However, there is a third position, which suggests that soaps are watched not primarily because of their content or sociological accessibility, but because they are conveniently scheduled, and that they are therefore watched by those for whom the scheduling is convenient. Accordingly, audience trends will shift as other social factors change, particularly patterns of adult employment. Accounting for soap's popularity in this way acknowledges that viewers may include elderly residents of retirement homes, college students or children, even while these character types may be underrepresented on the shows themselves. It may even encourage the gradual transformation of the genre's traditional interests, as producers work to repackage their product towards a new demographic. Most noticeably in the 1990s, this has involved the progressive introduction of teenage and twentysomething characters to US, British and Australian shows, with some US daytime shows reportedly going so far as to pension off their middle-aged cast members.

Thinking about soaps in terms of network scheduling resonates more neatly than earlier accounts with the current trend towards writing about television according to narratives of policy, economics, globalisation, marketing and media ownership. This trend often appears indifferent to the trivia of textual detail, yet it also signals a limited return to ways of thinking about texts in the context of genre. In this account, soaps are classifiable as such because they are a recognisably distinct type of product circulating in international import–export flows: their genre significance is economic as much as cultural, and their cultural significance is regionally specific. Paradoxically, however, analysis of scheduling points out the frailty of genre classification just as it offers a new, market-based justification for it. For as an ongoing serial screened daily at a regular time, no matter whether this is in the United Kingdom, Germany or Australia, a Grundy product such as *Neighbours* has as much in common with the daily news and weather in that regional market as it does with other soaps screening around the world, including other Australian soaps. It is repackaged by local scheduling and marketing: its significance is localised by the routines of television, domestic and public life which frame it, and the discourses of local politics, popular culture and publicity which make sense of it. According to this version, the success of *Neighbours* in Britain can be directly attributed to its being the first stripped show on British television, and to its shift from a lunchtime slot to a time more convenient for schoolchildren. Its transformation of British soap watching to a daily habit was thus wholly dependent on the launch of daytime television in Britain, even though the more obvious manifestation of this influence lay in the ways in which local television subsequently attempted to imitate it in terms of content, setting and casting (Cunningham and Miller 1994: 128–35; Cunningham and Jacka 1996: 131; Crofts 1994).[1]

AUSTRALIAN SOAPS AT HOME AND AWAY

Understanding that soap is an economic product as much as a cultural formation is critical when considering its short history on Australian television. O'Regan (1993) characterises Australian television culture as import-dependent, and the function of cheap imported drama, particularly soap opera, has been important both in the recuperation of start-up costs by the first commercial licensees, and in determining the viability of local drama production. Soaps are therefore central to the history of the Australian television industry and, as in America, they found an audience accustomed by radio to the daily habit of serialised fiction. The earliest local television serials, such as *Autumn Affair*, produced by ATN-7 in 1958, were fifteen-minute dramas which owed much to what Moran (1989: 73) calls the 'radio inheritance'. However, it was the cheap availability of American product, which had already recouped its production costs in the large American domestic market and could therefore be sold at attractive prices overseas, that allowed the early station operators to achieve financial stability as television exhibitors, which in turn encouraged the rise of the local production houses, such as Crawfords, who produced the highly successful crime series *Homicide* from 1964 (Moran 1989: 28; O'Regan 1993).

As Australian audiences became acculturated to locally produced television drama by the mid-1960s, Australian television entered what Moran describes as its second phase. During this period, the introduction of Australian content regulations, with a specific drama quota in place from 1967, was an important step in encouraging the development of local series and serials. Moran demonstrates, however, that the levels of local content required were initially so low as to reflect existing practice rather than to provide increased security for the local producers (Moran 1989: 33). The ABC's *Bellbird* began screening the same year, with perhaps the next most significant serial launch being the arrival of Cash-Harmon's 'sex serial' *Number 96*, made for Ten in 1972. By 1974, the local drama series was such a familiar part of Australian television that the television reviewer from *The Australian* was moved to complain that the 'domestic serials' were a failed opportunity, disingenuous in their claims to naturalism, structurally contrived and generally failing to criticise Australian consumerism (Le Moignan 1974). In the same year, the Grundy Organisation, then Reg Grundy Productions, entered the drama market with *Class of '74*. Reg Grundy Productions had been a primary producer of low-cost quiz shows for regional stations; Moran attributes its move into serial drama to the introduction of a points system to local content rating in 1972, which gave stations higher credit for screening drama than either quiz or variety programming (Moran 1989: 151). And in 1979 Grundy launched one of Australian television's most idiosyncratic serials, *Prisoner*.

The trend towards serial production lent vigour to the debate about what counted as a soap and what was a serious drama. A 1977 article in the *Nation Review* suggested that there was no local competition for the US soaps, with *Days of our Lives*, *Another World*, *Search for Tomorrow*, *The Young and the Restless* and *General Hospital* all screening on Channel 9 in Sydney. By comparison, according to this writer, the Australian shows *Number 96*, *The Box* and 'that imbecilic newcomer', *The Young Doctors*, were too fast-paced and plot-oriented to qualify as soap proper, and historical serials such as *The Sullivans* were 'either too pretentious or too intelligent to be soaps'. *Bellbird* was disqualified by its 'excessive Australianness' and *Certain Women* by 'prime time's quest for quality'. Thus the vexed but ongoing attempt to make local synonymous with quality saw particular risks involved in pursuing the key export success of the American industry. A local show could be incompetent as real soap on any number of grounds, yet could scarcely hope to be accredited as mere soap on any of the same grounds, given the already awkward position of such an import-dependent industry within the public discourse of protectionist cultural nationalism which sustained it.

Perhaps the show which most encapsulated this awkwardness of status was *A Country Practice (ACP)*, which made its debut for the Seven Network in 1981. *ACP* was technically a series, but so emphasised the ongoing storylines of its major characters as to make the distinction between series and serial more or less meaningless. Despite the efforts of its producers to secure for it some kind of moral high ground in terms of not-being-soap, many of its narrative high points form part of a kind of national folk memory of Australian soap. Unlike the more obvious generic imitators of American product, set in hospitals and suburbs, it was both profoundly and comedically local, and its highly successful performance in the Australian export market made it clear that it was not only domestic cultural nationalism that was satisfied by the sight of an Australian country town. Given the discursive tussle between the show's economic and emotive status, there is a particular reason to appreciate the delicately ironic titling of Tulloch and Moran's extensive survey of all aspects of its making and marketing: *A Country Practice: 'Quality Soap'*.

Meanwhile, in 1985, the drama that was to transform Australia's reputation in Europe, both as a television exporter and a tourist destination, made its famously inauspicious debut on Seven, where it was swiftly axed. *Neighbours* was then resold by The Grundy Organisation to Ten, which engineered its successful relaunch, and in 1986 it followed a number of other Australian soaps (including *A Country Practice* from 1983) into the expanding British television market, being purchased by the BBC as part of their move into daytime television. The stripping of *Neighbours*, followed by the ITV's purchase of the stripped Seven soap *Home and Away*, not only transformed the way in which British television managed and understood the potential of the soaps, but created a show which was, more obviously than others before it, a product. This was in part due to the way in which its teenage cast, then including Kylie Minogue, Jason Donovan, Guy Pearce and Craig McLachlan, were packaged by a vigorous promotional campaign. In a manner reminiscent of the astute management of fan culture by the Hollywood studios earlier this century, the lives and interrelationships of these young actors were staged and strategised to maximise the interplay between the fiction and the 'real'.

The targeting of the major UK women's magazines with publicity stories, and the use of promotional tours and pantomime gigs, consolidated the British fan base for the Australian shows, and furnished a number of associated retail opportunities: in 1989, for example, BBC Enterprises coproduced, under exclusive licence from Grundy, the *Neighbours Wedding Collection* video ('the memorable video all fans will want to keep'). Beyond the immediate production–exhibition nexus, a number of independent magazine publishing companies were able to capitalise on the shows' success: between 1988 and 1990, the London-based Octave View publishing company produced a collection of *Great Aussie Recipes: Personal Favourites Cooked by the Stars of Neighbours*; Century Magazines Pty Ltd, based in Sydney, produced for UK distribution a specialist magazine, *Stars of Oz* ('Win an autographed Vegemite bucket full of Summer Bay sand!!'); and the Star Magazine Group produced a short run of the monthly title *Neighbours: Who's Who*. This proliferation of official and unofficial spin-off productions made it clear that, whatever the moral or cultural impact of a soap, and whatever impact it had made on the viewing habits of a nation or two, its ultimate performance as an export product had been in the fruition of these further opportunities for local and overseas producers and distributors to trade up from its initial, rather more straightforward, popularity.

Perhaps more than any other show, *Neighbours* has garnered international cultural notoriety for the Australian television industry as a producer of poor-quality soap for export dumping. However, despite a fairly determined effort by both popular and academic commentators in Britain and Australia to explain *Neighbours* in terms of the show's unexceptional content or its briefly ground-breaking form, very little attention has been paid to this complex and co-opportunistic set of marketing strategies generated by the show both in its domestic and its overseas markets. This is where a fourth trend in writing about television soaps, anticipated by Tulloch and Moran (1986) but as yet to be fully developed, could learn to pay closer attention to the textual practices of the publicity industries, in the context of a limited return to the pragmatics of genre classification.

CONCLUDING COMMENTS

Since the evolution of policy-based television studies, it would seem that textual analysis has been relegated to a subsidiary role in understanding the management and marketing of these jet-setting pop culture products, not to mention the career trajectories of their jet-setting starlet casts. And yet, as Cunningham and Miller (1994: 10) suggest, neither the demotion of content analysis in the study of television, nor the fragmentation of established orders of generic classification, spells the demise of genre as a method of analysis. Rather, genre is the method of analysis which connects industry, academic, fan and promotional discourses about television: everyone uses some form of genre-speak when they describe what they make, sell, consume, enjoy or dislike. Take the practical example of the way in which the term 'soap' can be put to work by Australia's three soap magazines, which may differ quite markedly on the shows they cover, but which nonetheless agree that 'soap' is the relevant label by which they will attract their target readership. For their editors, market reach is achieved precisely by knowing how and when to apply the very generic labelling which seems so vexed in terms of the organisation of a book such as this one. Whether or not to include *Water Rats* or *Blue Heelers*, or *Beverly Hills 90210*, is far less important than keeping 'soap' in the magazine's title and using the classic US daytimers as the cover features, particularly in order to recover the relatively high costs of US picture content (Taylor, D. 1999, pers. comm. 2 February).

This, finally, is the reason to retain a modest interest in the kinds of textual analysis which originally furnished the critical stereotype of the 'typical soap'. Analysing texts rather than budgets is one of the ways in which academics have acquired the unenviable reputation of taking popular culture too seriously. However, it is in appreciating the ironic compromise between the discursive value of the stereotype of 'soap' and the specific analysis of what is tackled, and how, in any particular soap, that we can more fully appreciate the dynamic nature of these evolving shows, the fan cultures which they support, and the programming and publicity routines which continue to make such everyday, practical use of the contested term 'soap'.

NOTE

1 The incursion of Australian soaps into the UK market led to at least two British attempts to make a local imitation, explicitly using young, attractive casts and sunny locations, which had been considered to be the critical factors in the success of the Australian shows. Neither Granada TV's *Families*, set simultaneously in Sydney and the Derbyshire countryside, nor the BBC's highly promoted *Eldorado*, succeeded. The fact that they were produced at all, however, indicates the extent of the British television industry's attention to the unexpected and unsettling success of imported product.

Nine   David Rowe

Sport: The genre that runs and runs

ESTABLISHING AUSTRALIAN SPORTS TV

As Australian television enters the much-hyped new millennium, television sport—free-to-air, pay and online—seems as much a part of contemporary life as the Internet and the hole in the ozone layer. But it was not always thus. Barely half a century ago, sport—astonishingly—resisted the embrace of what Marshall McLuhan (1967) memorably called 'The Mechanical Bride'—and television wasn't so sure that sport was such a good catch either. How did these reluctant lovers become the Romeo and Juliet of the culture industries?

It is almost impossible to imagine today, but the intimate relationship between television and sport was once very tentative and based on a high level of mutual suspicion. To understand why this was the case—and is no more—requires an appreciation that media and sport, while they have a long-standing association in Australia and elsewhere (Cashman 1995), developed as essentially different divisions of the entertainment industry. In the pre-broadcasting age, newspapers reported on sport, describing the event and, increasingly, raising levels of anticipation before major sports contests. The print media also engaged in lengthening and deepening post-game (or post-mortem) analysis, visually supported by often striking still sports photography (Rowe 1999). Radio broadcasting of sport added another crucial dimension—'liveness' and a more immediate sense of 'having-been-there'. These new possibilities led, famously, to simulations of the live action from a 1934 Ashes cricket test match in England for Australian audiences, whereby ball-by-ball descriptions arrived in a series of individual telegrams, while the moment was recreated through pre-recorded crowd applause and a pencil striking a piece of hollow wood in order to sound like bat on ball! The arrival of television in 1956 ushered in the era of the moving sports image, enhancing the illusion of physically attending sports events in real time and space.

Yet, although the technological capability of covering sport in the media developed reasonably swiftly over the twentieth century, the willingness of the parties to cooperate and combine their efforts was slower in coming. As John Goldlust (1987), Garry Whannel (1992) and Steven Barnett (1990) have all pointed out, Australia at first followed the British tradition of regarding the television coverage of major sports events as an important aspect of nation building, helping to forge and foster a common national culture. Hence the Australian Broadcasting Commission (now Corporation) (ABC) dominated the TV treatment of Australian sport in the mould of the British Broadcasting Corporation's (BBC's) pioneering coverage of sport in that country. This influence of British public broadcasting had, as we will see, highly significant consequences for how Australian TV covered sport, contrasting sharply with the techniques developed in the United States by commercial broadcasters.

The founding moment in Australian TV sport was the 1956 Olympic Games, when for the first time Australians not only received television images, but their arrival was explicitly tied to Melbourne's hosting of the world's premier mass spectacle. Yet, as Brian Stoddart observes:

> At first, curiously enough, television had little structural impact upon media coverage of Australian sport . . . Australian Broadcasting Commission coverage continued the BBC practice of upholding the traditional, to the point of using English commentators such as Michael Charlton. Superb though such broadcasters were, they were concerned with maintaining past imported values rather than establishing new national ones. (Stoddart 1986: 99)

So, with the ABC following a stately British model (not helped, it must be said, by television's limitation to black-and-white images provided by a small number of mostly static cameras); the first commercial TV channels and their advertisers being a little unsure about sport's long-term audience appeal; and with most sports organisations concerned that TV coverage would reduce their revenues from gate takings, 'For twenty years [after the arrival of television with the 1956 Olympics] sport played a surprisingly modest role in Australian television and its consumption patterns.' (Stoddart 1986: 99)

But all this changed from the mid-1970s onwards, when colour television made the TV sports spectacle more vibrant and life-like. TV sport developed with innovations in camera technology and TV sports presentation techniques, especially in the United States, and with the dawning realisation that sport could capture some of the largest and most loyal audiences for advertisers, deliver excellent ratings to TV companies and provide extremely valuable opportunities for 'feel good' brand recognition for sponsors. Tobacco companies like Benson and Hedges, Rothmans and Amatil, which were now banned from directly advertising on Australian television, benefited particularly from 'incidental' advertising, still being permitted prominent signage at sports events (like Rugby League's Winfield Cup) which they sponsored and to which they had gained naming rights (Harris 1988). The most notable and dramatic shift towards a new domination of a specific type of commercial television over public sports broadcasting and earlier, relatively low-key forms of commercial sports broadcast came in 1977 with what is widely called 'The Packer Revolution'.

THE PACKER REVOLUTION

Kerry Packer's move on cricket broadcasting was a watershed in Australian sports television (Adair and Vamplew 1997), representing an unprecedented incursion of capital into a cultural space created by two institutions which, by their nature, were not in tune with the fully realised commodification of sport through television. The ABC, which developed the cricketing TV audience into a potentially valuable media commodity and held its broadcast rights, had a generally comfortable relationship with the game's controllers, the Australian Cricket Board (ACB), a governing body which fitted well McKay and Miller's (1991) typification of the 'old boys' who ran the most traditional of all Australian sports on patrician, amateurist lines. Packer's offers of higher broadcasting fees (the now laughably small sum of $500 000 in return for broadcasting exclusivity) by the Publishing and Broadcasting Limited (PBL) company he controlled to the ACB, and a promise to make the game more popular, were rejected in favour of 'Aunty' (as the ABC, either affectionately or contemptuously, was once widely known). Having failed to secure the crucial commercial advantage of exclusive broadcast rights, Packer established his own competition, World Series Cricket, which signed up most of the major stars of the day, paid them much more money than they had received before, and introduced innovations such as new camera locations and night cricket. In fairly quick time, the ACB capitulated to 'Packer's Pirates', officially 'running' the game while Packer's PBL Marketing promoted the test and other matches televised on his developing Nine Network, which was making a major play to be *the* TV sports network.

In Australia, Packer was at the leading edge of a new sports television order which already existed in the United States and which, in Britain, was in the process of changing first through a more assertive approach against BBC hegemony by the ITV commercial network (Whannel 1992) and then, in the late 1980s, by the much more aggressive manoeuvring of another Australian media baron, Rupert Murdoch, through his BSkyB satellite subscription TV network service. Australian cross-media ownership rules (which are subject to constant review in response to 'convergence') have for some time prevented Murdoch from controlling a free-to-air television network, meaning that in this country, too, he has had to concentrate on pay TV sport. It was, in fact, Packer's tight hold on the free-to-air and pay TV rights to the main winter sport, Rugby League, in the key New South Wales and Queensland markets that precipitated the disastrous 1995–97 'war of attrition' between 'Super League' and the Australian Rugby League that split the sport into competing media-aligned camps playing in rival competitions (Rowe 1996). This television-induced cataclysm, despite a Murdoch–Packer truce over broadcast rights sharing and a new, unified National Rugby League (NRL), is one from which the code is yet to recover (if, indeed, it ever does).

Packer's determination to protect his valuable TV sports assets (not only against Murdoch, but also against Channel Seven, holder of the key rights to Australian Rules Football and the Olympic Games) reveals the level of his investment in the overall 'project' of developing sports television and the profound importance of sport to profitability in Australian television. Packer can be seen as a significant international sports TV player, both copying overseas innovations and generating new techniques that have been taken up in other television systems. In the case of cricket, Channel Nine sought to make the game a more compelling TV spectacle, especially for less sport-committed viewers, in a manner that had repercussions far beyond the Southern Hemisphere. As Barnett states:

> Australian television allows a glimpse of how a very British sport can find itself transformed by commercial television. When Packer's Channel Nine finally wrenched Test cricket away from the Australian Broadcasting Corporation [sic], it invested considerable financial and technical resources into coverage. Some of the innovations—aerial shots of field placing, split-screen comparisons of respective bowling actions—were valuable contributions to a better view and a better understanding of the game. Others were little more than cheap production tricks that had little to do with explaining a complex game to the uninformed. (Barnett 1990: 169)

Barnett is particularly unimpressed by the 'ridiculous cartoon duck' introduced to escort a batter who had failed to score from the field—a device introduced clearly to appeal to children, just as the basic explanation of cricket's rules and tactics catered for female (and some male) viewers unacquainted with the game. The use of 'super-slow motion' replays, cameras placed in stumps and additional TV production enhancements was accompanied by other 'spectacular-ising' changes (described by Harriss (1990) as signalling a shift from 'modernism' to 'postmodernism') designed to accommodate sport more exactly to the demands of television. These adjustments included the promotion of one-day cricket as a more dramatic form of the game with guaranteed climaxes and results; the modification of rules to the one-day game to heighten the level of 'action'; the introduction of floodlit games with white balls in order to fit better into prime-time TV schedules; and the use of coloured uniforms to exploit the game's visual potential. The consequences of these new techniques went far beyond cricket and Channel Nine, with other sports and networks required by commercial and/or viewing logics to follow suit. For this reason, TV sports footage from barely two decades ago looks quaintly stilted and subdued to contemporary eyes.

The influence of Kerry Packer's PBL company (now in the hands of son James) on Australian sports television has clearly been substantial and, given that this chapter is concerned with notions of genre, we might consider whether the 'imprint' has been so far-reaching as to have created a Packer sports TV genre. Such a conclusion would be premature, however, for two reasons. First, Australian sports TV texts need to be located more carefully within larger traditions that have promoted different genres. Second, we need to assess the level of diversity and 'hybridity', such that that there may be several genres produced out of the different functions which sports TV programs discharge. As already noted in passing, 'live' action sports broadcasts have quite different structures and roles from those of preview and review programs. In examining past, present and emergent genres, we turn first to the most important in terms of viewer numbers and broadcast rights fees—live action.

LIVE-ACTION HEROES

It is unquestionable that the greatest advantage of sports television over other sports media is its capacity to simulate actual attendance at a sports event. The print media can offer acres of analysis and striking sports photography in dedicated sports magazines and, increasingly, in newspaper 'wraparounds' devoted to sports like Rugby Union, League, Australian Rules Football and to major events like the Olympic Games, the Australian Open Tennis Championship and the soccer World Cup. During sports contests, radio's flexibility can be demonstrated as listeners tune in while driving or going about their household chores. But, especially when something significant happens in a game—a goal scored or a wicket taken—it is the television set that provides the most comprehensive sensory experience. Numerous replays from a multitude of angles at various speeds are available to the viewer, with the unique sporting moment caught in real time by the 'live' TV eye. While this is not the only form of sports television, it is unquestionably the most prized and popular. It is, of course, a highly mediated experience and quite different from physically attending the event. The viewer's gaze is directed by the program producer, and their interpretations of events guided by commentators. There is none of the bodily experience of crowd movement and 'atmosphere', the sights and smells that arise from 'being there', and the sense of place and territoriality that make attending sports contests much less 'surgical' than remote sports watching (Bale 1998).

It is usual among sports *aficionados* to see the TV viewing experience as inferior to the 'real thing', and a great deal of emphasis is still placed on ground attendance by sports marketers (not least because, without crowds to provide atmosphere and ambience for TV viewers, they would be forced to simulate crowd noise electronically or to lure them in like live TV studio audiences). For example, much was made in March 1999 of the historic significance of being part of the largest-ever Rugby League crowd in Australia at the inaugural event at the Olympic Stadium in Homebush, Sydney. Well-known writer Thomas Keneally, whose 'New Season Ode' featured in the NRL's 1999 TV advertising and promotion campaign, self-consciously mythologised the moment:

> A child at the stadium last night will never have seen a more awesome venue for their heroes.
> And when they grow old, they will tell their children: 'I remember the day my father took me there.' (Keneally 1999: 2)

With over 100 000 people in attendance, the event was only relatively 'exclusive', but it is safe to say that even if, magically, the entire live television audience was given the opportunity to be there, many would prefer to watch at home. This is because, for those who are not 'dyed in the wool' sports fans, the entertainment choice they make to watch sports TV may not be recognised as inferior to actually being there. Rational calculations of the cost, time and (dis)comfort level arising out of attendance mean for many a preference for 'armchair' spectatorship. Indeed, the advantages of home viewing have been recognised by the operators of sports stadia through the installation of huge TV screens (two of which are installed at Stadium Australia costing $6 million each) with the same replay capacity as the home TV set. Both players and crowds routinely consult such replays, especially when used in the adjudication of controversial umpiring decisions, in an ironic simulation of the living room sports viewing experience (just as the latter is being brought closer to the stadium experience by more 'close-ups', directional microphones and the 'wiring' of sports officials for sound).

Irrespective of the competing attractions of physical attendance and remaining in the armchair, watching sport on television is now a much more economically important component of the sports industry than ground attendance, with the regular TV sports audience many times the size of the 'faithful' who go to sports events whatever the weather conditions, entertainment alternatives or other commitments. We need, therefore, to understand better the appeal of watching live sports TV rather than to disparage it as a necessarily second-best activity to going to the match. Live TV sport can constitute a compelling or distracting spectacle for committed and non-committed sports fans alike. There are many different ways in which to mediate sport through television, from leisurely long shots with laid-back commentary to the frantic intercutting of 'hyper close-ups' accompanied by the screamed imprecations of over-excited TV hosts. In Australia, as noted above, the former once dominated for cultural and technical reasons—the imported BBC house style and the small number of fixed cameras widely sweeping as much of the action as possible in a simulation of a single spectator getting the 'best seat in the house'. Its large-scale supplanting by the livelier and more upbeat US-style of televising sport (epitomised by the sports network ESPN) can be seen as a more extensive use of the 'grammar' of television to construct and shape rather than merely to show and report the event.

If we consider that sports programming is in competition with other televisual forms (such as soap operas or films), and that commercial free-to-air television is driven by an audience-maximisation imperative, then it is in the interests of sports TV producers to recruit casual viewers without alienating the committed. Key techniques such as the acceleration and personalisation of live TV sport can, therefore, discharge the dual functions of intensifying the interest of some and stimulating it in others. A heavily promoted, loud, pacy and highly dramatised live sports broadcast which caters for non- or casual sports fans, therefore, can generate a spectacular cross-audience appeal in a manner that a slow, reverential and highly specialised broadcast will not. The 'acceleration' of live TV sport can be briefly illustrated by my replication in 1998 of John Fiske's (1983) case study of televised cricket in Australia. I found that while the average (camera) shot-length of six seconds (similar, according to Fiske, to that in adventure and news programs) had fallen slightly (5.7 seconds), the average length of each six-ball over of cricket was only 166 seconds, about half of that sampled by Fiske fifteen years earlier (Rowe 1999: 155–56). While the sport tailor-made for live TV seems to be speeding up in the quest for broad audience appeal, the competition for the free-to-air and pay TV rights is hotting up, as the aforementioned Super League struggle between Packer and Murdoch revealed. But, in the abundant world of sports television, the live is but one genre among many, increasingly hybridised program types.

SPORTS TV: THE CONVERGENCE WITH COMEDY, CHAT AND THE QUIZ SHOW

Live action may be the most valuable genre (or sub-genre) of TV sport for programmers and fans alike, but it does not stand alone. As noted above, sport is a form of popular culture which is not just played and shown, but also endlessly talked about and over. Umberto Eco (1986: 162) describes this discourse as 'sports chatter': the endlessly proliferating talk about sport, followed by talk about sports talk, and so on, in an ever-ascending spiral. Many hours of broadcast time can be devoted to 'fleshing out' live action on free-to-air television. Most TV news bulletins include a substantial sports report (particularly at weekends, when 'hard' news is scarcer) and, given the greater prominence of sport in general news arising from developments like Sydney's hosting of the 2000 Summer Olympic Games, it is not unusual for a sports item to be the lead story (as in the recent scandals involving the International Olympic Committee). Late-night sports review programs like Channel Ten's *Sports Tonight* are under less pressing time pressures than the sports news segments in general news programs, although their staple fare consists of little more than moderately extended replays of the day's main sports events. From the late 1970s to the late 1990s, sports TV magazine programs typified by Channel Nine's *Wide World of Sports* (a formula based on an American program) stretched out over the weekend daylight hours, presenting a series of brief sporting 'highlights' including a disparate range of 'world' sports, and featuring dramatic moments (especially collisions), usually with the action synchronised with rock music and hosted by 'blokey' presenters like Max Walker.

In one of commercial television's cyclical cost-cutting drives, however, the successor programs to *Wide World of Sports*, *Sports Saturday* and *Sports Sunday*, were 'canned' in July 1999 by Channel Nine, leaving much of this TV sports field to Channel Seven programs like *Sportsworld* and *World Sports*, and to the Foxtel pay TV service in which Packer's PBL had taken a 25 per cent stake as part of its previously noted 'treaty' with the Murdoch-controlled News Limited. Nonetheless, more targeted, sports-specific free-to-air TV shows like Channel Nine's *The Sunday Footy Show*, Seven's *Footy Grandstand*, *Alive and Kicking* and *Sportsworld Footy Panel*, and Ten's *Extreme Games*, alongside live, delayed telecast and highlights sports programming on both public and commercial networks, ensure that there is little escape from sport for weekend daytime (and in some slots evening and late-night) viewers.

The advantage of such forms of sports programming from the perspective of TV economics (even if somewhat diminished in the eyes of James Packer) is that they are predominantly studio-based and so, instead of requiring elaborate outside broadcasts, involve pre-packaged material, familiar studio presenters, and regular and occasional guests. While the action is not live-to-air or even a 'delayed telecast' in sports news and magazine programs, there is still considerable reliance on the visual spectacle of the captured sports performance. However, the boundaries of sports television are now stretched further by forms of sports programming with much less concern with showing recent action highlights. TV sport has spawned several sub-genres which themselves derive from—and also combine and synthesise—other genres like variety, comedy, chat and quiz shows.

The movement away from an absolute dependence on live sports action is fairly long-standing in Australian television, but this was, in the 1970s and 1980s, a rather tentative and contained move which produced sports controversialists like Lew Richards and Bobbie Skelton in Australian Rules Football, and Rex Mossop in Rugby League, fulminating against some aspect of their respective football codes deemed to be objectionable. This hectoring style of sports TV discourse, appropriately, helped engender its own parody and *pastiche* in later forms of sports and quasi-sports television. For example, the sports 'ironists' 'Rampaging' Roy Slaven and HG Nelson, in *This Sporting Life* and in the variety shows *Club Buggery* and *Roy and HG*, picked up on the language of excess in sports discussion/post mortem programs and used them to considerable comic effect. The possibilities presented by taking established sports TV genres and 'tweaking' them somewhat have been to date most fully exploited in Australia in *Live and Sweaty*, a late-night comedy show on the ABC that ran for four seasons between 1992 and 1995.

Following its initial hosting by Andrew Denton, *Live and Sweaty* provided a rather unlikely TV site in which the highly conservative, male traditionalist Rex Mossop encountered current and former professional sportspeople, and also passing celebrities on the chat show circuit (including, notably, 'queer' singer k.d. lang). The particular irony of the later seasons of *Live and Sweaty* is that control of this televisual space (devoted to a key bastion of Australian masculinity) was exercised by three women—Elle McFeast, Karen Tighe and Debbie Spillane—in a calculated inversion of the prevailing sports gender order. As Jackie Cook and Karen Jennings put it:

> The postmodern playfulness of this television has re-articulated the patriarchal positioning of sports television. And with it has come a powerful eroticism, part conventional female objectification, part counter sexualisation of the male, part homo-erotic sexual fluidity, part high-camp parody. (Cook and Jennings 1995: 11)

If Cook and Jennings took this female appropriation of 'variety' sports TV to be a pointer to the future, it was not to be. Just prior to the publication of their celebratory article, the show's run ended, and there has been a reassertion of the predominant role of men. As noted above, the satirical *faux* sports commentary of Roy and HG has been a significant TV phenomenon which, in routinely subjecting various excessive displays of sporting masculinity to ridicule, has paradoxically reproduced the sport–masculinity nexus that has shaped most forms of sports television (somewhat attenuated, it must be recalled, by the belated 'discovery' of the large actual and potential female audience for live TV sports action—see Miller 1998).

Here a connection can be seen with developments over the last decade in British sports TV, which has supplemented live action, edited highlights and the long-running quiz show *Question of Sport* with several 'new laddish' sports shows like *They Think It's All Over* (a sentence from a famous snatch of TV soccer commentary from the 1966 soccer World Cup) and *Fantasy Football League* (an offshoot of which, *Fantasy World Cup*, was shown in Australia by SBS TV during the 1998 soccer World Cup Finals in France). Such shows also follow a parodic postmodern path spiced with a clear indulgence of the deep affective investment that many men have made in sport. In Australia, however, the current preference is for all-male 'footy' shows (devoted to Australian Rules and League, and themselves once parodied in the TV sketch comedy *Full Frontal* by an all-woman panel of sexist netball followers) which eschew ironic, even mildly reflexive comedy in favour of 'smutty' humour, bodily function jokes and 'matey' banter in front of a studio audience dressed mainly in football colours, 'revved up' by the studio band and mimicking elements of rowdy crowd behaviour at football matches.

The 1998 season of the Rugby League *Footy Show* on Channel Nine, for example, is described by journalist Heath Gilmore (1999: 6) as 'a raunchy show, great for a buck's night', the 'highlights' of which included:

> Mr Methane, an English performance artist, who used his bodily functions to blow out candles and play wind instruments . . .
>
> Peter Sterling reading a letter to Laurie Daley from a female fan who wanted to do all manner of lewd things to regions under his footy gear.
>
> The woman was then dragged from the studio audience to show various bits of her anatomy and leer seductively.
>
> And who could forget the Pick-A-Bum competition in which contestants were asked to identify which pair of quivering buttocks belonged to whom [?].
>
> The clincher would be the female who sucked the toes of a former player known far and wide as Crusher Cleal. (Gilmore 1999: 6)

To which can be added *The Footy Show*'s intense and lascivious interest in the transcontinental (and now defunct) relationship between footballer Solomon Haumono and Gabrielle Richens, the latter acquiring the nickname 'The Pleasure Machine' (giving Richens sufficient prominence to appear, among other media spaces, as an *Australian Playboy* centrefold). Its Melbourne-based Australian rules equivalent has gained similar notoriety, not least through host Sam Newman's 'blacking up' to impersonate a 'no show' guest, Aboriginal footballer Nicky Winmar (for which Newman was required to issue a public—and plainly uncon-vincing—apology).

This brand of 'boof headed' humour, loaded with sexual innuendo and lame jokes acted out in the League *Footy Show* by the expert footballers-turned-inexpert-TV presenters nicknamed Fatty (Paul Vautin), Sterlo (Peter Sterling) and Blocker (Steve Roach), is carefully designed to elicit a benignly head-shaking affection for the ordinary 'blokes' behind the desk largely indistinguishable from their everyday counterparts in the studio and lounge room (and seen as indulged by the everyday 'sheilas' in both locations). The genre also encompasses serious sporting matters, most dramatically during the aforementioned Super League War, when the show adopted a highly partisan advocacy role as loyal Packer employees. Here, and in the eruption of issues with wider social ramifications such as violence (including domestic), racism, sexism, homophobia, drunkenness and the use of performance-enhancing drugs, there is a highly evident uneasy relationship between the idealised sporting world and the 'social world' calling it to account. However, such controversies have their commercial uses, also auto-generating publicity for *The Footy Show*, as in the case of Peter Sterling's self-confessed 'outburst' against Rupert Murdoch's *Daily Telegraph*. Objecting to the newspaper's criticisms of the current state of League and of *The Footy Show* itself, Sterling described it on camera as 'an absolute disgrace' and 'a piece of rubbish', throwing the paper over his shoulder with the approval of Vautin, who described it as 'a heap of trash'. Less than forty-eight hours later, Sterling (1999) was explaining 'Why I blew my stack' exclusively in the pages of *The Newcastle*

Herald (1999), which carried a 'page one teaser' for the article, as well as its own descriptive news story about the incident, 'Sterlo defends tirade', immediately above it.

Such cross-referential and multimedia discourse, spread over Sterling's and others' appearances as 'callers' of live rugby league and hosts of 'review' programs like *The Sunday Footy Show*, and as commentators on radio and in print, generates an important publicity momentum for the key Thursday night *Footy Show*. But the balance between seriousness and carnivalesque humour is carefully maintained and monitored to the extent that, in 1999, the show claimed to be 'dumping bad taste', although: 'The boys will still resort to skit humour. And there is one final piece of good news for fans—the dresses stay on.' (Gilmore 1999: 6) This frequent deployment of 'cross-dress humour' is an instance of the carriage of the off-field leisure practices of male football teams on to the *The Footy Show* screen. It leads us, finally, to a consideration of what the social uses of the various genres of TV sport might be.

THE USES OF TV SPORT

We have discussed the extent to which sport on television performs many functions for different viewers, simulating the experience of attending sports events, distracting casual observers with bright, noisy spectacle, providing opportunities for unreconstructed male bonding, and supplying the pretext for the comic exploration of prevailing gender relationships and identities. Watching sport on television is a complex and diverse social activity, ranging from a 'default' activity when no better leisure options are available to greatly relished rituals of social engagement with family and friends (see various chapters in Wenner 1998). This 'plasticity' of social uses of television sport is matched by the many ways in which sports material can be presented and represented. In a television system that, following the arrival of multi-channel TV, is increasingly content hungry, sport provides much cheap and globally mobile program fodder. Even more importantly, as the age of free-to-air broadcasting hegemony passes, sport is perceived by media entrepreneurs as, in Rupert Murdoch's words, 'a battering ram' which can open up the private domestic sphere to the full range of possibilities going far beyond subscription and pay-per-view television to telephonic and information-based services. As Murdoch, Packer and other media moguls keenly appreciate, sport is consummately successful at attracting free-to-air audiences and, especially when key sports can be 'siphoned' off free-to-air and on to pay TV, represents the most potent means of building up a subscriber base (Rowe 1996).

In Australia, despite (according to Gareth Grainger 1996: 25) making 'the bravest effort at an effective anti-siphoning regime ever undertaken anywhere in the world', the pressures are building up to follow the example of Britain and New Zealand in permitting the best games in the most popular live sports like soccer and Rugby Union to migrate to pay TV. For example, after the BBC lost broadcasting rights to international cricket to BSkyB and the commercial Channel Four, the 1999 England versus New Zealand test series could only be seen live on pay TV, with one hour's early evening highlights on free-to-air television. Free-to-air television, then—finding itself outbid for prime live TV rights—will, if regulatory systems fail (as they seem to have with some overseas cricket tours), only be able to broadcast less popular sports live, or (as is now common) will have to resort to delayed telecasts and brief (often non-prime time) highlights packages. The sports talk and 'clip' shows like *The Footy Show* and *Sports Tonight*, from this perspective, will look even more like poor compensation for free-to-air television's loss of prime live TV sport to cashed-up pay TV companies.

Sport, then, is absolutely central to the economics of television in all its forms and modes of delivery. Sydney's hosting in 2000 of the most famous global television spectacle of all—the Summer Olympic Games—is a sublime manifestation of the alliance between sport and television, with its compulsively excessive opening ceremony consistently setting new world records for global viewing (Gordon and Sibson 1998; Wilson 1998). Live action, discussion and analysis programs, and comedies—not to mention the stock nostalgic imagery for future 'remember when?' programs—all demonstrate the protean nature of the TV sport. This television genre is set, literally, to run and run.

Ten

Alan McKee

Prime-time drama: 77 Sunset Strip to SeaChange

Drama is an important part of Australia's free-to-air television schedule. Estimates suggest that on the commercial channels, in 1959, drama was 81 per cent of prime time programming; in 1979, it was 71 per cent (Moran 1985: 9); and in 1993, 55.6 per cent (O'Regan 1993: 76). This decline signifies both a broadening of the genres which are broadcast in prime time and the costliness of drama, rather than a dramatic decline in the prestige or popularity of the genre. This drama is a mixture of imported (mainly American and British) and local product. Over the 1990s, there was between three and half and five times as much imported as local drama in prime time; in 1993 local drama made up 'only 10.4 per cent of Australian programming on metropolitan commercial stations' (O'Regan 1993: 76).

In the late 1990s, during ratings periods, an average of around eight Australian adult drama series were being shown on Australian television in prime time. Excluded from this figure are serials such as *Neighbours* and *Home and Away*, which are considered in Chapter 8. During the 1990s, these included programs such as *Blue Heelers*, *Water Rats*, *Murder Call*, *SeaChange*, *Wildside*, *Stingers* and *All Saints*.

Despite the fact that so much more imported than local drama is shown, it is Australian drama programs which are consistently the most popular examples of the genre—and some of the most popular programs on television. Drama programs appear consistently in the top ten national television programs each week: Australian programs in the top five, and imported drama series usually in the lower half of the charts. During 1998, the most popular drama series on television were all Australian. In the period from July to October that year, the two most popular drama series in every week of the ratings period were Australian. American programs appeared lower in the top ten programs. The only genre which was consistently more popular than Australian drama was imported American sitcoms. Australian drama is consistently more popular than imported drama (although *some* imported programs are more popular than *some* Australian drama series).

OUTLINE HISTORY OF AUSTRALIAN TELEVISION DRAMA

When Australian television first began in some eastern states in 1956, there was no local television drama. In Albert Moran's account of the period 1956–64, he notes that the most popular drama series of this period were all imported: including '[p]opular Westerns [such as] . . . *Rawhide, Wagon Train, Cheyanne, Sugarfoot, Wanted Dead or Alive* and *Bonanza* . . . [and] popular crime series [like] . . . *77 Sunset Strip, The Untouchables* and *Dragnet*' (Moran 1993: 11). The turning point for Australian television drama came in 1964, with the Crawfords police series *Homicide*. Within a year, it was the highest rating program in both the Melbourne and Sydney markets.

It is always problematic to try to explain the success of programs retrospectively. With 20/20 hindsight, any explanation can be made to seem convincing. Moran suggests that at least part of the program's success can be explained by looking at the context in which it was broadcast—a context in which the previously successful American drama imports were no longer able to dominate the schedule. He notes that with the introduction of a third network (0–10) in 1964–65, 'there were barely enough programs to go around . . . the market now favoured the seller . . . Relations between American program distributors and Australian commercial television stations deteriorated to the extent that in 1966–67 no American programs were bought for nearly twelve months.' (Moran 1985: 30)

Whatever the reason, *Homicide* became 'the most successful drama series produced for Australian television', and ran for eleven years (Moran 1993: 15). It led to a flurry of (Crawford-produced) police series on all the commercial channels, *Matlock Police* and *Division Four* being the other channels' versions. In this first phase of television drama, it was the police series which reigned.

In the mid-1970s, the situation changed. If cop shows dominated the first period of Australian television drama, it was more soapie-style dramas which dominated in the mid- to late 1970s. Moran suggests that there have been three 'formative genres' in the history of Australian television drama: 'police crime series, soap opera, and the historical mini-series' (Moran 1989: 238). The second of these genres is addressed in Chapter 8. It is worth noting that *Homicide* was replaced by such programs as *Number 96, The Sullivans, Prisoner* and *A Country Practice* at the top of the Australian ratings.

At the same time that the soap operas were moving to the centre of Australian television's drama production, the mini-series was emerging as an important form of drama. For Albert Moran, 1976–86 are 'the golden years of drama', when mini-series became particularly important (1993: 19), starting with programs such as *Luke's Kingdom* (1974–75). From 1978 in particular, with the broadcast of *Against the Wind*, the mini-series really took off (Moran 1993: 21).

With the introduction of 10BA tax laws in 1981 (see below), the mini-series was consolidated as a central part of Australian television drama production. Mini-series were a particularly expensive form of television (I refer to them in the past tense because, although a small number are still produced, they no longer hold the dominant place in Australian television that they did during the 1980s), and tended to consist of a short number of episodes (from three to about thirteen), telling a single narrative across this length (Moran 1985: 11). The most typical mini-series feature 'the insertion of (sympathetic) fictional characters into "real" historical and/or institutional settings "in times of tremendous stress"' (Moran 1985: 207, quoting Paul Kerr). Some of the most notable examples of the form in Australian television history are *A Town Like Alice* (1981), *The Dismissal* and *Return to Eden* (1983) and *Bodyline* (1984).

The cyclical form of cultural movements can be seen in Albert Moran's comments on the displacement of police series by mini-series. Writing in 1989, Moran suggests that television cop shows had suffered 'displacement' by the mini-series (Moran 1989: 241). It is now obvious, with the immense and continued success during the 1990s of police shows such as *Blue Heelers* and *Water Rats*, that the mini-series itself has suffered 'displacement' in this decade. In a way, however, Moran might still be correct. He suggests that in recent television, it is no longer possible to have the absolutely discrete episodes of the television *series* (see Tulloch and Alvarado 1983). In all television drama now, he suggests, 'there is an intense stress on personal relationships of one kind or another with a constant narrative variation of relationships' (Moran 1989: 247). This is indeed the case with all of Australia's most successful recent drama series—even the cop shows will focus on the continuing narratives of the cops' personal lives as much as they do on the crime solving.

LEGISLATING AND REGULATING AUSTRALIAN CONTENT

While the ABC has never been subject to specific Australian content provision— although its charter requires the station to: 'provide . . . programs . . . that contribute to a sense of national identity' (Cunningham and Jacka 1996: 57)— commercial television has worked under Australian content quota regulation since 1960. The 1960 quota system required that, overall, Australian content should be 40 per cent of television output, with four hours per twenty-eight days being in prime time. No genre quotas were set within this general Australian category.

However, by 1966, drama programs were privileged within regulation by having their own quota level set.

> In 1963 the Vincent Committee had recommended that by 1966 Australian commercial television should have a drama quota of about 9 per cent of airtime. However the Liberal-Country Party government ignored the report . . . in 1966, two members of the ABCB under the instructions of the Minister began a second investigation . . . Late that year a drama quota was announced, although it was not to come into effect until the following year . . . The quota required stations to broadcast thirty minutes of locally produced drama each week . . . (Moran 1985: 32)

Since that time, Australian drama quotas have been a feature of television regulation. The 'points system', which was introduced in 1973, required stations to meet a certain number of points related to their hours of transmission and allocated different amounts of points to different categories of program and an annual quota of 104 hours of drama (Cunningham 1992: 53, 54). (A detailed table of the various quota requirements in Australian television up until 1985 is given in Moran 1985: 33.)

An inquiry by the Australian Broadcasting Tribunal, running from 1984 to 1989, then resulted in a new Television Standard which began operating in 1990. In this, the 'Australian factor' was described as: 'creative control of production, as evidenced by key indicators such as . . . "nationality of the producers, writers, directors, actors, composers and editors"' (Cunningham 1992: 60). As a backup, if there was 'conflict about creative control', the Tribunal also set out a series of textual features by which 'Australian content' might be measured: 'theme; perspective; language and character' were to be 'recognisably Australian' (1992: 57).

Revisions to the standard were introduced in January 1996 and in March 1999. The version current in 2000 states that Australian programs must be at least 55 per cent of all programming broadcast in a year by the licensee between 6.00 a.m. and midnight and that:

> the drama scores for all first release Australian drama programs broadcast in prime time in any year must total at least 225.
> The 'drama score' for an Australian drama program is calculated using the following formula:
> drama score = format factor x duration
> . . . the 'format factor' is:
> (a) for an Australian drama program that is a serial or series produced at the rate of more than 1 hour per week—1; and
> (b) for an Australian drama program that is a serial or series produced at the rate of 1 hour or less per week—2; and
> (c) for an Australian drama program that is a feature film, a telemovie, a mini-series, or self-contained drama of less than 90 minutes' duration—3.2.
> (Australian Broadcast Standard, 1999, Sections 10, 11)

In the latest versions of the standard, the definition of 'Australian content' on television 'does not contain any form of on-screen test' (Australian Broadcast Standard 1999), but is still justified in terms of 'seek[ing] to promote the role of Australian television in reflecting a sense of Australian identity, character and cultural diversity' (David Flint, in *ABA Update* 1999: 6). The change which has occurred in the 1999 version of the Standard is the recognition of New Zealand programs as being 'Australian' for the purposes of fulfilling quotas (see below).

FUNDING AUSTRALIAN TELEVISION DRAMA

Many of the changes in Australian television drama over the years can be linked to funding arrangements for the medium. O'Regan notes that:

> Australian television is a medium-sized Western television service operating in the English language. Servicing 17 million people, it is not large enough to support local programming across the schedule . . . Nor is it large enough to support the scale of local production in higher budgeted . . . limited episode serial television. (1993: 11–12)

Television drama is a particularly expensive form. It is much cheaper to import drama. Australian television has a 'double face': 'its medium size makes it more outward looking' (1993: 59).

The international context is particularly important for the genre of television drama. As Cunningham and Jacka note, most television genres are 'locally specific and are not heavily traded' (Cunningham and Jacka 1996: 40). This is true of genres such as news, current affairs, quiz and game shows, infotainment, sport and variety programs. It is drama programs (including soapies) and sitcoms which are amongst the most 'exportable' forms of television. And it is against this background that the production of Australian drama must be considered.

To buy local television drama is much more expensive for the Australian networks than to import programs. Depending on the popularity of the program, 'US television programs cost the [Australian] networks between half and one fifth of local programs' (Molloy and Burgan 1993: 115), while for other countries Woods estimates that, compared with local long-form series drama costs of $160 000 an hour, imported drama costs can be as little as $30 000 per hour (Woods 1998: 10).

Despite this fact, Australian television drama has been a regular part of schedules since 1964. The three major factors contributing to this are the consistent popularity of such programs (see above); regulation which promotes such programming (see above); and government support mechanisms.

10BA

Cunningham and Jacka note that: '[u]ntil the tax concessions introduced in 1980, virtually every Australian . . . high-budget television drama was funded through the Australian Film Commission' (1996: 59). The introduction in 1980 of 10BA tax concessions for investment in film and television production was hugely important for Australian television drama production. The forms of drama production it promoted were quite specific: both the AFC and 10BA were primarily oriented towards feature films, and their involvement in television was almost an afterthought (O'Regan 1989: 15). Because of this, both forms of government funding encouraged the production of *filmic* kinds of television: telemovies or limited-run mini-series. Neither AFC investment nor 10BA concessions applied to investment in long-running drama series. In this way, the 10BA may indeed have led to 'the golden age of Australian television' (Cunningham and Jacka 1996: 60)—if golden-ness is defined as becoming more filmic. Indeed, the 'convergence' of the film and television industries promoted by these kinds of government support for drama production has been noted by many writers (Cunningham 1993: 33; Moran 1989: 238; O'Regan 1989: 19).

Australian Film Finance Corporation

10BA tax concessions were wound back in 1988 and in stepped the Australian Film Finance Corporation (FFC). The FFC is 'the Commonwealth government's primary agency for providing investment to the Australian film and television production industry' and aims 'to realise the Commonwealth's objectives of ensuring the Australian film industry contributes to the projection of diverse images of Australia locally and overseas by direct investment in film and television' (FFC 1999). It is a wholly government-owned company, which works with the marketplace to try to produce commercially successful projects by acting as an investor in them, on a commercial basis. Once again, it is telemovies and mini-series which are supported by this organisation. And, once again, the televisual has been added as an afterthought.

At least until 2001, the FFC will be a continuing part of the Australian television funding situation, with the Commonwealth government guaranteeing funding of at least $48.015 million per annum until the financial year 2000/01 (FFC 1999). For 1998–99, its investment targets are: features: 50–60 per cent; television drama: 30–40 per cent; and documentaries: 10–15 per cent.

Australian Commercial Television Fund

From 1995 to 1998, the AFC administered the Australian Commercial Television Fund—a fund established especially to promote quality commercial television drama production in Australia. The fund received up to $20 million a year, and its logic was to promote the production of television drama in excess to legislated quota requirement. Once again, it was non-series forms which were promoted: 'In its first year of operation, the CTPF assisted in the production of twenty-six hours of new Australian drama, comprising six telemovies, one mini-series, a half-hour anthology series, a children's telemovie and a family movie.' (AFC 1996: 5)

Although the Fund was not renewed past June 1998, a number of projects have gone on to further series.

It should be noted that the tendency for government investment not to fund long-form drama is based on the assumption that it is a more commercial product that can work unassisted in the marketplace. As Albert Moran notes, the long-running drama series 'offers certain advantages in terms of the organisation of both production and reception/consumption' (Moran 1985: 10). The reuse of sets and actors, and the regularised production schedule for writers and directors, mean that longer-running series are more financially efficient than one-off drama productions, while the regularity of series broadcast well suits the 'dailiness' and everyday familiarity of the television medium (see Scanell 1996: 155).

According to figures produced by the Australian Film Commission in 1996, 'production [of series and serials] has been reasonably stable, an average of sixteen titles totalling $100 million have been produced per year since 1988/99' (AFC 1996: 62). As to financing, the AFC notes that: '[i]n the five years to 1994/95, according to the ABA, annual expenditure on drama and children's television by commercial networks fell from nearly $127 million to $85 million' (1996: 4). This can be explained with reference to the financial crises experienced by all the commercial networks in the early 1990s—since that time, 'they have generally been wary of spending money on high-quality drama . . . long running soaps have been seen as a safe way to reach Australian content quotas' (AFC 1996: 5).

The companies

One of the most visible effects of this decline has been a major reduction in the number of independent production companies working in Australia. Molloy and Burgan note that the number of independent producers fell by 43 per cent in the period 1988 to 1993 (1993: 41). Now 'the production of Australian television drama is highly concentrated: the vast majority of programs in this category are produced by relatively few . . . firms' (Molloy and Burgan 1993: 37). The AFC notes that 'the mid-1990s saw four big players consolidate their positions, namely Southern Star, Village Roadshow, Artist Services and Beyond' (AFC 1996: 5).

Particularly important in the 1990s was Southern Star. The importance of this particular production company is undeniable: by the end of 1998, Southern Star was producing the three most popular drama series on Australian television: *Blue Heelers, Water Rats* and *Murder Call* (Southern Star 1998: 7). By 1994, *Blue Heelers* had established itself as the highest rating Australian drama and held that position for half a decade. By the end of the decade, Southern Star entertainment was 'Australia's leading producer of television programs' (Southern Star 1998: 7).

Part of the success of Southern Star may be explained by its international marketing presence. The combination of less money available from local networks and an increasingly global television market has encouraged television drama producers to seek coproduction deals, and international pre-sales for their product. In the 1990s, Southern Star International and Beyond International were 'the only two significant Australian-owned independent international distributors' (Cunningham and Jacka 1996: 108).

DRAMA AS GENRE

Albert Moran and John Tulloch have written on the production of drama series (Moran 1982; Tulloch and Moran 1986). Albert Moran has also written on production contexts and provided some analysis of the programs (1985). Some of the articles in John Tulloch and Graeme Turner's collection *Australian Television: Programs, Pleasures and Politics* address drama series (1989). The best reference work on Australian drama is Albert Moran's *Moran's Guide to Australian TV Series* (1993)—which only lists drama series and serials and sitcoms, and does not include any current affairs, game shows, infotainment or other genres. A number of articles on soap operas, drama series and mini-series are scattered across various collections and journals (see, for example, Moran 1985; Cunningham 1984; Stern 1982; Moran 1989).

Attempting to survey writing on television drama, it quickly becomes apparent how imprecise the category is. For Cunningham and Miller, 'genre is often said to be the essence of TV' (1994: 9). However, the category of 'drama' is an odd one. Whereas cinema can boast a number of relatively stable and obvious genres (Western, horror, action movie, for example), television's genres are much less obvious. Indeed, television programs often seem to be categorised by *format* more than by genre: for example, a sit-com is half an hour long and has a laugh track, but its content can include anything from the Korean War (*M*A*S*H*) to a blended family (*The Brady Bunch*). The category 'drama' is particularly porous. The classification 'series and serials' can include everything from *A Country Practice* to *Bananas in Pyjamas*. Albert Moran uses the category 'drama'—but includes within it sitcoms and soap operas. In this book, we separate 'drama' and 'soap operas', although the boundaries between the two of these are not clear.

It is no longer possible to make a simple distinction between programs, as Tulloch and Alvarado previously did, on the basis of whether episodes of the program have discrete narratives (in which case they are series) or ongoing ones (serials). As noted above, almost all Australian drama programs now contain serial (continuing) elements from one episode to the next.

One of the ways in which we might try to make sense of drama, however, is by appealing to a sense of seriousness, gravitas or importance that seems to adhere to the title—in short, 'quality'. Bruce Best, for example, the executive producer of the ABC's series *GP*, insisted that the program was not a soap opera—it was drama because it dealt with 'serious issues' (Best 1993). It is such a formulation—whereby the genre of drama is defined by 'quality' (in opposition to, say, soapies)—which makes sense of comments such as that by the Vincent Committee, which reported to the federal government on Australian broadcasting in 1963:

> Of all types of television programs, drama is recognised, said the senators, as having the greatest sociological, psychological and emotional impact upon the audience. Drama is the most powerful weapon of all in its effects upon the moral standards of the community and in influencing its attitudes . . . (quoted in Docker 1991: 13, 12)

A similar suggestion is propounded by Paterson, when he argues that:

> television drama plays a major role in all television systems because it aspires, even without self-conscious reflection, to address the cultural identity of its audience . . . [it] can act as a national theatre devoted to representing nations to themselves. (Paterson 1998: 62, 64)

As John Tulloch notes, the question of deciding what counts as 'drama' on television is an important (and ideologically informed) one (Tulloch 1990: 1). He notes the tendency to collapse 'drama' into 'serious drama' (1990: 4). In attempting to make sense of the category, however, this seems to be a necessary step for deciding what distinguishes 'drama' as a genre.

Within cultural theory, some writers see genres not as collections of texts so much as 'historically and culturally variable systems for the regulation of reading and writing practices' (Bennett, quoted in Cunningham and Miller 1994: 11; see also Neale 1990: 46; Jameson 1981: 106–7). From this point of view, genres exist as interpretive systems, used by audiences to make sense of programs (i.e. if this is a horror film, then the basement must be a dangerous place to be; if this is a cop show, then crime must be punished, etc.).

For other writers, genres are symptomatic of wider cultural moods and concerns (Kitses 1969; Schatz 1981; Grant 1986; Noriega 1987): they are like myths, which reconcile problems in social experience in order to come to a hegemonic conclusion (Tulloch 1990: 63); they are 'both adaptive and conservative' (1990: 65); they deal with novelty in social experiences by 'paper[ing] over contradictions', trying to establish consensual positions and create workable discourses about how society functions. Genres 'wor[k] . . . ideological tensions, anxieties and fantasies into fictional forms' (James Donald, quoted in Tulloch 1990: 71), in order to 'bind together fragmented social order' (1990: 72).

From this latter, mythic, perspective, writers on one particular kind of drama have argued that 'the police series is principally concerned with negotiating the boundaries between a familiar, predictable world and another more anarchic, more twilight one' (Moran 1985: 174). Cunningham and Miller suggest that more recent cop shows are quite different from those in the first phase of drama production:

> Police shows of the 1960s, notably the archetypal *Homicide*, concentrated on the social landscape and the professional specifics of policing—its public face. By

contrast, later programs tend to construct an interiority for their characters. A set of emotional tendencies merges with action and office life to produce soap-operatic forms such as *Police Rescue*. Police stories, like other dramatic genres, increasingly work to broker the relationship between the private and public spheres. (1994: 14)

Moran argues that one continuing element of cop shows is the lack of courts—and this is ideologically important. 'The complexities of social order, law and criminality are reduced to crime, identification, pursuit and capture,' he argues. 'Instead, detection and apprehension become synonymous with guilt; the police become agents not only of law, but of justice too.' (Moran 1985: 162) To focus on the courts, he suggests, would necessarily make the issues of criminality less black and white—for law is about rhetoric, reasonable doubt, convincing jurists of the guilt of suspects. By contrast, in cop shows there is little doubt as to the guilt of individual criminals by the end of the show—thus the overplayed device of the criminals confessing to their crimes, even though the cops have not 'proved' that they did it.

Despite this, the ideological conservatism of Australia's currently dominant form of television drama should not be overstated. In many ways, Australia's drama programs are particularly (small 'l') liberal in their attitudes towards social issues. This can be traced as a common factor in Australian drama since at least *A Country Practice*.

A Country Practice is probably the ur-text of the Australian television drama which has entered the 'televisual memory'. Broadcast from 1981 to 1994, the program was, throughout the 1990s, still being played daily on daytime Channel Seven. And, as Tulloch and Moran's account of this program makes clear, episodes of the show were often constructed around 'social issues' (Tulloch and Moran 1986: 38). A social issue can be defined as a matter raised in the media as being something of public concern, and whose provenance is in the area called the 'social' (not the political, not the individual). This is a governed realm, overseen by 'qualified personnel' (Deleuze 1979: ix) such as social workers, police, nurses and doctors and so on. It is these 'qualified personnel' who have often been the heroes of Australian television drama: the social has been their arena, and the 'social problem' has been their means of engagement with it.

Blue Heelers is not the most 'social issue' oriented television drama program in 1990s Australia. *All Saints* and *State Coroner* are much more in the tradition of the 'issue of the week'. Nevertheless, it does deal with social issues on a regular basis: police corruption, business ethics, arranged marriages, suicide, infertility, HIV infection, fostering, environmental pollution, vigilante justice and heroin use are just some of the issues which have been addressed. In the cop shows (although not to the same extent as other dramas), there is an identifiable (small 'l') liberal impulse—much more so than in news and current affairs programs, for example. In television drama, there is often an explanation for crime, an oppressed group to be defended, or a matter of cultural relativism to be respected. This is not true for news and current affairs programs, where criminals are simply 'they', against whom 'we' must be protected (Hartley 1992: 206). For example, the *State Coroner* episode 'Assumptions' (2 November 1998) deals with gang membership and drug dealing in the Sydney Vietnamese community, concluding with the magistrate's solemn summing up:

> While the majority of the Vietnamese community is law abiding and productive, a significant proportion of our young migrant population becomes marginalised. I urge the relevant authorities to continue to address the problems of such youngsters.

Drawing attention to wider social trends and explanations rather than focusing solely on final events, the social analysis of television drama is quite different from that of news and current affairs. It functions as an important 'liberal' area in Australia's public sphere (with, of course, the limitations that such a political approach suggests).

CULT TELEVISION

Cult programs are those which are: 'set apart from the mainstream . . . Cult programs are the objects of special devotion . . . [and] passion' (Lewis and Stempel 1993: 8). Examples on Australian television in the 1990s include *The X-Files, Buffy the Vampire Slayer, Xena: Warrior Princess* and *Star Trek: Voyager*. It is immediately apparent that these programs have something in common: they are all American imports (*Xena* is made in New Zealand but is American).

Reeves et al. (1996) argue that the emergence of cult television programs can be traced to the original *Star Trek* series in the 1960s, and that the phenomenon is closely linked to economic formations:

> the emergence of cult TV [is] one of the chief manifestations of the most extreme shift the American mass-communication 'complex' has experienced since the 1950s . . . the drift from the mass marketing of the 'Fordist' manufacturing economy to the niche marketing of the 'post-Fordist' service economy. (Reeves et al. 1996: 24)

They see cult television as a 'post-Fordist' phenomenon: programming which does not attempt to gain the largest audience possible, but rather seeks to claim a smaller, devoted audience within a particular demographic, which will then consume the program and its related paraphernalia and merchandising.

There is a shift from 'TVI' to 'TVII'. 'TVI' describes 'network era television':

> once [the three networks] commanded over 90 per cent of the audience, today the major network audience has decreased to about 60 percent . . . CBS's 'rural purge' in 1971 [saw] the cancellation of highly rated shows . . . because they did not attract segments of the population that were most valued by advertisers . . . 'Popularity' came to mean high ratings with the eighteen- to forty-nine-year-old urban dweller rather than popularity with the older rural audience. (Jane Feuer, quoted in Reeves et al. 1996: 30)

Facing the loss of the 'mass' audience in the face of competition from other forms of television—primarily pay TV—the networks were forced instead to chase 'quality demographics'. It is to this factor that Reeves et al. attribute a shift in forms of television: 'the networks' pursuit of sophisticated viewers . . . has provided economic incentive for supporting other narrative innovations that are often labelled "postmodern"' (1996: 30).

The shift to TVII has happened in Australia in particular and limited ways. Australian television does offer examples of cult drama, but they are all imported (usually from America). Channel 10 is the strongest example of TVII in Australia, explicitly aiming for a youth demographic rather than mass audiences—and it does so by programming far more American drama in prime time than any other station. While Australian drama remains resolutely in the realm of 'TVI'— attempting to reach the largest possible audience, with little in the way of 'postmodern' innovation—American 'cult' programs have a strong presence in the Australian mediasphere. Australian programs which have attempted to inno- vate in such a way (the final episodes of *Chances* or *Good Guys, Bad Guys*) have not had the public presence of the American examples. Gwenllian-Jones and Pearson (forthcoming) address many American and British 'cult' television pro- grams: *Quatermass, Xena, Star Trek, The X-Files, The Prisoner, Babylon 5, Twin Peaks, Doctor Who, The Avengers, Batman*: there are no Australian examples in their collection.

Many of these programs have been successful in Australia. Programs such as *Xena* are never in the top ten listings, but their cultural presence can be immense. *Xena*, for example, has offered new cultural material for making sense of social relations in Australia: the figure of the competent, strong, but still very sexual and feminised heroine. In an article in *TV Week*, for example, the possible retirement of Lucy Lawless from the role of Xena leads to a discussion of suitable replacements from within the Australian public sphere—Lisa McCune, Sigrid Thornton, Kathy Kinney and Pauline Hanson. All of these Australians have their faces pasted on Xena's famous leather and metalwork costume (*TV Week* 1998: 9). Xena is used to mock the last of these: 'does she suffer from Xena-phobia? Please explain?'—a reference to an infamous incident in a *60 Minutes* interview during which Hanson, asked if she were xenophobic, failed to understand the term and asked 'Please explain?' This phrase was widely disseminated, not least in the song 'I'm a Backdoor Man', a collection of choice Hanson phrases, recut and rearranged by Sydney drag queen Pauline Pantsdown. This familiar part of the Australian political sphere is melded with the figure of Xena.

New Idea similarly draws Xena into the Australian mediasphere, and again into the area of politics. Asked who she would like to 'swap lives with for a day', Natasha Stott Despoja, Australian Democrats Senator, replies that Xena would be her ideal: 'I want to wear that breastplate in the Senate!': as with *TV Week*, Stott Despoja's face is here pasted on to 'that breastplate' (*New Idea* 1998: 21). Here, Xena is called upon to represent a feminised version of power (armour and breasts, all in one), in order to make sense of the role of an Australian political figure.

TV Week links the gay community with Xena via the 'Please explain' of Paulines Pantsdown and Hanson—but there are more direct links as well. Xena has become an important part of the self-identity of Australian lesbian and gay communities. For example, the Gay and Lesbian Mardi Gras has become an important part of Australia's national identity in recent years. Indeed, in an article entitled 'The Sum of Us' (Carey, 1995), trailed with the question 'Who are we?', the *Age* places this celebration squarely at the centre of Australia's national imaginary. On the cover of the *Age Good Weekend* magazine, a range of 'Australian' images are juxtaposed: the Mardi Gras dancing boys are mixed with unreconstructed suburbia (Noeline Donahue), Aboriginality (Cathy Freeman), the bushman (*Crocodile Dundee*), Asia and surfing and Anzac Day to provide a mosaic of what 'Australia' might mean in the 1990s. 'What does it say about Australia's national identity that one of our most popular grassroots festivals . . . is a celebration of homosexuality?' asks the article (Carey, 1995: 30). The Mardi Gras has made queer sexuality a central part of 'Australia'. And a part of this particularly queer national identity is *Xena: Warrior Princess*—famously, at the last two Mardi Gras parades, the 'marching Xenas' (one hundred lesbians in Xena costumes) have marched down Oxford Street in Sydney. This is a television program produced in New Zealand, by an American company, appropriated by a subculture, and returned to the nation via a commercial television channel.

Programs like *The X-Files, Melrose Place* and *Xena: Warrior Princess* have been important in Australia as examples of imported cult TV drama which have not scored top ten ratings, but have nevertheless become important parts of the Australian mediasphere.

Many thanks to John Rapsey for his suggestions and advice in preparing this chapter.

Eleven John Hartley

The television live event: From the 'wandering booby' to the 'death of history'

BORN UNDER A WANDERING BOOBY

In its early years, TV was transmitted live as it was produced. This was a technical requirement before the advent of videotape. Liveness therefore applied to drama, comedy and variety acts, not just to outside broadcasts and actuality. Indeed, at the launch of the BBC Television Service in 1936, drama was live but news was not. Instead of news, the BBC transmitted *British Movietone News*, newsreels made for cinema exhibition.

By comparison with cinema, television's ability to do fiction and light entertainment from the studio in real time was remarkable. But its achievement was also the reason why it was doomed. A flavour of the vicissitudes of live drama transmission can be had from this passage by Nigel Kneale, legendary writer of the *Quatermass* 'science fiction' series of the 1950s:

> Control . . . precision. These are the elements that until recently were always unpleasantly lacking in live television.
>
> Weeks of rehearsal would culminate in the studio on transmission day. Now the filmed and live scenes would join for the first time. All the actual sets, props, effects were there at last. Now and only now could the actual effect of the play be assessed—when it was too late to alter anything. Not only that, but disaster could strike in many forms. Your leading man could fall sick or drop dead. It's only remarkable that more haven't done so . . . Most destructive of all, to the production and the author's intentions, was the wandering booby. Appearing in his

dust-coat at the court of Henry VIII, or outside a 40th-floor window of a skyscraper. One play of mine had what was intended as a tense, penultimate scene in a Himalayan ice cave at 22 000 feet. Two heavily clad actors were acting hard on transmission when a figure appeared outside the cave. It wore a dust-coat and was busily sweeping up the eternal snows. A booby, it turned out, who was in a hurry to get home and thought he would clear up early. In those days plays were repeated live a few days later, so at the second transmission he was firmly warned. To make sure, the cave was rendered booby-proof with a black sky-cloth and a large stack of boxes. But with a waywardness that had something wonderful in it, he managed to appear again. They should put up a statue to him at the Television Centre, a monument to the old days.

Now video tape enables the whole production to be pre-recorded . . . The day of the booby is almost done. (Kneale 1959)

Live drama gave way to pre-recorded performances, in order for directors and producers—not to mention the hapless actors—to establish the kind of 'control and precision' that was already familiar in film. So *unfamiliar* did the spectacle of actors making a mess of things in front of cameras eventually become that it spawned an entirely new genre of television entertainment—the out-take 'blooper' shows done as comedy, such as *It'll Be Alright on the Night* and *Auntie's Bloomers*. The 'wayward booby' was back, starring in its own show.

'LIVENESS' AS A RITUAL OF IMPROVABLE COMMUNITY

But even as live transmission gave way to videotaping, a myth of 'liveness' was assiduously cultivated within the TV industry itself. 'Liveness' was a marketing advantage, a property of the new technology that could be used to encourage *governments* to liberalise the licensing of TV stations, *investors* to support TV's very costly infrastructural development, and *viewers* to buy or rent the expensive decoding apparatus.

Nevertheless, even in actuality and the 'OB' or outside broadcast, television was not really all that 'live'. Outside broadcasts were expensive and required major planning. They were reserved for events that were themselves major exercises in live presentation. It seemed obvious that OB trucks (one for the scanner, one for the transmitter, one for the generator) would be sent to places where something was guaranteed not only to occur but also to be of existing interest to a large number of ordinary people. OB was not sent to shops, streets, beaches, private dwellings, or other haunts of 'the' people themselves, nor was it seen in the public sphere, at local government meetings, in the boardrooms or factories of industry, in classrooms, laboratories, churches or ports. TV took a long while to relax sufficiently to go out and about into an unrehearsed, unstaged version of live reality. TV's 'liveness' was that of the theatre—the performative kind. Compared with radio (even patrician BBC radio), live television actuality was over-produced and unspontaneous.

But what made the 'liveness' of television more than a delusion of critics habituated to the oedipal dark of a movie theatre, or a self-serving marketing slogan for commercial exploitation, was that television as a medium eventually crossed the boundary from technology or industry to become a *cultural* form. As 'culture' (rather than invention or investment), television had a combination of characteristics that other media couldn't match. It was public—unlike telephony—and visual—unlike radio. Unlike cinema, television's public visualisations could appear *now*. This lent them an 'unauthored' quality—if something was live, it may not simply represent the intentions of the broadcaster, be they commercial, political or ideological (never mind artistic). Viewers could imagine that 'television' wasn't a creation of the television institution itself. Film and television addressed their 'readers' in different *tenses*—film discourse was done in the past-perfect tense; TV narrated in the present tense. Film was literally a *fait accompli*; TV could nudge up against 'nextness'. No one—neither producer nor audience—knew what would happen next. This was what made 'liveness' appealing for the audience.

Furthermore, these un-authored public visualisations of the 'here and now' appeared in the domestic environment of the private home, to be seen in the context and perhaps even the company of intimate family. In 1952, British documentarist Michael Clarke suggested how this combination of characteristics might improve society. He thought that television could be 'an influence which would help to abolish the atomic concept of society which grows more and more powerful and seductive.' 'Atomization' was 'a potentially appalling situation; for our culture encourages individualism, and our political and economic behaviour in the mass is inevitably conditioned by appeals to individual, not group, self-interest.' TV could lessen the 'isolation of the individual . . . For the television set in hundreds of thousands of homes ought to be a tremendous influence to make us better informed about the fascinating detail of the complex, modern world.' (Clarke 1952: 184–85)

What's more, TV could exercise this benign 'influence' 'in our homes, where we are least vulnerable to the illusions to which, in the group, we might succumb'. Television was hailed as something *less* ideological, because it was less produced, than other media. It would signal the end of 'mass' political persuasion and the baleful influence of the demagogue (a quite proper nightmare for mid-twentieth century imaginations). Instead, thought Clarke, 'we all need the easy, informal education that television can provide' (1952: 186). For him, the positive potential of television was its ability to bring 'isolated' or 'atomised' individuals together, in their homes (away from undue influence), as a community, to experience live events that would inform, educate and improve the whole society.

Here was a 'theory' of the 'live event' that went on to be put into practice. The television live event was developed and used around the world as a secular ritual of community-building. What made all this important was broadcast television's eventual popularity—its ability not simply to bring live events into 'the' home, but into *everyone's* home, linking a nation together in front of one event, or one show. It wasn't long before television could link people from different nations together as well; it was able to domesticate a sense of global belonging, and equate its audience with *humanity*, never mind 'our country'. Clarke's optimistically imagined 'hundreds of thousands of homes' became billions.

TV could *visualise* people's sense of 'imagined community'—the confidence most people had of belonging to a country, even though they had not met and never would meet more than an infinitesimal proportion of its actual inhabitants, their co-citizens (Anderson 1991). Such a sense of community was nurtured via:

- *institutions*—for example, national sporting bodies and teams, schools, government, national arts and cultural organisations;
- *discourses*—for example, nationalism, a national language, patriotic rhetoric and images, celebrity;
- *rituals*—for example, traditionally associated with collective religious observance, but modernised into rituals of secular 'communion' with others inside a specific time/space context (e.g. watching on TV the same event that millions of others were 'known' to be seeing simultaneously).

TV combined all three of these. Institutionally, in Britain and Australia, legislation produced the 'national broadcaster': the BBC and ABC. This pattern was common throughout the Commonwealth, such as Doordarshan in India, SABC in South Africa, CBC in Canada and STV in Singapore. In free-enterprise America, the institutional form of television was established uniformly across the nation, but not as a monopoly, rather as Network TV + local affiliates, a very stable arrangement that survived unchallenged for nearly fifty years.

Discursively, television excelled in a national mode of address within daily programming such as news, sport and weather forecasting. In this context, the myth of 'liveness' was particularly strong. News was always presented as-if-live, even when it contained film from foreign parts that may have taken three days to be flown to the TV station, processed, edited and voice-overed. The important thing was not the newsgathering, but the population-gathering: news *presentation* was live, and the nation was gathered around the act of disclosure not origination. News was *discursively* (if not temporally) live because the 'liveness' allowed something that was not literally true to be understood, accepted and acted upon as if it were true—namely, that 'the nation' was self-conscious.

Ritually, like radio before it (and alongside it), television proved ideal as a site for daily private family rituals of reconsumption, via fanship for given genres, especially news, drama series and soap opera. The 'TV altar' may have been public, but observances at it were private. The connection between them was 'the nation'. In its broadcast heyday (the late 1950s to the 1990s), TV also exceeded the reach of any prior communications technology. Watching TV (not all of it broadcast) became the most popular pastime the world had ever known. Thus TV was ritualised as an institutionalised discourse of national togetherness. TV became *seriously* popular, and its visual capacity within a domestic environment made it ideal for ritualised acts of imagining, organised around the symbolic connectivity between person, home (i.e. family) and country.

NATIONAL IDENTITY CRISIS (LIVE, ON TV)

TV performed the feat of bringing together an imagined community for many modern and modernising nations during a period when it was getting less and less obvious what that community was. With migration, multiculturalism and globalisation, and with the fragmentation of national identity away from ethnic and territorial markers, it became harder to answer with confidence the question 'how—by what evidence—do I know I'm Australian (or British or American)?' at a personal level. And at a collective level, with the emergence of new identities based on gender, non-indigenous ethnicities, sexual orientation, age, religion—even taste—it became difficult to specify definitively what counted as Englishness, Australianness, Americanness.

What had once seemed 'natural'—for instance, that the 'normal citizen' was a male, white, Anglo-Saxon Protestant or WASP—came to be seen as sexist, racist, sectarian and exclusionary. National communities included people of colour, migrants, Indigenous people and sub-national ethnic minorities. It was not safe to extrapolate from any particular lifestyle to pronounce on what was appropriate for anyone else. Indeed, terms that had once seemed full of meaning—like 'Englishness'—became a joke, conjuring up not common images, but caricatures.

At best what they meant was contested. In the 1960s and 1970s, 'Englishness' was a site of struggle between a traditional 'officer class' image and a subcultural, Carnaby-Street version (The Who, skinheads, 'swinging London') that started out as a piss-take and went on to become a commercial life-saver, outliving the 'authentic' national iconography on which it was initially a kitsch ironic comment. This unequal contest between 'substance' and 'style' even had its own TV show—*The Avengers* (style 'won'). In the same period, 'Americanness' became as much a term of horror as of patriotism for some of its own citizens because of the Vietnam War and the growth of various counter-cultures. For a time, there was a vogue for altering the very spelling of the country's name to 'Amerika' to signify the alienation of the younger generation from the aggressive expansionism of the 'military-industrial complex'.

People from within its own core community were ridiculing or rebelling against the very idea of 'national identity' and turning to cultural identities associated with personal characteristics (age, gender, sexuality, ethnicity) or even 'do-it-yourself' identities associated with taste constituencies (music, clothing, lifestyle). 'Subcultures' became more prominent than the 'parent' culture from which they were nominally derived. At such a time, if national communities were to avoid balkanisation into internally warring and segregated 'tribes', they needed to identify themselves with something completely different from the traditional markers of nationality—that is, territory and common ethnic descent. They needed to 'virtualise' the idea of a national community, making the name of the country completely devoid of any 'intrinsic' meaning, and able to bear whatever meaning anyone from any group wanted to ascribe to it.

National identity shifted from unity based on land and blood, to diversity based on difference. It was vital, in such circumstances, to settle on *symbolic* markers of nationality, derived from *institutions* rather than land, from *discourses* rather than ethnicity, and from *rituals* not neighbourhoods. People had to be brought together by *doing* things together rather than *being* something in particular. This was where TV scored highly.

TV was a good barometer for these variations in the political and cultural climate. Comedy shows, sitcoms and drama serials were able to use their story lines, gags and situations to discuss seasonal hot topics, to bring conflicts into the open, to explore and expand the sense of difference among the variegated audience. TV took identity out of the political arena—of contestation for rights or competition for resources—and into the cultural arena. It communicated difference across demographic groups, but simultaneously gathered populations together rather than splitting them into their constituent groups.

TV news, current affairs, chat shows and sport became vehicles for quite disproportionate attention to the tension between 'we' and 'they' identities. These 'live' genres were used as mechanisms for thinking through the question of 'how do I know I'm . . . Australian, American, British (etc.)?' Factual television addressed that question negatively, most of the time. 'Our' national identity was confirmed by being contrasted with a series of 'they' identities, usually in some kind of conflict or competition. 'We' were identified by negativisation: 'We are what others are not.'

In this context, the live event became a kind of collective cultural calculator, thinking though the question of national identity and personal citizenship in a positive way.

'LIVENESS' AS IDEOLOGY

During the era of broadcast television, critics on both sides of the Atlantic began to argue that so great was television's *ideological* investment in 'liveness' that the idea coloured everything that was broadcast, not just live segments or shows. In other words, and particularly from the point of view of the viewer's experience, broadcast television as a whole came across—or was promoted—as live, no matter how it was shot or transmitted.

This idea gained critical-theoretical credence in the screen theory of the 1970s, oddly enough just after the time when transmissions had ceased to be live for most purposes. Screen theorists Stephen Heath and Gillian Skirrow set out what might be regarded as a paranoid version of the 'liveness' myth. They noted that: 'Transmission "live", "as it happens", unrecorded, *en direct* (the

French expression)' was 'very far indeed from representing the bulk of the television seen'. Nevertheless, within what they called 'normal assumptions', live TV was 'taken as the television norm, as the very definition of television'. They argued that 'within the terms of those [normal] assumptions, *the television programme is then effectively identified with the "live" television programme*' (Heath and Skirrow 1977: 53).

Most of what was seen on TV was not live, but Heath and Skirrow argued that 'liveness' was a 'generalised fantasy of the television institution', that 'the image' was *'direct*, and direct *for me*'. Through this effect of immediacy—an effect that belonged to broadcast television as an institution rather than to any particular image on screen—all sorts of heterogeneous material could be ordered into a 'present continuous' sequence. 'Liveness' infected, as it were, the whole shebang.

Meanwhile, the 'me' for whom 'live broadcasting' was 'direct', said Heath and Skirrow, was 'a citizen in the world of communication'—television was 'here and now, for me personally, for me as the unity of everyone' (1977: 56). For Heath and Skirrow, this was the general 'ideology' of television.

Applying this generalised (paranoid) perspective to the American context, Jane Feuer analysed the 'ideology of liveness' in ABC's *Good Morning America* show, anchored at the time by David Hartman. She wrote:

> *Good Morning America* is constructed around the most extreme fragmentation—a mosaic of film, video and 'live' segments emanating from New York, Washington, and Chicago, with features on how to clean fireplaces and how to use an electric blanket, news of the Iranian crisis and the Olympics, ads for Sears soft contact lenses and Lucky's pinto beans, not to mention Rona Barrett's review of *Cruising*, Joan Baez' visit to Cambodia, and the last in a series of 'great romances'. (Feuer 1983: 16–17)

All this in one morning; there have been many mornings since 1980. Feuer identified two forces that worked to unify this 'variety of content' and the 'extreme spatial fragmentation' of the show across the United States. First, patriarchy: 'All this is unified by the presence of David Hartman—the ultimate father figure—in the anchor chair.' Second: 'The show is obsessed with its own liveness . . . David acts as custodian of flow and regularity, the personification of a force which creates unity out of fragmentation.' (1983: 17) For Feuer, the anchor united both time and space in the service of 'family unity': 'Television, in its liveness, its immediacy, its reality, can create families where none exist.' (1983: 20) In all this the 'event' was TV itself.

NO SOONER DONE THAN SAID: LIVE HISTORICAL MEMORY

Many commentators have noticed the difference between different kinds of time, not only on TV but 'anthropologically', as it were. Everyday time could be measured incrementally as a 'banal', 'profane' or ordinary sequence. Special time, on the other hand, was marked by the interruption of 'fatal', 'sacred' and extraordinary events. Weekdays were differentiated from weekends; Sundays were secularised 'holy-days'. In people's lives, some events were of 'lifelong' significance rather than belonging to ordinary time. Births, weddings and funerals were obvious examples.

At a wedding, people observed strange rituals clearly marked off from ordinary life, and made great efforts to slow time down to a standstill. They dressed in special costumes, with clothes from a bygone (Edwardian) age. The 'event' was out-of-time (not much 'happened' but it was 'the day of a lifetime'). The wedding was compulsively photographed to make a permanent record, although people stopped what they were doing to assemble in timeless immobility for this purpose. The formal ceremony and informal goings-on both displayed elements going back hundreds of years. People gathered from among families, friends and neighbours who might otherwise never have met or barely spoken. The community became self-conscious, for an instant.

Like people, television needed both types of time. Normally, it babbled away happily in 'present continuous,' banal, profane, everyday time. But sometimes it switched to fatal, sacred time. This was where the live event came into its own: weddings, funerals, anything—so long as they were on a national scale or greater.

The 'big' live event has had a bad press from critics. Aesthetically it was criticised for taking a very long time to say very little—it seemed to be characterised generically by distended semiotic excess. Ideologically it was prone to other kinds of excess—the political evils of populism and nationalism, the commercial exploitation of culture, the commodification of identity. It has even been seen as contributing to 'the death of history'.

Meaghan Morris has written about the excesses of a typical four-hour 'live event' show broadcast on Australian television to mark the Bicentennial celebrations in 1988—the show *Australia Live: Celebration of a Nation* (Morris 1993). Morris argued that *Australia Live* 'produced a landscape without *shadows*', in which 'capital (mobility) was the basic theme,' rather than historical analysis, despite the historical pretext for the whole event. But she warned against 'paranoid' conclusions: 'An event like *Australia Live* is no more representative of a mythic "television-in-general" than it was reflective of life in Australia.' (Morris 1993: 20, 26)

A more difficult problem for analysis, she argues, is what might be meant by 'live' in live-event TV:

> The 'live,' in this frame of reference, has a rather peculiar meaning. Live television is an operation guaranteed, and yet contested, not by an opposite or a negation (the not-live: the prerecorded, the archival, the simulacrum, the ghostly, the 'dead') but an array of vague possibilities associated with *life*: unprogrammed events, breaks in continuity, accidents, missed connections, random occurrences, unforeseen human and technical recalcitrance. (Morris 1993: 52–53)

The interruption of 'the live' by 'the living' was nothing less than the return of Nigel Kneale's 'wandering booby'. Morris made the wandering booby not a symptom of the death of history, nor of the collapse of critical distance, but a precondition of the live genre—and in fact a reprieve for history:

> The ceremonial 'present' became, for the official script on the day [of *Australia Live*], a field of suspense and evasion. Speech after speech from the dais skipped hastily from the 'mistakes of the past' to expressions of faith in 'the future'. The *significant* present was elsewhere: with people lying in the sun, having picnics, watching boats and milling about, but above all with the insistent critical accompaniment of the Aboriginal protest. Audible and visible in most telecasts on the day, extending later into media commentary, news items, current affairs shows and the television archive of future Aboriginal images—that protest effectively historicised, on Aboriginal terms, an entrepreneurial 'national' event. (Morris 1993: 54–55)

Morris concluded: 'Only by beginning to think of media as accompanying experience, and as time (not just 'space') for action, can criticism respond to an event.' (1993: 54) The live event had not supplanted history, but in its relations with a 'significant present' that was 'elsewhere', it allowed criticism, both activist and reflective, to become 'live'.

THE 'PRODUCED' AND THE 'NATURAL'

During television history, there have been broadcasts of many live events. Although each one was unique, the 'TV live event' displayed generic regularities that can be typified. They have tended to be of two kinds, which can be characterised as 'produced' and 'natural' respectively.

The 'produced' category approximates anthropologically to a wedding. 'Produced' live events included actual celebrity weddings, but they also included a genre unique to television, the live coverage of temporal markers of national (sometimes super-national) history: anniversaries, centenaries, millennia. TV usually covered some aspect of annual Foundation Days (Fourth of July in the United States, May Day in the Soviet Union). Beyond this seasonal stepping out of banal time into holiday time, there was a vogue for very much more elaborate celebrations of significant anniversaries of national foundation in countries with modern constitutions. There was a spate of bicentennials that were primarily TV events: the United States in 1976, Australia in 1988, France in 1989. Not wanting to wait so long, the People's Republic of China pulled out all the plugs for its 50th in October 1999, as did India and Pakistan in 1997. Countries with pre-modern constitutions had to make do with Royal Weddings—Britain liked to have one or two of these every decade.

The 'produced' type of 'live event', like early live TV, could seem a bit of a con. So heavily stage-managed was the 'liveness' that the best the audience could hope for was interruption by a 'wandering booby'. More interesting in many ways was the other type of live event: the 'natural' variety. These were live transmission of events that were actually happening. It would be too much to claim that they would have occurred even without the TV camera, although this could be the case, but they could not be reduced to television presentation alone. However, what made them interesting was that their 'natural' qualities were precisely what made them memorable television, and then they entered social memory (if not history) as *television* events, not as 'natural' ones. Such events could be characterised as 'fatal' as opposed to 'banal' in Baudrillard's terms (see McKee 1997: 192). They approximated anthropologically not to the 'produced' wedding but to 'natural' birth and death events, especially death.

The number one event in this category happened to be a 'birth'. The moon landing of July 1969 was certainly hailed as the harbinger of a new era in human history. Gregor Goethals provided a classical comparison:

> We saw images 'live from the moon' and heard the voice of the astronaut as he lowered himself onto the moon's surface. Television transformed the human heroism and scientific success of those memorable, fleeting moments into public, symbolic records for all citizens to witness.
>
> In recalling these moments it is important to remember that political and economic institutions have always been conscious of symbolism. One comparison that comes to mind is the building of the Parthenon in fifth-century Athens. In the years after the defeat of the Persians, Athens was the most powerful and influential city-state. What better way to celebrate and underscore that position than to construct a magnificent temple? No matter how much disorder was manifested at the time, citizens could see tangible evidence of Athens' grandeur embodied in the Parthenon. (Goethals 1981: 83–84)

The citizens were gathered to the 'magnificent temple' of the moon landings by television. Using the most expensive and convincing empirical evidence, the Apollo program live on TV, it was possible to *imagine* human order, power and progress as a 'giant leap for mankind', done by means of the 'small step of a man'.

People remembered the moonwalk 'out of time', as it were—if it was a 'real' or 'historical' event, it was as much a television one. McKenzie Wark recorded various Australian writers' recollections of their experience as part of 'generation moonwalk'. One recalled being aged ten when '"the world" watched with bated breath, fuzzy grainy pictures in which very little happened over what seemed like hours and hours cramped five in a double desk in the grade five and six classroom'. Another remembered:

> We had a portable TV set brought into the class especially . . . There was a very strong sense of occasion about it, that we were watching something very special . . . There was a sense that it was a television event, as much as a historical one.'

Another confessed:

It was a real bonding moment for me and dad. He sat there with a glass of beer and affected a suitable silent *gravitas* while the whole damn thing took place. I admit I was impressed too . . . That it was happening live, right at that very minute, it was real impressive. (Wark 1999: 235–37)

But 'natural' events were perhaps typified more frequently by interrupting normal programming with live coverage of negative, literally 'fatal' events. These included high-status political assassinations, such as Americans John and Robert Kennedy, and Martin Luther King (but not Norwegian Olf Palme or Egyptian Anwar Sadat). They extended to the aftermath of certain disasters, like coverage of bombings in Oklahoma (but not in Algeria or Angola). They included celebrity crashes—JFK Jnr and Diana Princess of Wales (but not Robert Hughes). The 'live-event' format colonised entire battles, like the Gulf War (see Wark 1994: 3–46) (but not Chechnya). Many other incidents of socially sacralised violence (newsworthy conflict) have turned into live-event spectacle, from the SAS storming the Iranian Embassy in London in 1979, up to the aftermath of massacres such as Port Arthur in 1996 or Columbine High School in 1999. In a class of its own was live coverage of the entire OJ Simpson trial, lasting a full year and provoking intense internal, and indeed global, meditation on what 'America' might mean now.

It was pretty clear from these examples that fatality was a compelling pretext for live-event TV. Normally the 'natural' event emanated from or went to the national agenda of the United States of America. The United States seemed less sure-footed about blowing its own trumpet in the 'produced' category. The 500th anniversary of Columbus's 'discovery' of 'America' in 1992 was embarrassing even to the participants, provoking the 'wrong' sort of national self-consciousness. National togetherness and self-reflection have seemed more readily sparked by 'natural' events in the United States, especially if they were literally 'fatal' to a suitably high-status celebrity.

LIVENESS WAS AMERICAN—AMERICA WAS EVERYONE'S INDIGENOUS

The American live event on TV became everyone else's live event. There was a very important consequence to this, one that has been noted in relation to American national fictions by Scott Olson, writing primarily about movies and TV-drama:

Due to a unique mix of cultural conditions that create a transparency, the United States has a competitive advantage in the creation and global distribution of popular taste. *Transparency* is defined as any textual apparatus that allows audiences to project indigenous values, beliefs, rites, and rituals into imported media or the use of those devices. This transparency effect means that American cultural exports, such as cinema, television, and related merchandise, manifest narrative structures that easily blend into other cultures. Those cultures are able to project their own narratives, values, myths, and meanings into the American iconic media, making those texts resonate with the same meanings they might have if they were indigenous. (Olson 1999: 5–6)

Olson used this insight not to trot out the well-worn accusations of American domination of the world via media-colonialism, but to argue something that was very nearly the opposite:

Transparency allows such narratives to become stealthy, to be foreign myths that surreptitiously act like indigenous ones, Greek gifts to Troy, but with Trojan citizens inside the horse . . . The process [of cultural change] is causally the reverse of what is generally assumed—the indigenous culture actively reaches out, haggles, and does not merely absorb in hypodermic needle, magic-bullet fashion some set of injected cultural values. The readings of indigenous text are indigenous, but the images and sounds are transplanted. (Olson 1999: 6; see also Lotman 1990 and O'Regan 1996: 213–26, for the transmitter/receiver relations of import/export cultures)

'Perhaps,' Olson argued, 'despite alarms to the contrary, the world is not being melted down into a single, hegemonic, more-or-less American monoculture, even though American cultural products dominate the world' (1999: 5). The 'Greek gifts to Troy' turned out to be a Parthenon after all, and everyone inside was a Trojan (even the Americans).

These issues applied not only to US fictions but also to those 'foreign myths' that came in factual form, whether as news or as more expansive 'live events'. When people from middling or small countries watched their own national television, they *saw* a great deal of American programming. Viewer participation in or identification with 'live events', whether 'natural' or 'produced', was very likely indeed to entail participation in or identification with *American* events. But the identification would not necessarily be as-an-American; the participation would not be within the polity of the United States (see Wark 1994: 14).

Australian critic Graeme Turner has described his own 'first contact' with American live coverage via CNN. He found its Americanness and its liveness both strangely liberating. The 1997 British General Election on CNN was 'visually dull', minimally edited, 'poorly structured, repetitive and predictable'. But that was the point: as a result of its very liveness, 'it seemed to have moved slightly beyond the reach of the discursive conventions of television news' (the booby was wandering close by). And Americanness offered a dual benefit. Contact with it, from suburban Brisbane, provided a 'metropolitanising buzz', but the 'Indigene' who watched from outside the United States also experienced 'exemption from complicity' in the national ideologies encoded into CNN's 'discursive regime' (Turner 1997: 116–17). Seeing the moon landings, the death of a Kennedy, or any other ceremonies of American national television, including *British* elections followed in *Australian* homes, did not make people from around the world into Americans. It may not even have made American citizens themselves into 'Americans'.

The 'transparency' Olson analysed allowed citizens of all countries to become what I have called 'citizens of media' (Hartley 1996: Ch. 3; 1999: Chs 12–14). The live event was one of the most important devices for gathering those citizens together out of their 'normal' everyday time and space. When 'we' watched the ecstasies of lunar landings we were fleetingly human, not national; when 'we' saw the agonies of assassination, or even the lunacies of the Monica Lewinsky saga, we were 'haggling' for meanings about ourselves however construed, not about our relation to the United States.

FATAL BANALITIES

'Suicide is painless, it brings on many changes.' So said the title song of the American hit comedy series *M*A*S*H*. One of the changes it may have introduced among competing US TV executives, at least momentarily, was doubt about their uncritical enthusiasm for the live television event. The cause for concern was the death of Daniel V. Jones just before 4.00 p.m. on Thursday 30 April 1998.

The problem posed by Mr Jones was apparently editorial. It wasn't the fact that he blew his brains out on a Los Angeles freeway, but that he did this while a number of competing news helicopters were following his every move, two of them in especially tight close-up at that moment. These pictures were broadcast live, following the chase of a deranged person with a gun, 'OJ-style', and reporting on the traffic gridlock the chase had caused. Thus there was no time for newsroom debate about whether or not to broadcast the act of suicide itself. In the words of Howard Rosenberg, TV critic for the *Los Angeles Times*, 'No time to ponder. No safeguards. In an age valuing media speed over reflection, the Jones shooting happened and was transmitted simultaneously.' (Rosenberg 1999: 70)

A banal suicide could assume world-historical significance if it happened in America. For Rosenberg this was just such an occasion:

> The TV shot heard throughout much of the world was a seminal moment in newscasting excess, one representing the ultimate horror of knee-jerk live coverage that in recent years had been careening across the televisionscape like fugitives fleeing police in those familiar Southern California police chases. (1999: 70)

Interestingly, Rosenberg's discussion of this 'seminal moment' was part of a special issue on the 'future of journalism', portentously entitled *What's Next?*, in the house journal of the Freedom Forum. If 'Man Commits Suicide—LIVE!' was indeed 'what's next?' then Rosenberg found himself wondering 'whether some of the authority of journalism died that day in Los Angeles along with Jones'.

The professional doubt turned on whether 'viewers should have been shown' Jones' suicide. But this case represented more than the familiar debate about public-interest news versus private-gratification entertainment. It even went beyond the more technical problem of live production/transmission, which was to remove editorial decision-making powers from editors. The deeper disquiet felt by journalists suggested that here was a perceived limit of what the 'live event' was supposed to do. The whole point was that the death of an anonymous man was not 'the ultimate horror' at all. Suicide may be fatal to the perpetrator, but it is nevertheless a banal, private, everyday, profane matter. Here it seems the real issue was professional squeamishness about using *broadcast television* for this kind of 'live event'.

LIVE ONLINE—AND IN A FIELD OF COWS

But it was already too late for such worries. *Broadcast* television may increasingly have concentrated on the 'fatal' and sacral live event, as opposed to the 'banal' and secular. There may well have been a glut of community-building, population-gathering, citizen-calling live spectaculars, from the Millennium to Olympic opening- and closing-ceremonies. And these may indeed have become more international and more global (based on the 'Olson' formula that American = the universal subject position). But none of this meant that such live events as the Jones suicide had gone away. Everyday liveness was only 'fugitive' as it migrated away from broadcast television, first to non-broadcast forms such as cable-TV, but perhaps more decisively to the Internet.

It was never clear what 'live television' encompassed; now it was no longer easy to be sure what was meant by 'television' either (see also Chapter 5). 'Television' without qualification tended to refer to the era of national network broadcasting. But television was already passing out of this era. Multi-channel cable, satellite and digital TV meant that it was increasingly hard to gather whole populations to witness and participate in any one ritual of national togetherness. The Internet, with 'JenniCAMs' proliferating in their thousands, meant that the 'live event' could be private not public (see http://www.jennicam.org/).

One of the Internet's more popular innovations was the camera sited in someone's bedroom, allowing users to check out domestic banalities (with a promise of intimacies normally banned from broadcast TV) in real time, all done for nothing by private individuals in their own homes. As well, 'live' could also be interactive, a feature exploited by the porn industry to allow clients to specify exactly what they'd like a model to do, and to share their fantasy with its object. Of course, different kinds of interactive liveness could be combined: a Net-search for JENNYCAM yielded, among others, 'Young Voyeur Jennycam Cams Nude Girls', on the one hand and 'Navigating the Image of Woman Online—A feminist approach to the JenniCAM', on the other. Then ('for the voyeur of discriminating taste') there was The Peeping Moe's JenniCAM Fan Page:

Jennifer has graciously allowed us a live, 24 hour-a-day portal into her life . . . In one sense, Jenni is a pioneer. Since her debut, many more have followed the trail she blazed . . . Somehow she answers a ton of email, and still keeps her sanity. Her live presence cannot last forever, but maybe the lesson of her open and unassuming sharing of it, will.—The Peeping Moes. (http://peepingmoe.com/netcams/jennicam/)

'The nation' was fragmented, 'liveness' was privatised. This posed quite a challenge to the very idea of an 'event'—someone in a bedroom, whether or not engaged in activities designed to arouse sexual excitement, was not *doing* enough to qualify the proceedings as an 'event' by the definition established over the previous forty years of broadcasting. In short, 'liveness' was shifting from 'sacred' to 'profane' time/space and participation. However, what Jenni was *not doing* nevertheless became international news: she was interviewed on the *Late Show with David Letterman*, on *E! Entertainment News*, and in a *Penthouse* 'Women of the Net' story.

Because it was rich and full of creative people, broadcast television could still reflect on and even play with these developments. One interesting example was shown on BBC television in Britain, in the days leading up to the 1999 Glastonbury music festival, which attracted over a hundred thousand people annually. As part of its nightly continuity (i.e. the TV that is broadcast between programs, often taking the form of a station ID or an announcement about an up-coming show), the BBC sited a camera in a field with a 'Live from Glastonbury' caption. For several nights, the picture showed nothing more (but also, bizarrely, nothing less) than a few cattle nuzzling the verbiage in the darkening hues of the long northern summer evening. Only as the festival itself took place did this unwonted vision of 'liveness' (where nothing was happening) transform into its spectacular, festive, teeming, sacred opposite, filling the same field.

'Liveness,' 'television' and 'event' were all, it has transpired, doubtful terms. In the gloom of the Somerset farmland they went beyond doubt and scepticism to achieve self-reflexivity. Meaghan Morris thought that 'the live and the living' (live TV event and living people) 'interact in a mode of hostile complicity' (Morris 1993: 54), which could certainly be the case. But the BBC's Glastonbury joke—a 'trailer' for a 'live' event (impossible, if you think about it . . . and was the trailer *really* live?)—relied on viewer literacy about both television-continuity and the accompanying 'living' world. It showed that 'complicity' could be post-paranoid and mutually playful too.

In fact, the live and the living were connected not by either hostility or playfulness only, but also by what was called in communications technology 'convergence', whether or not they supported a personal Netcam site. Or, as Nigel Kneale presciently put it, understanding in the language of the 1950s the integration of technology, narration and life: 'I don't like the term "science fiction", but if we're going to bandy it about, it could be applied just as well to the world we live in.' (Kneale 1959)

The audience

Twelve Sue Turnbull

Figuring the audience

SETTING THE SCENE

Sir Robert Menzies: (upon the opening of commercial television station TCN9, 16 September 1956):
Well, now that we have offered our good wishes and congratulations to this new station, congratulating them on their enterprise and hoping they will have great success, you'll remember that I said something about housewives, the women in the home. You may not agree—perhaps you'd like to say something about that—would you?

Dame Patti Menzies:
Well, I should be very interested to know how many housewives will have the time to sit and watch television. But I do think that it will be a wonderful thing to help us educate and amuse our children, and it will also help the housewife in the home to entertain much more easily. And as long as we can sit, learn, and then get up and give Australia the benefit of that learning, then television, I'm sure, will be a great thing for this great young country.[1]

Invited by her husband Sir Robert, the then Liberal prime minister, to comment on the future of television, Dame Patti seems compelled to speak on behalf of the busy Australian housewife and mother. Expressing her high hopes for the new medium in terms of entertainment, education and its role in nation formation, but also her reservations about its implications for the domestic management of time, Dame Patti proved remarkably prescient about the future of television audience research, which would be preoccupied, especially in the early years, with these very same issues.

Dame Patti's comments also signal the optimism with which the advent of television and its potential impact were imagined by some, although there were those who were equally pessimistic about the possible cultural and moral effects of the new medium (Curthoys 1991). The arrival of television in Australia (just in time for the Melbourne Olympic Games) was heralded by a wealth of public debate about the possible implications of the new medium and the difference it might make. Debates which took place formally (in a Royal Commission of Inquiry) and less formally (in forums like the television column of *The Australian Woman's Weekly*), were fuelled for the most part by similar debates in the United Kingdom and the United States where television was already entrenched. Thus, like other media technologies before it (the printing press, photography, the telegraph, the telephone, the cinema and radio) and to follow (video, electronic games, mobile phones, pay and digital televison), television was introduced on a wave of contradictory rhetorics and hype.

Of course, television did make a difference to family life, although the initial impact may have been neither as sudden nor as unrelated to other factors as might be imagined. As Hartley and O'Regan (1992) reveal, on an October night in 1959 when television eventually opened in Perth, only 3300 television sets were in operation although an estimated 70 000 people were watching them. Nevertheless, they argue, by 1961 television was well ensconced in the home and had begun to change the ways in which people ate their meals, managed their time and organised their domestic spaces. It should, however, be noted that the arrival of television coincided with a postwar housing boom in the United Kingdom, the United States and Australia, the subsequent growth of suburbia, and an emphasis on the home as the site of consumption for all manner of consumer goods—goods which television avidly displayed in its advertisements or as the essential accoutrements of the affluent middle-class lifestyle, as portrayed on the set of the domestic sitcom (Spigel 1992).

GENEOLOGY OF AUDIENCE RESEARCH

If the consumption of television as a medium should therefore be considered in the context of postwar economic growth and social change, then television audience research should also be considered in the context of already established media audience debates and research. What these debates tended to have in common was the ways in which they were framed: either the mass medium was considered in terms of its 'effects' on the consumer, or it was considered in terms of the 'functions' it might serve, and often in terms of both. In each case, those posing the question usually did so from a position of moral and critical authority.

One of the most interesting examples of early audience research, which was to establish a set of research practices and mode of inquiry for the future, was an American project known as The Payne Fund Studies. Conducted over a three-year period, from 1929–32, these studies marked the moment when public concern about a particular media form—in this case, the burgeoning popularity of the Hollywood film and cinema attendance—coincided with developments in social science methodologies which might be used to investigate this phenomenon (Lowery and de Fleur 1983: 31–54). In these various studies, questions were asked and research initiated which endeavoured to provide 'scientific' data about the effects of movie going on social attitudes, general conduct and delinquent behaviour, with a particular emphasis on children.

Another significant pre-TV research project focusing on a particular media text and its audience is Herta Herzog's study of daytime listeners to radio soap operas (Herzog 1941). Herzog's inquiry, which involved interviewing some 100 daytime soap listeners living in the Greater New York area and asking them to fill out a questionnaire, presented its findings in terms of the 'gratifications' which these women gained from these serials. It came to the rather superior conclusion that, because these women's lives were 'uneventful', they found the soap operas helped them cope with the 'drudgery' of their lives by providing 'ideologies and recipes for adjustment' (Herzog 1941). This study, one of the first to be described as 'uses and gratifications' research (McQuail 1991: 233–7), thus anticipates many of the concerns about female television soap opera viewers in the home which were to occupy a significant number of feminist researchers during the 1970s and 1980s (Brunsdon 1997: 29–43).

It is possible, therefore, to sketch out the parameters of the debates and research about media audiences which anticipated the attention directed to the new medium of television in Australia, as in other countries. First, the ways in which the relationship between television and its audience was constructed depended to a great deal on the rhetorics of utopianism and dystopianism associated with earlier media forms and their imagined social impact. Second, debates about the impact of the mass media had already been framed in terms of a moral concern about the possible effects or functions of television for a mass audience imagined as somehow more vulnerable and less critical than the researcher. And third, because of the nature of television's domestic location and consumption, the research agenda was already established with regard to those who had been identified as most at risk from other forms of media influence: women and children.

Indeed, it has been argued that the audience for television as a whole has been consistently 'feminised' and rendered 'childlike' by the producers of television and critical commentators alike. This feminising practice is noted by Lyn Joyrich in her survey of television audience research in America (Joyrich 1996: 39–42), while the 'paedocratising' impulse has been discussed by John Hartley (1987). Hartley, along with Ien Ang and others, has also pointed to the possibility that television 'audiences are literally unknowable' since they exist only as a discursive entity in debates about television, and that their viewing practices may be impossible to track or understand in all their social and cultural complexity (Hartley 1992: 110; Ang 1991: x). People watching television in their living rooms, kitchens or bedrooms are not members of an audience in the same way as people watching a film in a movie theatre. Yet people have been, and still are, imagined as audiences for television in a variety of ways by those with an interest in investigating the nature of their viewing practices, including academics, government policy-makers and the media industries themselves.

Television audiences have therefore been identified in relation to a range of social and cultural categories (including class, ethnicity, gender, age); in relation to their shared taste for particular genres or television texts (from soap opera to World Federation Wrestling); or with reference to shared practices of watching or using the medium. Television audiences have been identified as passive in terms of effects, or active in terms of the ways in which they might be imagined to 'read' television, taking from it what is of value in the construction of their personal identities and management of their social lives. Research methods have included the experimental laboratory experience borrowed from the natural sciences; the survey questionnaire and interview techniques borrowed from the social sciences; participant observation and the use of ethnographic research strategies borrowed from anthropology; as well as attention to the practices of making meaning derived from reader response theory and semiotics.

If academic research has been concerned with trying to identify the nature of the television viewing experience in all its complex social and cultural manifestations, what of the television industry? Clearly knowing what audiences are watching and why would seem to be of considerable interest to those in the business of producing television, since as far as commercial networks are concerned, their revenue depends on selling air time to advertisers at the best possible rate. In Australia, information about television audiences has been sold to advertisers and networks by AC Neilsen, an international market research company which produces daily television ratings based on the viewing patterns of a 'sample' television audience. (From 2001, the major ratings contract has been won by AGB Australia.) For the purposes of AC Neilsen's research, a viewer is simply identified as a person who is in the room when the television is switched on. The 'viewing' figures thus produced, commonly referred to as the 'ratings', constitute the 'currency' which networks and advertisers use to sell and buy air time. As Jacka has suggested, limited though the information produced about television audiences by these means may be, this may not be important as long as those involved in using it consider it 'good enough' for their purposes (Jacka 1994: 48).

So while the ratings might tell us how many people of what age, sex or social demographic may have the television tuned to particular program at any moment of the day, they cannot tell us whether this person is actually watching, or why, or with what possible outcomes. These are the kinds of questions which have continued to occupy academic audience research—which, it should be remembered, is by no means completely disinterested or objective. Even the framing of a research question, the choosing of a particular audience and the choice of methodologies, may reveal a particular bias. Moreover, academics have frequently been employed as consultants or advisers in research which has been commissioned by industry, governments and policy-makers who may have a particular objective in mind. This is particularly evident in any review of research concerning the relationship between children and television, and the issues which usually arise in this context, including censorship and the representation of violence in the media.

TV KIDS

Children have consistently been identified as a very particular audience for television, commanding special attention and concern. As Hodge suggests, there may be many reasons for this, not least the construction of children as either impressionable innocents needing protection, or as wilful ferals needing control (Hodge 1989: 159). In each case, such constructions legitimate various forms of social intervention on the part of those who profess concern about children's welfare. What can be identified in a necessarily brief overview of this research here is a contradiction, and indeed a tension, between research framed in terms of the question 'What does television do to children?'' and its alternative 'What do children do with television—and why?'

Even though one of the very earliest studies of television advocated approaching the issue of children and television from the perspective of the child:

> What television is bringing to children, as we shall show, is not essentially different from what radio and movies brought them; but what children bring to television and other mass media is infinitely varied. So when we talk about the effect of television we are really talking about how children use television. A child comes to television seeking to satisfy some need. He [sic] finds something there and uses it . . . Something in their lives makes them reach out for a particular experience on television. This experience then enters into their lives, and has to make its way amidst the stored experience, the codified values, the social relationships, and immediately urgent needs that are already a part of those lives. (Schramm et al. 1961: 2)

This complex and holistic approach was not always observed. Indeed, one of the striking features of a great deal of research on children and television is that it has continued to be framed simply in terms of the logic of cause and effects—that is, television does things to children. Furthermore, much of this research has been instigated by state bodies in response (or so it is argued) to public concern about the medium and its effects. This is particularly true of what has come to be called the media violence debate (Cunningham 1992: 137–67). Thus, in the 1960s, public concern about civil unrest in the United States, which included vigorous student protest against American involvement in the Vietnam War, a spate of political assassinations (including that of President

John Kennedy, his brother Robert and the leader of the equal rights movement, Martin Luther King), was translated into a hugely expensive government-funded research program seeking to investigate the effects of the television on children (Surgeon General's Scientific Advisory Committee on Television and Social Behaviour 1972). Similarly in Australia during the late 1980s, after a series of very public crimes involving young men (including the Hoddle Street and Queen Street massacres), the Labor government of the day requested that the Australian Broadcasting Tribunal conduct a public inquiry into the relationship between children and television violence (Australian Broadcasting Tribunal 1990).

This Australian inquiry, which involved scrutinising some 1100 submissions from interested groups and members of the public (as well as conducting a review of television content, and a series of nationwide public conferences), produced a set of controversial recommendations. These included an implicit rejection of the perceived causal connection between representations of media violence and violence in the community, pointing instead to the 'many factors which may facilitate aggression away from the television screen' (Australian Broadcasting Tribunal 1990: xviii). These many factors were identified as poverty, stress, unemployment, low self-esteem, family breakdown and challenges to traditional values and prejudice. What the report therefore advocated was not more censorship of TV, but a push for more media education, debate about industry practices and an industry-wide, self-regulatory code on the representation of violence (Cunningham 1992: 152–5). These conclusions, as Cunningham suggests, were regarded by some as 'scant and meek', a perception which indicates the pressure placed on those working in the area of publicly commissioned media audience research to produce outcomes which will satisfy a public policy agenda drawn up elsewhere.

This tension is also evident in an account of the research conducted by the newly constructed Australian Broadcasting Authority (which replaced the Australian Broadcasting Tribunal in 1992), which sought to canvass what people thought about the possibility of showing 'R' rated material on pay television (Spurgeon 1994: 55–60). In this particular instance, the Senate Select Committee on Community Standards was highly critical of the research design and its findings, which seemed to suggest that Australian television audiences were relatively relaxed about the prospect of sexually explicit material being made available on pay TV. Thus, despite the recommendations of the ABA, based on the results of their wide-ranging processes of community consultation, the Senate Select Committee chose to disregard the findings in making their own recommendations for policy. This outcome points to the persistence of a very real anxiety about the relationship between images and audiences which refuses to be allayed by even the most comprehensive and methodologically rigorous academic research.

One reason for the persistence of this anxiety may be a consequence of the ways in which this debate *about* the media and its audiences continues to be represented *by* the media. Thus immediately after the Port Arthur massacre in

Tasmania in April 1997 when 28-year-old Martin Bryant murdered thirty-five people with an automatic machine gun, the Melbourne *Age* newspaper published an article entitled 'Do Movies Make Mass Murderers?' (Turnbull 1997: 41–9). Similarly, in May 1999 after the Columbine High School murders involving two young men in Denver Colorado, newspaper articles immediately attributed their actions to a cult-like following of pop media persona Marilyn Manson, their playing of the computer game *Doom* and their 'dangerous' navigation of the Internet (Rowe 1999). Whatever the other motivations and causes of these young men's behaviour—and there were obviously many—the media representations of the events continued to play upon public anxieties about the effects of the media on the young, impressionable and potentially out of control.

Meanwhile, a more progressive approach to children and television has proceeded along the lines earlier identified by Schramm et al. (1961), seeking to investigate children's relationship with the medium in terms of how they make sense of television, and how it matters to them in the context of their own lives. Thus Patricia Palmer's Australian study, *The Lively Audience* (1986a), approached the relationship from a number of different theoretical angles (including symbolic-finteractionism) and using a variety of different research methods. Firstly, sixty-four children were interviewed about their television habits and asked to draw themselves in front of the TV set. Secondly, twenty-three different children were observed watching television in their own homes and the variety of their viewing styles and activities around the television set noted. Lastly, 486 students were surveyed about their attitudes towards the medium. These various results were then incoporated into an account which endeavoured to account for children's television usage in and on their own terms.

Another significant Australian study of children and television (Hodge and Tripp 1986) investigated children's understandings of the medium by showing them a particular TV cartoon and examining the ways in which children made sense of this program when asked about it. Hodge and Tripp argue that their approach is based not only on earlier theorisations of media uses and functions as described above, but also incorporates the application of semiotics and a 'cultural studies' approach, taking into account 'theories of ideology, culture and acculturation' (Hodge and Tripp 1986: 7–9).

CULTURAL STUDIES AND ETHNOGRAPHY

While some television audience research has been influenced by the tradition of American mass communications research (including projects like the Payne Fund Studies and that of Schramm et al. mentioned above), other significant developments in the field have resulted from encounters with different research traditions, including that of British cultural studies. Emerging out of the theoretical and political engagement of a group of scholars based at the Centre for Contemporary Cultural Studies at the University of Birmingham in the late

1960s and 1970s, British cultural studies was primarily concerned with questions of class, ideology and control (Turner 1990; Fiske 1992). Building on Marxist critiques of capitalism, incoporating lessons from European structuralism and semiotics, cultural studies was interested in the relationship between people's class-based social context and the ways in which they might make meaning of their cultural experience, including that of television.

Thus, in 1980, David Morley undertook a project to see how different audience groups might (on the basis of their different class and social contexts) read the same current affairs show. Using Hall's essay 'Encoding/Decoding' (Hall 1980) as a theoretical model derived from semiotics, Morley established a set of criteria for evaluating audience responses to the same television text based on whether or not the different groups read the news item in terms of: a) its dominant meanings (what the producers—and Morley—considered to be the intended meanings and political position advocated); b) a negotiated set of understandings (taking on some but not all of the intended meanings and political positions); or c) in oppositional ways (refusing to accept the meanings or positions offered at all). In a subsequent re-evaluation of the project, Morley (1981) acknowledged that his results had been over-determined by the fact that he himself had established what the dominant meanings might be (and had created the audience groups which might be thought to share those meanings) recognising that this hardly reflected the experience or meaning-making processes of watching television in any ordinary domestic context.

Hence Morley's next project, which involved interviewing eighteen South London families in their own homes about the role of television in their lives, their tastes and viewing habits. *Family Television: Domestic Power and Cultural Leisure* (Morley 1986) is a significant project in the history of television audience research because it vividly reveals the importance of gender for the consumption of television as a medium in terms of control over program choice, styles of viewing and taste. Morley's study also contributed to a growing body of research which attempts to understand the functions of television and other media technologies, such as the video recorder or home computer, in relation to the politics of their domestic context and everyday use (Gray 1992; Silverstone and Hirsch 1992). Relying primarily on interview data, Morley demonstrated the complexity of television viewing as a cultural practice—and, ironically, the difficulty of making sense of this as an outsider.

Morley's early television research has been associated with what is often described as the 'ethnographic turn' in media audience research, though this description has been strongly contested (Nightingale 1989). It is possible that the research methods employed in cultural studies research such as Morley's were as much influenced by the 'qualititative' methodologies emerging out of American social science and mass communications as they were by ethnography (Lindlof et al. 1987; Lull 1990). Nevertheless, with its origins in anthropology, where ethnography has been understood as a way of studying and writing about the way of life of a people (Clifford and Marcus 1986), this research approach was originally incorporated into the British cultural studies project through the work of Richard Hoggart (1958) and Paul Willis (1977), whose concerns were more broadly sociological and not particularly focused on media texts. However, because of the desire to understand how people might relate to television in the context of their lived experience, quasi-ethnographic methods were appropriated into television audience research with a cultural studies focus—projects including those of Morley (1980, 1986); Hobson (in her 1982 study of the female audience for the television soap *Crossroads*); Ang in her discussion of the television audience for *Dallas* (1982); and David Buckingham in a study of the British soap *Eastenders* (1987).

In Australia, the influence of cultural studies has also been apparent in studies which relate to television. For example, In 1980 Claire Thomas (clearly influenced by Paul Willis's cultural studies approach to the youth sub-cultures referred above) conducted a study of working-class girls in schools in order to demonstrate how their oppositional school sub-culture might adversely affect their academic success (Thomas 1980). Using ethnographic methods such as participant observation, discussion and interviews, Thomas found that the Australian soap opera *Prisoner* (known as *Cell Block H* in some overseas markets) figured prominently in the girls' metaphoric construction of school as a prison and themselves as victims (Thomas 1980: 43). In a similar vein, Patricia Palmer's research into the role of television in the lives of thirty Sydney schoolgirls took as its focus the ways in which soap opera viewing might relate to the ways which the girls talked about themselves, their lives and their futures (Palmer 1986).

While the label 'ethnography' may indeed be a misnomer, it is clear that television audience studies which embrace a cultural studies approach have in common a desire to consider television usage in relation to the social, cultural, economic and political context of the viewers concerned. To this end, methods borrowed from ethnography, including participant observation, may be employed in an endeavour to obtain a more comprehensive account of how television viewing might relate to a broad range of other social factors.

TELEVISION TEXTS AND THE 'ACTIVE' AUDIENCE

While ethnographic approaches to the study of television reception have therefore constituted one productive direction for television audience research, it is apparent from the examples cited above that there has been a tendency in cultural studies to focus on the television audience called into being for a particular genre or particular texts. Such studies have varied from those which discuss the potential effects of the text in terms of an imagined reader (what we might call the author's text), and which never directly engage with actual TV viewers and what they say, to those which engage with audience members directly and the meanings which they construct from the text in question (what we might call the reader's text). An example of the former might include Tania Modleski's discussion of the television audience for daytime soaps in America (1992), which deals only with a hypothetical audience, while an example of the latter might include Mary Ellen Brown's empirical study of soap opera and women's talk in Australia which is much influenced by John Fiske's theorisation of the 'active audience'.

Although Fiske's account of audience activity has been much criticised over the years, it has played a vital role in correcting the opposite assumption (held by both the political right and left) that media consumption is passive and over-determined in its effects by the ideological formation of the text. In *Reading the Popular* (1989), Fiske outlines his theory of semiotic resistance, arguing that while the power of the dominant within capitalism may be economic, the dominant class has no control over the productive work of readers who are free to interpret the signs of that power (in the media and elsewhere) in ways which may subvert their intended meaning (1989: 9–10). Fiske therefore imagines the reader (or viewer) as a kind of semiotic guerilla, fighting micropolitical battles in a struggle for meaning—and ultimately winning. Thus young women read Madonna's videos in ways which enable them to see that 'the meanings of feminine sexuality can be in their control', and that their subjectivities 'are not necessarily determined by the dominant patriarchy' (1989: 107).

With its origins in reader response theory and the semiotics of the open text, the concept of the active audience therefore builds on already established principles of 'uses and gratifications' which have sought to identify how people interpret and make use of the media in specific social contexts. At its most extreme, however, the concept of the active audience calls into question the power of those social determinants previously thought to matter most in the production of meaning. In this construction, the active reader, far from being constrained in their meaning-making by the experience of social class, ethnicity and gender, is therefore imagined as being able to transcend these social determinants in and through their reading of the media text.

Other Australian studies which have focused on a particular text and the activity of its audience include that of Tulloch and Moran (1986), who were particularly interested in the success of the television soap/series *A Country Practice*. While Part 1 of their study is devoted to a substantial study of the show, dealing with all aspects of its production process, performers and content, Part 2 considers the show's reception by its audience. In order to address the latter, the authors employ a variety of different methods including a discussion of the show's demographics as revealed by the ratings, an account of the experience of watching the show with different families in their own homes, and an analysis of letters sent by fans to the program's producers. This last tactic points to another development in the history of television audience research, which is specifically addressed to fan activity.

In this regard, fans for television science fiction shows have received particular attention, although other kinds of fan activity have also been studied in the Australian context, including Nightingale's account of Rugby League followers watching televised matches, or the activities of Elvis and Marilyn impersonators (Nightingale 1994). However, studies of *Star Trek* fans, such as those of Jenkins (1992), Tulloch and Jenkins (1995) and Bacon-Smith (1992), are of particular interest because of a marked shift in the position of the researcher doing the research: no longer is he or she divorced from the audience experience under consideration, but actively engaged in it. The researcher as fan is therefore a recent development in television audience studies which, while welcome in that it marks a departure from the position of moral superiority assumed in earlier audience research, nevertheless bears its own limitations and constraints. Indeed, the more avid the researcher as fan, the more committed they are to the text under consideration, then the more danger there is of a solipsistic move assuming the researcher's own relationship with the text might stand for that of the audience as a whole. To their credit, academic fan researchers of fan activity (such as those mentioned above) seem only too well aware of this possibility, trying to negotiate a position somewhere between critical and engaged, thereby enabling a more comprehensive and productive understanding of particular audience–text relationships.

POSTMODERN POSITIONS

At its most extreme, the concept of the active viewer merges with the concept of the postmodern viewer of the postmodern television text. The postmodern viewer has been imagined in both dystopian and utopian terms. From a dysto- pian perspective as outlined by Baudrillard (1980), the postmodern viewer could be said to exist in no particular time or place, to have no particular social or political affiliations and to be the product of a media-saturated culture where the worst effect is no affect. The more utopian version of this figure is to imagine he or she as an ironic and knowing consumer of television texts which acknowledge this irony through their self-referentiality. This is the view of the audience espoused by Australian commentators such as Catharine Lumby (1999), who proposes a media-literate audience participating in a democratic public sphere enabled by a proliferation of media forms to which many more people have much more access than ever before. And yet, the postmodern viewer in this 'virtual republic', as McKenzie Wark describes it (1999), exists essentially as a discursive trope, a figment of the research imagination, since attempts to study him or her inevitably necessitate that this free-flowing entity be anchored in terms of gender, ethnicity, social context and/or their relationship to specific texts.

While attractive as a proposition which seeks to move beyond the social determinism implicit in television audience studies which imagine audiences as always already constituted social groups, always condemned to make sense of television in terms of their cultural and economic constraints, the concept of the active, postmodern viewer therefore runs the risk of ignoring the social context of viewing altogether. But, as Ang (1997: 15) reminds us, people are not simply or always media audiences: the context of their viewing still matters in terms of issues of access, economics, politics and power. This is clearly apparent in a major study of Australian cultural tastes by Bennett et al. (1999), who demonstrate that all aspects of access and taste, including media use in the home, can be related to issues of gender, class, age and the economy of the household (not to mention ethnicity and whether or not the family lives in rural or suburban/ urban Australia). Television audience research at the end of the twentieth century therefore continues to face the problem of how best to imagine the relationship between the medium and the viewer. But now this relationship has to be considered in the context of economic and cultural globalisation and in a multi-channel environment enabled by the proliferation of digital forms of communication technology. The free-to-air network television service cautiously welcomed by Dame Patti is facing some stiff competition.

FUTURE DIRECTIONS IN TELEVISION AUDIENCE RESEARCH

Cross-culturalism

When discussing the possible role of television in the globalisation of culture, it is usually agreed that the medium may have already played, and still be playing, a significant role in this process. Ang's study of the Dutch audience for *Dallas* in 1985—although the audience's Dutchness was not a major issue at the time— might be regarded as the forerunner of a body of television audience research which has attempted to assess how people might make sense of a TV production from somewhere else—for example, Liebes and Katz's study of the cross-cultural audience for *Dallas* (1990), Gripsrud's study of the television audience for *Dynasty* in Norway (1995) or Wober and Fazal (1994) on the reception of the Australian soap *Neighbours* in Britain. The international career of Australian television exports in a global mediascape from 1985–94 has been discussed in detail by Cunningham and Jacka (1996). In this study, Cunningham and Jacka deal not only with the relative success of the suburban soap *Neighbours* in the United Kingdom, but also with the reception of the Australian bush-medical soap *The Flying Doctors* in the Netherlands, as well as that of short-lived glamour surf-soap, *Paradise Beach*, on American TV. Although no original audience research was conducted for this project, the reasons why specific audiences might have been attracted (or not) to the Australian product are certainly addressed.

To different degrees, what these studies have in common is an underlying concern with the ways in which television might be implicated in the construction of cultural identity and ideas about nationhood in a global context. If much of this research is premised on an anxiety about how local, national identities might be erased by a global (principally American) popular culture, then studies such as that of Kolar-Panov (1997), which demonstrate how Serbian communities in Perth used video tapes of imported television news reports of war in the Balkans to confirm their ethnic allegiances, demonstrates that the opposite may also be true. The possibility that diasporic communities may use their access to video, satellite and cable television from their country of origin in order to reinforce their sense of cultural and national identity and to resist the forces of cultural globalisation is also evident in research into the media habits of Vietnamese communities in Australia. The work of Cunningham and Nguyen (2000; also discussed in Chapter 14) discusses the ways in which videos of live variety shows and music videos, specifically produced for the Vietnamese diaspora around the world, may facilitate not simply some form of cultural maintenance, but also a degree of adaptation to Western culture. This is so because the videos consumed by these diasporic communities are produced, for the most part, by Vietnamese living in America, and are already a product of a cultural fusion, bearing the hybrid markers of their Vietnamese and Western origins. Indeed, the study of Asian diasporas and media use of which this work forms a part (Cunningham and Sinclair 2000) demonstrates the extent and dynamism of 'global narrowcasting' of a wide variety of media materials to dispersed ethnic communities.

While previous studies have therefore framed the relationship between television audiences and the processes of globalisation in terms of the circulation of specific television texts in particular cultural settings, it could be argued that such processes need to be examined in relation to the use of other media forms. For example, as Ellen Seiter points out, the success of the American television series *The X Files* depended to a large extent on the establishment of an Internet home page and the subsequent stimulation and interest of an audience with both computer access and the high demographic profile attractive to network executives (Seiter 1999: 119). Clearly, the relationship between viewers and television screens can no longer be considered in isolation from other media forms in the home—if indeed it ever could. The use by networks and program producers of Internet access to stimulate viewer interest, provide information, market different products—and to track the profile of their most valued viewers—is rapidly becoming standard practice in Australia, as is demonstrated by the deployment of Channel Nine's Internet site, ninemsn.

New behaviour with the Internet and pay TV

Visit the Website for ninemsn and you are immediately invited to set this as your default home page where the information (and advertising) will change every day, even as your visit to the site is being tracked by the presence of an electronic 'cookie' which records information about your computer and its venue. In the banner across the top of the page, you are offered free email and a button on the right offers you an immediate $10.00 shopping voucher if you click on it and visit ninemsn's related shopping site, wishlist, where, on 26 August 1999, you are encouraged to buy your Father's Day gift from the suggested items (always assuming you are prepared to surrender your credit card information via a 'totally secure' encrypted message). Ninemsn also presents their visitor with the latest news and weather, and an invitation to vote on the issue of the day: click on the picture of Senator Natasha Stott Despoja and you can join in an online chat room for one hour in the evening discussing Internet censorship and Australia's role in the digital revolution. You can also win $5000 in lighting installation if you visit the site of Channel Nine's infotainment show, *Our House*. Other featured program sites include that of *A Current Affair*, where you can vote yes or no on the issue of whether or not violence on video and TV may directly affect kids' behaviour, and learn of Channel Nine's own research conducted by a child psychiatrist, Brent Waters, who filmed children's 'free play' after they were 'required' to play a range of video games. Thus visitors to the ninemsn site are invited to participate in some version of an online consumer democracy, where they can simultaneously shop, vote and acquire information about research into children and video games.

Meanwhile, your visit to the site, how long you stayed, what links you clicked on, what purchases you made, are all being recorded in ways which deliver to the owners of the site a considerable amount of very personal and specific information. If, as has often been suggested, commercial television shows only exist as a way of delivering potential consumers to advertisers, then what of the ninemsn site? Not only can this site deliver visitors to advertisers, it can do so personally and instantly, enabling direct contact between seller and buyer in ways which can be tracked, monitored and pursued. As Winton has pointed out (1999a), this is niche marketing of the first order, and with advertisers currently scrambling to get online, the revenue from online advertising is projected to be worth some $400 million by the year 2003.

There is so much to do and so many places to go on the ninemsn site, it is no wonder that television viewing practices are reportedly changing. An article in the Melbourne *Age* by Karen Kissane on 15 May 1999 posed the question 'Does free-to-air television have a future?' and suggested that people were turning off their television sets in the early evening to do other things, including 'play' with computers. But what sorts of play? A study by Cubitt and Stockbridge some three years earlier suggested that playing computer and video games accounted for only 3 per cent of young people's time, as compared with the 33 per cent of leisure time devoted to watching television (Cubitt and Stockbridge 1996: xi). Perhaps people are turning to the Internet instead? An Australian Bureau of Statistics survey of household computer use suggested that in February 1999, of the 45.3 per cent of Australian households in which there was a computer, just over 18 per cent of all households (or 1.3 million) had home Internet access, a 50 per cent increase over the February 1998 figure (ABS 1999: 5). If this rapid rate of growth in Internet access seems surprising, there is some precedent for suggesting that Australians have always been quick to take up new technologies, as was the case with the successful penetration of the domestic video in the early 1980s (Cunningham and Turner 1993: 342) or the recent proliferation of mobile phones, which is one of the highest rates amongst OECD countries (Bennett et al. 1999: 58).

As if to contradict this argument about Australians and their enthusiasm for new technology, the takeup of pay television in Australia has been rather slow, resulting in an enormous $898 million loss for pay TV operators in their first two years of operation (CEPU 1999). Figures from Pay TV News (10 February 1999) suggested that, in February 1999, only 13.7 per cent of homes in Australia were subscribing to pay TV (some 930 000 households). On 2 August 1999, AC Neilsen released its first ratings report for pay TV in Australia, revealing that while the audience for pay TV accounted for only 7.3 per cent of Australia's total television viewing audience, in those homes where pay TV is watched, this accounts for 46.3 per cent, or almost half of the total television viewing time (Winton 1999b: 9).

As Winton suggests, these figures have not been lost on advertisers, and in the twelve months up to August 1999, pay TV was able to glean some $30 million dollars of advertising revenue (Winton 1999b: 9). Furthermore, despite the relatively small numbers involved, the enormous profits to be made from pay-per-view services make pay television an extremely lucrative operation (Winton 1998: 9). And when evidence is forthcoming about what people do in fact pay to watch—boxing, wrestling and music concerts (1998: 8)—then another set of issues presents itself. The fact that it is women who are reportedly turning into the music concerts, while men are paying for the boxing and both are watching the wrestling, reminds us of the continuing significance of gender, taste and class in these new developments.

While evidence from other countries such as the United States and the United Kingdom, where pay television is more firmly established, would suggest that there is a distinct class basis to the take-up of satellite and cable services (Brunsdon 1997; Seiter 1999), there is little evidence in Australia as yet to support this argument. However, given that debates about television as a medium have always tended to migrate to Australia somewhat after the fact, it may be that questions about the preferences and practices of the pay television consumer are just around the corner. As Seiter points out, television viewing may then become considerably more stigmatised as an activity. Even now, she suggests, while sitting at the computer is considered a worthy enterprise, free-to air television is becoming the ghetto of the underprivileged and excluded (Seiter 1999: 132). Given that all the evidence on computer and Internet use in the home seems to point to the fact that it is mainly the males in the household who are booting up and logging on, are women doomed to be the most underprivileged and excluded of all (ABS 1999a; ABS 1999b; Bennett et al. 1999: 57–86)?

NEW METHODOLOGIES?

If television viewing as a practice is changing, then clearly television audience research must also change. The growing interdependency of television and computers in the home, likely to be accelerated by the introduction of digital television, indicates the continuing need to consider television viewing in relation to the entire matrix of domestic communication technologies. For some time it has been apparent that it is impossible to study television watching in isolation from other forms of media consumption—including, most obviously, the newspapers, magazines and Internet sites which interact with the viewing experience. A viewer's experience of their favourite TV show may be augmented by purchasing the magazine tie-in, reading an article about the show or its stars in another publication, or visiting the program Website. Television viewers may also form their own 'international' fan groups on the Internet, forging strategic allegiances based on nothing more than their shared enthusiasm for a particular television product, possibly leading to other forms of mutuality and information-sharing which cross international boundaries. Globalisation indeed.

But how to study these practices? Questions of methodology remain a fascinating problem in television audience research. While there are those who continue to advocate ethnographic methods as the only way to understand the complexity of media consumption in terms of the life experience and media usage of the consumer, ethnographic methods continue to present the researcher with all sorts of problems in terms of access and understanding. How is it possible to 'know' enough about a person in order to understand the nature of their viewing experience? Will observation, self-report and interview ever give the whole picture? Can observing what people do around the television set provide any insight into what their doing might mean to either themselves or others (Bausinger 1984)? And what of the interview, formal or informal, structured or unstructured, or the focus group discussion? What of the ethics of 'listening in' to such discussions on the Internet? What can be said to whom about what and where?

One of the primary ways in which information about television viewers has been gathered in the past is by asking questions and/or 'listening to' what people say or write to each other or to the person asking the questions. But those being studied about their television viewing, or media habits in general, already have some knowledge of how such activities might be regarded by different groups in society and their remarks are usually framed to take account of this. As has been frequently demonstrated, how people talk about their media practices constitutes a significant aspect of their self-presentation and impression management (Seiter 1990; Turnbull 1993). Even in Bennett et al.'s major study of Australian taste cultures, it is evident that the ways in which people reported their use of the personal computer (stressing its educational function) or their television viewing practices (describing most of what is on as 'rubbish') clearly demonstrate their perceived need to present their media practices in what they might consider to be the 'best' light (Bennett et al. 1999: 57–86). One productive branch of future audience research might therefore be to investigate the relationship between these different discourses of value—who uses them and in what ways—in order to explore the social construction of taste which is implicit in how we represent our television and media consumption to others and even to ourselves.

But such representations may, of course, be at one remove from what people are actually doing with television—or rather, the various screens which now figure in their lives. In the future, it is likely to be the media industries themselves (or their agents) who will be tracking this activity in ever-increasingly accurate detail, but with a very specific set of motives in mind: how best to profit further from this relationship. And this is why, as our experience of the world and our position in it becomes increasingly dependent on mediated forms of communication, we still urgently need to know how and why, on what or whose terms this experience is negotatiated with what social implications for all. This is the continuing challenge of academic audience research: how to investigate and account for media practices in ways which will help us understand more clearly the proliferation of mediated forms of communication in relation to the practice of everyday life in all its social, cultural and moral complexity.

In 1997, watching television or videos still accounted for the majority of people's use of leisure time in Australia (87.6 per cent), well ahead of the next most popular activity described as 'socialising' (74.7 per cent) (ABS 1999b: 173). In 1999, some 99 per cent of Australian homes owned at least one television set (many have more) and 86.6 per cent of households owned at least one video recorder (Bennett et al. 1999). Meanwhile, at least half the homes in Australia had acquired at least one one computer (ABS 1999a: 5). It is therefore clear that how and in what ways that screen in the corner may affect our lives (or not), as it quietly mutates into something other than broadcast television, will continue to present a set of pressing issues for the future.

Note

1 The text of this exchange is taken from the documentary film 'Glued to the Telly', shown in the *True Stories* series on ABC Television, 2 July 1995. There is also a book of the film of the same name written by Cate Rayson (1998).

Thirteen Sally Stockbridge

The strategies of audience capture: The case of Network Ten

This chapter is concerned with the methods used by the commercial television industry to both measure and maintain an audience, with the focus on Network Ten as the 'underdog'—a case study of the first free-to-air TV network in Australia to cultivate a specific audience demographic.

Industry measurement includes ratings, surveys, focus groups and lifestyle research. Chief among these is ratings. The word 'rating' refers variously to:

- the percentage of households that are tuned to a particular station at a particular time;
- Target Audience Rating Points (TARPs), the percentage of the target audience tuned to a particular station at a particular time; and
- share, the percentage of households or audience tuned to a particular station at a particular time, when calculated against only the homes that have a television switched on. The statistics used in this chapter refer to shares. For example, a share of 32 for *Dawsons Creek* means that 32 per cent of those watching TV in that area are watching *Dawson*.

SHORT HISTORY OF TEN

In 1960, Australian broadcasting legislation was changed to allow for a third commercial station in Sydney, Melbourne and Adelaide. In November 1963, the Postmaster General issued a licence for United Telecasters Sydney Limited to operate a commercial television station in Sydney. The main programs purchased by the company were *Bonanza*, *The Flintstones*, *Petticoat Junction*, *Astro Boy*, *Gunsmoke* and *Hazel*. The Postmaster General advised that the station was to have 50 per cent Australian programming after the completion of twelve months of operation. Ten's Sydney station commenced operation in April 1965 followed in July by TVQ-0 in Brisbane. ATV10 Melbourne commenced in 1964 and its first Australian program was a pop music show called *GO*. By 1972, ratings for the stations broadcasting as 10 and 0 respectively were going down but this was the year the Australian adult sitcom *Number 96* was purchased and it marked a turning point for both ratings and profits. Other successes like *The Box* were launched in 1973 followed by *The Mike Walsh Show* in 1974.

In 1979, News Corporation acquired a controlling interest in Ten in Sydney and Melbourne until 1985 when it sold out to Network Ten Holdings Limited. In 1987, News Corp sold its shares in Network Ten Holdings to Westfield Capital Corp who already owned 20 per cent of Northern Star Holdings. This was followed by Northern Star's purchase of NEW Perth, ADS Adelaide and CTC Canberra, making the company Australia's only five-metropolitan-city network. This put the Lowys in charge of the network (see Chapter 3). The previous year saw Ten take over the rights of *Neighbours* from Channel 7, turning it into a ratings winner. The Brisbane station TVQ was purchased in 1989 and all stations in the network changed their frequency signal from 0 to 10 by the same year.

Record amounts were paid for broadcast rights, including $40 million for the Rugby League, decisions which led to the demise of the network. In September 1989, Channel Ten stations in Adelaide, Perth and Canberra were sold to Capital Television. The network was not re-established until 1995 with the re-purchase of ADS Adelaide and NEW Perth from Capital.

In 1990, Ten was placed in receivership and was regarded as the basket case of the TV industry. It was locked in a losing ratings battle with Nine and Seven, with all three networks going flat-out for the same viewers, spending huge amounts to do so.

YOUTH DEMOGRAPHICS, AND POSITION, POSITION, POSITION . . .

What do you do when you're third and can't hope to compete with the resources of the others in maximising audience numbers? That was the question. Going after a specific part of the audience, an emerging lucrative demographic, was the solution.

Network Ten's current ownership structure was initiated in 1992 when a consortium, including Canadian broadcaster CanWest Global Communications, purchased the network out of receivership. (Canwest holds a 14.99 per cent shareholding interest and a 57.5 per cent economic interest in Ten.) While Nine and Seven were battling it out to be number one across the board, Ten set out (under CEO Peter Viner) to target a younger audience (16–39 years) with a mix of innovative Australian and international programming. Since 1992, Ten has consistently held the largest commercial share of the 16–24-year-old audience and aims for the 16–39 group. This tactic was introduced to restore the company to a viable economic footing. The 16–39-year-old demographic was considered a good revenue focus and another way of being competitive on a low-cost base.

The 16–39-year-old age group has become the holy grail of commercial television. The other commercial networks, Seven and Nine, also recognise the appeal of this group. Its members are perceived as being big earners, big spenders, quick to adopt new products and having little brand loyalty. However, Ten also attracts large numbers of the 16–24-year-old group, a group least attached to television viewing. Examples from the late 1990s included *Good News Week* and *Good News Week Night Lite*, which had their highest ratings in this demographic, as did *The Panel*, with particularly high ratings among male viewers. *The Simpsons, The X-Files, Party of Five* and *Charmed* also rated extremely well with 16–24-year-olds. This group is normally the highest rating component of the 16–39 demographic for Ten.

The 16–39 demographic is more open to new products on the market and its members:

> are a lot more adventurous and willing to try new things, including products. Advertisers are also doing more to build long-term brands with this group . . . A big winner for Ten in 1999 was US drama *Dawson's Creek*; it has attracted 70 per cent of the core youth demographic watching television. *Party of Five, Xena, Cheez TV,* and *Video Hits* are also growing in audience and advertiser support. Advertisers who are putting money behind the youth market with Ten include convenience food brands, cinema distributors, and fashion. (*B&T*, 9 February 1999: 35)

The press also clearly admire the 'underdog' network for its strategy and tenacity:

> Ten runs a steady third in the ratings, but comes first in comparative financial terms. Its profit margin pips Nine and trounces Seven, a triumph of owner Canadian businessman Izzy Asper's decision to make Ten not the best, but the best at what it does: targeting the youth audience and delivering that crucial demographic to eager advertisers. It is the polar opposite of Seven which, in a futile attempt to topple ratings leader Nine, secured expensive programming and sent costs soaring, decimating its bottom line . . . Both Nine and Seven privately admire the Ten model, which has seen virtually all in-house production outsourced to Television and Media Services and its subsidiary, Global Television. (*Australian Financial Review* 7 June 1999: 1)

Since that analysis, Nine has bought shares in Television and Media Services and Seven, on a rapid economising drive, has moved to outsource programming more significantly.

Cost management strategies were implemented at Ten through developing relationships with independent production houses and outsourcing the majority

Figure 13.1 Broadcasting profit of networks and affiliates in multi-station markets, 1992–97 ($m)

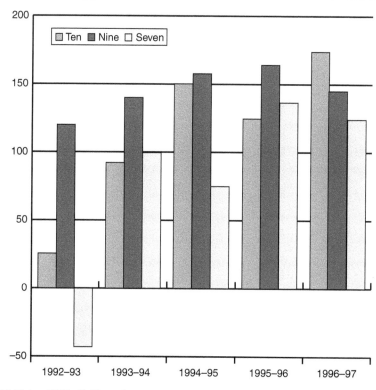

Source: *ABA Update* (1998: 6), Figure 8.

of production. Much of Ten's production is outsourced to Television and Media Services and its subsidiary, Global Television, which is housed in the old Ten premises in North Ryde, Sydney with Ten acquiring an 8 per cent stake in 1995, rising to 12 per cent in 1999. Studio productions include *Neighbours* (for Ten) and *Water Rats* (for Nine), while broadcast events have included *Indy Car, Melbourne Cup, World Swimming Titles* and *City to Surf* for Ten. *Good News Week* is produced at the Global Studios, as was *Breakers*. Beyond Productions in Sydney produced *Sex/Life, Beyond 2000, Mardi Gras* and other material for Ten.

The youth focus of Ten is also reinforced by the way in which it sells itself to the chosen audience: through station IDs and slogans. The first ID specifically targeting the youth market was 'Give Me Ten'. This worked successfully for two years. It featured active young people and was based on a catchy, hip, American-style greeting—American culture is popular with the young.

The emphasis shifted in programming when Kristen Marlow (1994–October 1996) left and was replaced by Ross Plapp as Programming Head. The station ID took on a 'arty' look with no catchy slogan and turned attention back to a general audience. While the ID won an award—the 1997 US Promax International Gold Medallion—it didn't assist in consolidating a market. Plapp was replaced in October 1997 by his second in command, David Mott, and the focus returned to youth with a new station ID, 'Turn Me On'. This slogan was devised for Ten by Clemengers advertising agency, which also developed station promos featuring 'crazy' scenarios around successful Ten programming such as *The Nanny*, *Melrose Place* and *Seinfeld*. The 'Turn Me On' ID has also attracted a degree of complaint, from an older audience offended by its sexual implications.

Station IDs are crucial marketing tools responsible for moulding the network's image. 'They convey an image or attitude . . . For Ten it's a way for people to see that where Nine is celebrity-based (and Seven is family-focused: 'Everyone's Home on Seven'), we're younger.' (Cree Stevenson, Ten Promotions Manager, *Daily Telegraph* 12 November 1998: 7)

Program promos are as important as station IDs in reminding audiences of the program line-up and its focus. In prime time they take up twelve minutes of non-program time. The network remit here is to make them fun, quirky and memorable. Teen program promos emphasise 'action' or 'the kiss' and there is greater use of current popular music. Music has an even greater role in programs themselves. Ten also uses a promo production and placement strategy where an audience is allowed 'to find' a show, rather than being hit over the head by a hard sell. This strategy worked very well for programs like *The Panel* and it helps differentiate Ten from the other commercial networks. Thus a program is not necessarily pulled after three weeks if it does not rate well initially.

RESEARCHING THE AUDIENCE

Ten uses a variety of means to assess programs in relation to likely audiences and potential popularity: outside consultants with computerised assessment systems; market research/telephone surveys; focus groups; and of course ratings (people meters), which remain the chief method for testing whether or not programming decisions are paying off.

Outside consultants

As consultants, Ten uses TAPE, a British group with a computer-based system that can assess formats for shows. This includes age, gender and type for characters; actors with track records; domestic and overseas market viability; and age group appeal. It is basically a risk-management process into which can be fed a range of program attributes based on past experiences in Australia and abroad. TAPE is able to use British and American scheduling strategies as an efficient method to ascertain which programs to acquire from overseas. This operates as another set of eyes and ears in overseas territories. Network Ten has had a ten-year association with this group, which is also used by the production company Grundys in its effort to attract a broader overseas sales.

Market research and focus groups

Another method used by networks is market research: telephone surveys followed by focus group sessions. This can be used in a couple of ways:

- A producer or production company wanting to pitch to a network could add weight to their argument by having used focus groups to ascertain viewers' interest in their project or format.
- A production company could co-sponsor the research with the network. For example, Grundys, the producer of *Neighbours*, will use this method for both Australian and overseas markets. This is a very common practice in the United States where the researcher–producer relationship is more highly developed.

It is clear that overseas sales are important to the longevity of Australian programs. *Neighbours* and *Home and Away* have succeeded where *State Coroner* and *Breakers* did not. Because the Australian market is relatively small, production companies need external markets to cover production costs and generate profits. But the overseas market has changed since *Neighbours* commenced screening in Britain in 1986. Recently, output deals with US producers have swamped the British and European markets, making it harder for Australian productions to find buyers. *State Coroner* rated well in Australia but couldn't achieve the overseas sale it required to continue production. Research is just one factor that may assist in maintaining an audience.

Focus group research is being utilised more frequently by the networks, particularly the work of 'TV Doctor' David Castran (*The Australian* 15 July 1999: 14). Seven makes extensive use of Castran's methods and Ten also works with him to test Australian drama programs. This research is used to trial new programs or to find ways to reformat and increase ratings for longer-standing shows. Focus groups are used to test the general premise of a show, and its attractiveness for Australian audiences. Castran worked with Seven to test the pilot of the Australian drama *All Saints* which resulted in rewrites and reshooting of some scenes before the series was broadcast. Hal McElroy, creator of *Water Rats* and *Blue Heelers*, and a series that commenced production in October 1999 for Ten, *Above the Law*, uses focus group research to find out what the target audience thinks about the program. Production companies are keener users of this form of research than television networks, which are often more sceptical about its potential.

Above the Law focus group members were asked: 'Do you understand the show?' 'Is *Above the Law* an appropriate title?' 'Who is your favourite character

Table 13.1   Ratings for *Neighbours* compared with other stations

Seven	Nine	Ten (Neighbours)	
22.3	17.3	60.4	Teens 13–17
22.5	26.8	50.7	Men 16–24
19.2	20.0	61.1	Women 16–24
27.2	36.1	36.7	People 16–39

Source: Metro All 18 January–25 June 1999, AC Nielsen.

and why?' 'Do the storylines interest you?' Other questions were also asked, all designed to ascertain beforehand whether or not the series would work in two senses: whether it would be liked and whether it would appeal to the right demographic.

Neighbours commenced with a general audience focus but now targets a younger demographic. In 1998, David Mott, together with the network's Head of Drama, Rick Maier, and Grundys, spent considerable time developing strong storylines that targeted a younger demographic. Significant research was carried out in both Australia and the United Kingdom, since it was vital that future storylines appealed in both countries. Mott also focused attention on promotion and marketing to give it a hip, younger feel through the use of contemporary music. The BBC were so impressed with Network Ten's approach that they requested copies of the on-air campaign to develop their own version. To our knowledge, this is the first time this has happened. *Neighbours* now regularly achieves a 40 per cent share of the 16–39 audience in Australia, but is pitched to a slightly different market in the United Kingdom.

In general terms, Australian drama tends to skew old, as far as audience ratings are concerned. *State Coroner* rated well with an older audience. *Big Sky* and *Medivac* were deliberate attempts to attract a younger audience but they failed. Young audiences in Australia are not used to watching 'Australian'—even though, by regulation, 55 per cent of programming on all three commercial networks is Australian. But *Neighbours*, like *Home and Away*, is successful in attracting Australian youth and, according to the ratings, the 16–39 demographic (see Table 13.1). As can be seen from these statistics, *Neighbours* is winning hands down with those in the 13–24 age group, and still winning 16–39, though fewer older people aged 25–39 watch the program.

Ratings

The ratings provided by AC Nielsen are of importance as a measure of likely success when acquiring a program from another network. The ratings received by *Good News Week* in the 16–39 demographic were key in the decision to bid for the program that saw it change from the ABC. This was also the case in the battle with SBS over *South Park*, though in late 1999 it was no longer doing well in the United States.

Table 13.2   Ratings by program and age group

Neighbours			
Seven	Nine	Ten	
28.3	45.5	26.2	Total people
24.8	35.7	39.5	People 16–39
Party of Five			
Seven	Nine	Ten	
39.0	38.6	22.5	Total people
24.7	42.3	33.0	People 16–39
Dawsons Creek			
Seven	Nine	Ten	
29.9	44.3	25.7	Total people
25.8	41.4	32.8	People 16–39
Charmed			
Seven	Nine	Ten	
25.2	34.9	40.0	Total people
26.0	29.3	44.7	People 16–39

Source: AC Neilsen, Year to Date, 2 February–15 June 1999, Metro All.

Different departments within the network use ratings in different ways. The programming department clearly uses them in decision-making about program purchases—to judge whether or not a target demographic is being reached and what the actual viewership of a program is. Ratings can be broken into various demographics to obtain specific data. The statistics can be provided as five-minute brackets, to gauge viewer retention levels against all other programming; they can be divided into standard age and gender groups as follows: Total people, Children 5–12, Teens 13–17, Men 16–24, Women 16–24, Men 16–39, Women 16–39, Men 25–39, Women 25–39, Men 40–54, Women 40–54, Men 55–64, Women 55–64, Men 65+, Women 65+.

These data facilitate niche marketing and provide performance measures of target audience reach, for the purposes of sales—obviously of crucial importance to the network sales division. The ratings are commissioned by the television stations—in this case, all the commercial television stations. But as of August 1999, ratings are also available for pay TV.

Below are some examples of how ratings provide information to Ten about its audience. If you were to look at the ratings across a set of programs on a given night, it could well appear that the youth-oriented programs on Ten were not in fact rating and that Nine and Seven were leaving the network way behind. But break the ratings into age groups and the picture looks quite different (see Table 13.2). The programs are Ten youth-oriented shows, and their share of the total audience and then the 'young' audience can be compared against the other commercial networks for Sydney on 7 September 1999.

Ratings can further be divided by gender, this time across the first half of the ratings year (see Table 13.3).

Table 13.3 Ratings by program, age group and gender

Party of Five—women			
Seven	Nine	Ten	
21.2	25.2	53.9	16–24 years
30.9	33.1	36.1	16–39 years
Dawsons Creek—women			
Seven	Nine	Ten	
20.3	19.0	60.8	16–24 years
30.2	32.3	37.5	16–39 years
Melrose Place—women			
Seven	Nine	Ten	
29.0	26.5	44.5	16–24 years
34.0	31.2	34.9	16–39 years

Source: AC Neilsen, Year to Date, 2 February–15 June 1999 Metro All.

The general purpose of ratings is to enable licensees and advertisers to arrive at an agreed value for advertising time. This is correct, but they also enable programming to make important decisions. If you know who is watching—or not watching—you can determine the success of a program or a program schedule. It is also crucial for the placement of program promotions. For example, you wouldn't promote a male-oriented program during another show where women dominated the viewing. There are also regulations governing what you can promote during children's viewing times and G programming where child viewers predominate.

The ratings data also provide programmers with the information needed to 'counter program'. Counter programming is a strategy used to maximise audience while not going head to head with a rival network. David Mott regularly goes through the schedule using the ratings data to see who is watching which network and who is unserved—where there is an opportunity. Although it is Ten's remit to go after the 16–39 group, it is not worth programming two such programs against each other. Through a deal with Twentieth Century Fox, the Seven Network received *Ally McBeal*, which had a certain appeal for a younger audience. Though *Charmed*, one of Ten's new programs, could have been broadcast against *Ally McBeal*, it would not do as well as it in fact does on a Tuesday night. Because the ratings showed that *Ally McBeal* appealed to a young, predominantly female audience, Ten elected to televise *Law and Order* in that timeslot, a program which appeals to an older, predominantly male audience. This resulted in Ten obtaining a very solid second place for the timeslot.

Another case of counter programming occurred for the launch of the program *Dawson's Creek*. Mott wanted this program to slot into Tuesday night and discovered that Seven and Nine both had sporting commitments on its first night of broadcast. This was an ideal opportunity when many viewers would be looking for a light entertainment alternative (*Daily Telegraph* 14 January 1999).

Table 13.4 Ratings for *Video Hits*, compared with other networks

Seven	Nine	Ten (Video Hits)	
30.7	13.7	38.0	Total people
18.7	10.8	46.2	People 16–39

Source: AC Neilsen, Year to Date 3 January–4 September 1999 Metro All (Saturday).

WHAT WORKS WITH YOUNGER AUDIENCES: CROSS-PROMOTION, MUSIC, COMEDY AND REAL LIFE

It is clear that it is cheaper and less risky to buy tested youth drama from the United States than to produce it here. There are also strong cross-promotions between US youth programs and popular music, making them even more attractive. TV soundtracks are directed at young audiences and are released to coincide with the series as they are broadcast. The CD *Songs from Dawson's Creek* has been a big hit in the United States and was at the number one spot on Australia's ARIA album chart (*Daily Telegraph* 2 September 1999: 29).

Music programming itself is still a constant with youth audiences, but only Ten and the ABC have any popular music programming in the 1990s—a vastly different situation from the 1980s when this kind of programming was prolific (Stockbridge 1994). This reduction in music programming has been noted as one of the reasons younger people now watch less TV (*Weekend Australian* 13 December 1997). Ten's *Video Hits* and *Groundzero*, with its own Website, rate well with younger audiences (see Table 13.4).

Apart from American drama and Australian soaps, young Australian audiences prefer comedy and playful programming. News also suffers from the same desire of the young to be amused and irreverent. Focus group research with 16–28-year-olds by Lee Burton of Victoria College of the Arts suggests that they are getting their news and current affairs from the Internet and rejecting the usual style of news and current affairs (*The Media Report* 3 December 1998).

There are also links and cross-promotion with other youth media. For example, *The Panel* is simulcast on radio Triple M and so also was *The House from Hell*. *The House from Hell* rated well and is an example of a new trend in TV programming called 'Docusoaps', which 'can be produced for a fraction of the cost of drama and score considerable ratings'. Examples of this growing genre include: *RPA, Changing Rooms, Airport, Taxi Cab Confessions, House from Hell, Weddings, Learners* and *Hot Property* (*Herald Sun* 23 June 1999: 10).

In recent years, free-to-air commercial television has come under significant pressure from the 'communications revolution' and the fragmentation of the audience base for audiovisual and related services. Already, even before television enters the digital era, there is proliferating competition from other media and communications developments, including pay TV, the Internet, computer and video games. It is argued that younger people are now watching less television and that television viewing is an ageing pastime, with young males watching the least. Some cite the Internet as the substitute for television viewing, especially among young well-educated professionals. However, although there has been a marginal decline in free-to-air viewing, it still has 90 per cent reach in a given week. Free-to-air remains the only way to reach large audiences. The first television ratings survey to include pay TV, released in August 1999, appears to support this argument. To date, pay TV only captures 7.3 per cent of the total TV viewing audience in Australia, and while this is larger than some expected, it has to be divided by the 54 channels available.

CONCLUSIONS

As markets become more fragmented, niche marketing, or pitching to specific demographic groups, appears to be the way of the future. Network Ten was the first free-to-air television network to attempt to differentiate in this way. It was clearly a successful strategy to pull the network out of the dire straits of the 1980s and a useful way of differentiating it from the other commercial networks.

Ten is the more comfortable network when it comes to youth programming. Not being concerned with knocking Nine out of its top spot, it is not so anxious to capture the total population in its ratings. Cross-promotion with radio, pay TV and Internet Websites and tie-ins with other foci of younger people's leisure time are key strategies.

Research is another strategy of a much more recent vintage. Unlike the United States, Australian television programmers have been more inclined to rely on experience than research. While ratings have always been used, the use of focus groups in particular was a 1990s phenomenon. The need to maintain audience reach in the face of increasing competition could well be one of the reasons networks have joined with producers to take research more seriously.

Many people at Network Ten assisted with the provision of information essential for this chapter, including David Mott, General Manager Network Programming, Rick Maier, Head of Drama, and Jim Buchan, Network Program Scheduler.

Fourteen Tom O'Regan and Stuart Cunningham

Marginalised audiences

Differentness is functional: it cannot willingly or easily be relinquished. (Morley and Robins 1995: 167)

When we speak of 'marginal audiences', we are typically dealing with people or groups on the edge of society who are not addressed by mainstream television. These are communities, groups and individuals who, by virtue of disability, geographic location, race, ethnicity, taste, values, income or their particular social and cultural capacities, are under-served or poorly represented within our television system.

John Hartley (1992) and Ien Ang (1991: 3) have variously suggested our very conceptions of audiences are shaped by the institutional needs and purposes of those who imagine and produce them: the critical, industrial and regulatory institutions of television. Audience-making—defining, constructing, imagining and in some cases inventing audiences—is a permanently unfinished business which is undertaken by a variety of players ranging from advertisers and marketers to special-interest activists, government officials and the like (see Ettema and Whitney 1994 passim). Crucial to this business is having 'the audience' in question recognise itself as an audience so that others can address it.

Such theories suggest that how we understand and identify marginal audiences is inevitably produced by the intersection of the television industry with a variety of governmental processes, activism and critical discourses. Consequently, exactly who counts as a marginal audience varies—it is dependent upon these broader processes and discourses. Often this means that public recognition of marginal audiences is tied in with broader social or political campaigns. These might be in pursuit of social, cultural or political recognition of particular groups, or they may have been called up as a consequence of government policies in support of, for example, multiculturalism, Indigenous self-determination, anti-discrimination protocols, or principles of access and equity. So, for example, the case for SBS-TV and for greater accommodation of ethnic minorities in the programming and makeup of the ABC and the commercial networks is helped by policies which stress meeting Australia's cultural diversity: Australia is the second largest immigrant nation after Israel, 40 per cent of the population are either born outside the country or with at least one parent born outside the country, and one-third of households in Sydney and Melbourne speak a language other than English in the home.

Obvious candidates for inclusion as marginal audiences include: Aboriginal and Torres Strait Islander audiences; ethnic minority audiences; audience groupings formed around values, orientations and lifeways that are perceived to be outside the 'mainstream' (for example, gays and lesbians); audiences with disabilities—the hearing and sight impaired—who access television services under difficult conditions; and rural, regional and city audiences who may be too economically marginal to sustain the provision of adequate television signals or live in areas with poor reception owing to topographical features or distance. We can so readily identify all the above groups as marginal audiences as they are also the groups which are afforded some (usually hard-fought) public recognition as marginal in adjacent social, political and cultural fields. In many of these cases, activists take their 'difference' to the point where it can be claimed and increasingly recognised as a human right that needs to be met rather than as a claim of disadvantage to be met through welfare provision (Hartley 1999: 164).

Characteristically, a variety of schemes have developed to accommodate these audiences. These range from the development of an additional national broadcaster in SBS-TV to provide multicultural programming to the development of closed captioning for those 1.7 million Australians with significant hearing loss. Typically, all these groupings have to a greater or lesser extent voiced concerns about the services available to them. The exceptions to this pattern are those marginal groups—young teenagers, the poor or those with low media involvement, for instance—who are so economically disadvantaged that they lack articulate public voices to speak on their behalf.

This chapter begins with a discussion of what forms marginalisation can take in the context of broadcasting audiences. It is concerned with more than the audiences of free-to-air mainstream television. We examine the informal television services developed by particular cultural groups in circumstances where the formal television system does not—and is not likely to—meet their self-identified needs. The chapter continues by dealing with some of the policy interventions which have developed to secure better services for marginal audiences and, in concluding, suggests areas where further development needs to occur.

DEFINING MARGINALISATION

We (regulators, governments, activists, critics, television industry personnel) think of processes of marginalisation in several ways. Sometimes a dominant group actively marginalises minority groups, and cheapens their values and identities through active and passive processes of exclusion and even discrimination. Aboriginal and Islander, ethnic minority and gay and lesbian spokespersons routinely complain about just such *cultural discrimination*, which either renders them invisible in television or creates visibilities which diminish their own self-understandings.

Cunningham and Sinclair (2000) show that while mainstream media is in many instances consumed widely amongst the Asian communities of their study (and admitting that this is subject to people's degree of comfort with the English language), the communities also expressed widespread dissatisfaction with the likely effect of what the authors call *monocultural* maintenance. Precisely this dissatisfaction, registered as the failure of existing television services to address ethnic minorities and minority language groups as an audience, was recognised by the creation of SBS-TV in 1980 (O'Regan and Kolar-Panov 1993: 131). Such dissatisfaction has also motivated the creation of other kinds of parallel services. These can be formal services, as in the case of the Broadcasting for Remote Aboriginal Communities Scheme (BRACS), SBS-TV or pay TV services in Chinese and Italian; or they can be informal as in the case of the community video networks described by Cunningham and Sinclair (2000) for Asian ethnic minorities and by Kolar-Panov for Croatian and Macedonian minorities (1997).

Often such marginalisation is also linked to the choices marginal audiences themselves make about their own media and television consumption. Such choices are as much about cultural maintenance and sustaining their distinctiveness as cultural groups as they are about responding to a single, powerful, coercive mainstream—whether it is in the guise of its society, its culture or its television. Rarely do we encounter circumstances in which active discrimination is simply the whole story.

Take a Taiwanese-Australian family in Sunnybank in Brisbane whose members turn to Hong Kong and Taiwanese videos for their audio-visual diet. They might do so because mainstream Australian television and society force them to, by providing so little for them. Chinese movies and drama programs are simply screened too intermittently on SBS-TV to have the place of the regular nightly series and movies on the schedule available to the mainstream television audience. The news services, including the more internationally focused SBS *World News* and ABC *News*, only cover Taiwanese and other regional news stories as a part of a broader international remit. Within existing commercial and ABC services, people like them are rarely included on-screen or addressed as part of the 'we' implicit in television's mode of address. Their needing to substitute mainstream TV with the more informal circulation of the video library, community networks and the morning Mandarin news service on SBS-TV demonstrates neglect amounting to discrimination on the part of the existing televisual system in failing to usefully incorporate them and their aspirations.

But for this family, the Taiwanese videos and the cultural setting in which they are delivered are important to logics of cultural maintenance, intergenerational transmission of values and identities, carving out a 'separate' space for themselves, and simply 'being at home' (surrounded by familiar things and situations which include a domestic experience of television). What is important about this activity is precisely its 'private' and non-public dimension. Sometimes there is no desire for this consumption to become a matter for public debate and policy as it would turn unwanted attention to informal community networks and their practices (including, in some communities, extensive VCR piracy). Their activity here might be no different than that of the many expatriate Australians in Europe and Asia who turn to the Internet, ABC Online and the occasional Australian movie or TV news item to 'go back home' to Australia.

In any discussion of the processes of marginalisation, it is important to recognise the extent to which groups often make conscious choices to pursue their own distinct communication pathways and logics. This kind of separate (though not separatist) logic is itself part of the process of audience-making (see Hartley 1999: 164–7). The last decade has seen the development of niche services and marketing and an increasing fractioning of media audiences. The absence of additional free-to-air services or suitable pay TV programming has led to the use of video as a de facto pay TV service both in ethnic communities and in regional Australia. It has also led to the development of niche cultural product which has been sufficient to sustain minor seasons of gay and lesbian movies on SBS-TV and a domestic cycle of gay porn featuring titles like *Jackaroos*, *Going Down Under* and *Boys of Koala Beach* which queer traditional 'legends of the nation' (McKee 1999: 120).

Another development which reflects this interest of forging and repairing group collective identities in the face of the onslaught of mainstream television is the community television experiment at Yuendumu in Central Australia in the late 1980s. Here what was envisaged was nothing less than the 'Aboriginal invention of television', in Eric Michaels' (1986, 1994) words, designed to secure 'a cultural future' for the Warlpiri people (Michaels 1994: 98–124). The project involved the development, broadcasting and video circulation of programming constructed according to Aboriginal cultural protocols and dreaming tracks.

Sometimes marginalisation occurs when groups of people are physically prevented from participating in basic social amenities. This may be due to difficulties of access (perhaps by virtue of their location), or the very way the service is constructed in the first place may restrict their capacity to participate (as in the case of people with disabilities). When the development of remote satellite television services was canvassed in the early 1980s, still 2 per cent of the population (around 300 000 people) in remote and regional Australia were outside the reach of television services. Once satellite transmissions began, the access problems for this cohort remained. They needed to invest in expensive satellite dishes and decoders. Many of those on stations found their viewing times were limited to when the power generator was being run (Green 1998).

The hearing- and sight-impaired, and people with poor or in some cases no television reception, often complain about what amounts to social discrimination because it limits their participation in and access to existing services. These groups mostly don't want a different or more specialised service: they simply want the existing free-to-air content delivered in different and better ways. The hearing- and sight-impaired seek more extensive captioning of existing programs (for those who can read but not hear well) and 'video description' to inform what cannot be conveyed on the soundtrack (for those who can hear but see imperfectly). The only option is to seek compulsory captioning (as exists in the United Kingdom and the United States) and video description, as is being contemplated in the United States (see McConnell 1999). The hearing-impaired have had some local success: from January 2001, all prime-time news and current affairs programs must be captioned (Australian Caption Centre 1999).

Those with poor reception seek improvements often through local government and the Australian Broadcasting Authority. This category includes a substantial population on the fringes of reception in capital cities and regional areas. Being able to get 'decent television signals' becomes for them a priority and its absence a problem. The problem of television reception is also a major problem for caravaners, as evidenced by the success of publications such as *TV Across Australia: The Caravaner's Guide to Television Reception* (Haverfield and Haverfield 1998), now into its second edition.

There has been surprisingly little critical attention paid to television reception issues despite their continued relevance given the size of Australia's landmass. It was a significant problem affecting reception of the third commercial television service until the conversion to colour in 1975 (a significant number of television sets could not receive what was then called the '0/10' network). It was also a problem for SBS and affected its capacity to deliver its service into some of its core markets until the late 1990s when it developed the kind of extensive terrestrial translator service employed by the other networks. Indeed, the whole community television sector has always been bedevilled by its low-power transmission capability, which makes it impossible to receive a watchable signal in all but a handful of suburbs in any major city in which the service exists. A critical difference between Australian and North American thinking on cable TV services is that the North Americans approached cable TV as a means of delivering free-to-air television signals to poor reception areas. So cable was envisaged as part of the mix of provisions designed to secure 'access' to basic services. The Australian approach has been to see cable services as a separate medium capable of compromising the integrity and amenity of free-to-air services rather than as an alternative delivery mechanism.

Sometimes, marginalisation occurs when groups of people with common needs do not amount to a sufficiently large section of the market to justify the provision of adequate levels of service to meet their specific requirements. This process—often called a 'market failure'—can affect many different audience cohorts within what is primarily a commercial marketplace. Examples within the current media climate could include arts audiences, cosmopolitans, Aborigines and Islanders, regional and remote Australia, youth, the poor and the various minority ethnic communities. The history of Australian television shows that this problem has been addressed in one of two ways: through changes in the marketplace such as, for example, pay TV services providing channels in languages other than English or free-to-air television serving a wider program preference distribution; or through the development of additional services specifically designed to accommodate these 'special' needs—as in the SBS. Both are able to provide more specialised programming for more closely defined targeted groups.

Marginal audiences typically present practical difficulties for the television industry. They are difficult to cultivate, they are expensive to cater to, and they yield little profit once they are catered for. In some cases the industry runs the risk of alienating or losing core audiences should competing specific needs be too explicitly addressed. Catering specifically to remote and regional audiences often gets defined out of core business. *Countrywide*, for example, was taken off the air in the early 1990s despite its continued popularity in the country—it did not fit the ABC's profile for its predominantly urban audience. In a similar fashion, too much programming 'in language' drives down ratings; too many black or Asian or Southern European faces and situations are thought to limit a program's general appeal.

Marginal audiences getting something approximating an adequate, if not 'normal', provision of services will be dependent on their capacity to both construct their own usually informal parallel television services and to mobilise themselves and other actors to act on their behalf to develop policy interventions capable of delivering additional, often publicly funded, services.

INFORMAL AND ENTREPRENEURIAL TV

Various measures are taken by marginal audiences to provide themselves with an experience of television. The sight-impaired often enlist the service of someone to describe what is happening on screen; the hearing-impaired may rely on their capacity to lip read or might become a consumer of SBS-TV because of its subtitling service for programming in languages other than English. With an ageing population significantly swelling the number of hearing-impaired people, the amenity provided by SBS-TV's subtitling service becomes of particular significance, as too does the increasing volume of American and British programming supplied with closed captioning.

Regional audiences outside the reach of terrestrial television services in the early 1980s relied on family, friends and (illegal) video businesses advertising through the regional newspaper, *Queensland Country Life*, to provide them with tapes of prime-time television. In some cases, TV viewing became shifted to specified times of the year: holidays and visits to the city. In regional areas in Western and South Australia, with access to only one commercial station and the ABC, the video sector is more extensively used as a means to provide something approximating an alternative television service.

Cunningham and Sinclair (2000), in the most in-depth qualitiative study of media use among Asian communities in Australia, found that, faced with the cultural narrowness of broadcasting, these groups have constructed a popular cultural environment that significantly displaces broadcast media. There is intense viewer demand for news from the homelands among Chinese populations in Australia, which is addressed through SBS's *WorldWatch* news programs taken direct from satellites overnight and rebroadcast, without subtitles, each morning, and through the pay TV channel New World TV: 'As many studies of the migrant experience have shown, news from or about "home" has special status and value. It is a privileged form, watched avidly and intently and often in a state of what Naficy (1993: 107) terms "epistephilic desire".' (Sinclair et al. 2000: 44) In addition, for the well-established and highly cosmopolitan Chinese diasporas, there are distribution firms handling both cinema and television globally. This is seen as well in the case of Indian communities.

Creating a 'parallel' tele-video schedule, in the case of the Vietnamese diaspora, involves accessing the output of United States-based small business entrepreneurs producing music video for a globally dispersed but small diaspora. This displaced 'indigenous' output—along with the intense engagement (in the case of Vietnamese-Australian young people) with Hong Kong action film and (with older people) Hong Kong television series and serials—makes Euro-American cultural influences 'almost insignificant' in Vietnamese-Australian households, according to cultural anthropologist Mandy Thomas (1996 email communication with Stuart Cunningham). For other, less numerous, groups, the media environment is created through middleperson initiatives including flying in tapes of recent series drama on a weekly basis, film nights or concerts featuring community-based stars. The Cunningham and Sinclair study shows that the mainstream media environment has barely begun to take account of the million-plus Asian-Australians in the community.

The research into informal television shows that there are significant limits within the model of broadcast media in addressing marginal audiences in Australia. Even SBS-TV, a broadcaster programmatically committed to advancing cultural diversity across several fronts (NESB, Indigenous, regional and 'special'-interest) simply cannot successfully program to meet the diverse and incommensurate needs of Australia's multifarious communities within the con-straints of its single-channel free-to-air service (at present, over 150 ethnic groups speaking over 100 different languages originating from 200 countries).

Entrepreneurial initiatives in subscription television are the strongest devel-opments in broadcasting in Australia in response to these needs. With about

18 per cent of total households signed up by 1999, and reasonable expectations of further growth, and with more than 60 channels available on one or more of the services (Foxtel, Optus, Austar), there is corresponding growth in languages other than English (LOTE) and ethnic-specific programming. The Optus subscription package in 1999 in the largest cities offers up to seven non-English language channels and many of these offer programming specifically designed to address interests not catered to by SBS. Indeed, SBS itself has spun off a successful pay TV channel, 'World Movies', from its extensive back catalogue of movie broadcast licences. However, subscription-based specialist services will remain highly volatile areas of the market for the foreseeable future. The precarious financial position of such services will not improve until the costs of delivering specialist and narrowly themed channels are driven much lower.

POLICY-LED INTERVENTIONS

Characteristically, marginal groups develop sophisticated and articulate self-understandings or highly explicit cultural identities to deal with their situation. This helps them sustain political activity which expresses their interests and priorities at whatever political level (local, state or federal) is possible. However token, most of the marginal audiences have been afforded some explicit acknowledgement of their difficulties, their needs and their 'rights' to an equivalent television service as that available to the mainstream. To be sure, such recognition of the marginalising dynamics of television and attempts at redress have only intermittently preoccupied policy-makers and the public discussion of television in Australia. This preoccupation, though, has not been without its force.

The policy of localism in commercial television which was in operation up until the mid-1980s directly encouraged the provision of some commercial free-to-air programming to meet 'local' audience needs within a geographically defined television service area. After the mid-1980s, according to the new policy regime, regional Australia's 'needs' were no longer those of a distinct geographical community. Instead, regional Australia was the name given to a broad, underserved audience whose needs could be met by access to more free-to-air channels. The regions' needs were acknowledged as 'equivalent' to the needs of metropolitan audiences, and thus were able to be met through the television aggregation scheme which brought three commercial stations and SBS-TV to the more settled areas of eastern regional Australia.

As the growing divide between urban and regional Australia has shown, this strategy did not erode cultural and political differences. Indeed, it may have precipitated (through the everyday evidence of difference Sydney-delivered network television provided) the growing sense of political and cultural difference on the part of regional Australia. For Lelia Green (1998: 28), satellite-delivered television to remote audiences did not lessen 'the experience of rural or regional life'; quite the reverse, it 'represented to remote viewers a multitude of differences between city life and life lived in remote and rural areas . . . in many senses [it] heightened the sense of difference'. This sense of an embattled minority was mobilised for political ends by One Nation and the various independent candidates from regional areas (much as the 'ethnic vote' was in the 1970s by Labor when they won power after twenty-three years of Conservative rule, and in the 1980s by the Conservatives when they set up the SBS).

SBS-TV, with its international orientation and half of its schedule given over to programs in languages other than English, has come to occupy the position of the 'national broadcaster' for those born outside the country. AC Neilsen research showed that, in the five major capital cities in 1996, some 32 per cent of the SBS audience was born in a non-English speaking country whereas this group represented only 17 per cent of the potential audience; and 11 per cent of the audience was born in an English speaking country whereas this group represented 9 per cent of the viewing audience (SBS 1999).

The Broadcasting for Remote Aboriginal Communities Scheme (BRACS) was designed to contribute to an Aboriginalised television service by having the communities frame, filter and replace incoming television programs with their own Indigenous programming. This scheme was designed to ameliorate the negative effects upon remote communities of the delivery, for the first time, of broadcast television services. In this way, the BRACS scheme addressed Aboriginal community fears of significant cultural erosion stemming from the access to mainstream broadcasting services (Department of Aboriginal Affairs 1984; Michaels 1986, 1994) while establishing a culturally appropriate management system for broadcasting (see O'Regan and Batty 1993).

The revision of the ABC charter in the 1980s and 1990s included, belatedly, some reference to the diverse nature of Australian society, thus requiring the ABC to become more multicultural in its orientation. What is capable of being delivered by such policy settings is inevitably limited: marginal audiences can never hope to get a fully equivalent service; what is contested is how far along the continuum it is possible to go.

Alongside these policy measures is an ongoing and often unsuccessful lobbying process that has itself been marginalised in the wake of the removal of public licence renewal hearings for commercial broadcasters in the *Broadcasting Services Act* 1992. Activists have been involved over the late 1980s and 1990s in various campaigns to 'shame' network television for their non-inclusion of ethnic minority characters in television programs. The Communications Law Centre (1992) found considerable disquiet among people of a non-English speaking background (NESB) because their invisibility in the medium. This research was used to prosecute a dual agenda of mainstreaming ethnic faces in ordinary roles and creating spaces for the recognition of cultural diversity.

Vociferous public debate has surrounded the suspension of regionally specific editions of programs like the ABC's *7.30 Report* and Seven's state-based regional current affairs programs in favour of national versions produced out of Sydney in the mid-1990s. To get stations to extend 'text-captioning' to the whole schedule is an ongoing campaign pursued by various government departments and spokespersons for the aged and the hearing-impaired. Such campaigns rely on appeals to television networks as good corporate citizens and to politicians on equity grounds. Australia lacks the well-organised disability lobbying of the United States which has secured significant gains in the compulsory captioning of services.

Treating Aboriginal and Islander audiences as part of the community of viewers—the 'we' community rather than the 'they' community of victims, threats and social problems (Hartley 1992: 206–7; Mickler 1997)—is ongoing and has required the intervention of a high-profile Royal Commission into Aboriginal Deaths in Custody (Dodson 1991), with its specific attention to remediation of news and current affairs practice (see Hartley and McKee 1996). It is also the basis for an Aboriginal employment strategy which has focused on getting Indigenous faces into the production process.

Policy-makers and governments need good political reasons for recognising marginal audiences. A political case has to be made and this depends on the extent to which policy-makers and governments are prepared to see a collectivity as having grievances needing redress. Typically, this depends on the extent of political recognition of the 'marginal audience' in other social policy arenas. For this reason, discussions of audience marginalisation are often attached to the broader campaigns designed to highlight social and cultural disadvantage by the cohort in question. When multicultural policy-making was at its height during the late 1980s and early 1990s, this generated some attention to criticisms by ethnic and Aboriginal spokespersons of the bias of television programmers and the inflexibilities of the television system.

The contemporary attention on youth is focusing attention on the kind of service available to them and the youth audience has become a particular worry for all television networks, both public and commercial. As we have seen in the discussion of news and current affairs in Chapter 6, there is qualitative evidence that young people find conventional information formats boring, conservative and disdainful of youth cultures and attitudes. While program makers can and do innovate to address this issue (*Attitude*, *The Times* and *The Panel* instead of *Nightly News* and *A Current Affair*; *Heartbreak High* instead of *A Country Practice*), with varying degrees of success, the data show that the upper teen and early twenties demographic watch television least of all age groups, and that trend is accentuating with the prime uptake of television substitutes like the Internet and computer games amongst this age group.

However, despite much evidence that youth are a poorly addressed audience demographic in mainstream television, the fact that it is the key focus of a whole commercial network's strategy, namely Ten's—and that this strategy, as we have seen in Chapter 13, has been significantly successful—means that it is difficult to sustain an argument, alongside those for other groupings discussed here, that youth represent a marginalised audience. This is principally because young people constitute a sufficiently large and (now) attractive spending demographic to sustain 'marketisation' and in a sense to be taken out of the public policy domain, at least in terms of the provision of audiovisual 'leisure services'.

The reliance on a political, policy and social constituency defined as much elsewhere as in the lobbying for television services goes some way to explaining the gaps in our knowledge of marginal audiences. We can give a good rundown of the policy instruments implemented, recommended and lobbied for to meet the needs of the child audience, minority ethnic audiences, Aboriginal and Islander audiences, the hearing- and sight-impaired and regional and remote audiences. We can, at times, indicate programming designed to specifically meet their needs and identify a body of criticism calling for the on-screen representation of those needs. We can outline the pattern of ethnic minority consumption of SBS-TV. As befits this pre-eminently political logic of demonstrating need through the weight of numbers what we often get is the routine citing of population proportions, demographic trends and an indication via the weight of numbers, that 'something ought to be done'—much as we have done in this chapter. Consequently, the study of marginal audiences and their consumption patterns of audio-visual media is fragmented and often ethnographic (see Bednall 1988; Michaels 1994; Kolar-Panov 1997; Cunningham and Sinclair 2000).

CONCLUSION

The key issue for media policy raised by marginalised audiences is the need to structure screen services for both majoritarian and minoritarian populations in the interests of equity, access and the acquisition of social and cultural capital. The development of policy for marginal audiences has been seen almost exclusively in Australia through the prism of:

- limited transformation of the commercial television and principal national broadcaster, the ABC, via education campaigns and the development of limited obligations whether expressed through codes of practice in the case of commercial television or through the Charter, employment practices and the like in the case of the ABC;
- additional 'special services' whether through the national broadcaster model of the 'Special Broadcasting Service' or facilitating community-based television as a means for minorities to better manage their media futures;
- a tendency to construct and evaluate 'marginal audience' claims via a cultural calculus which recognises distinct cultural communities and interests. This has prioritised the affirmation of identity as an end in itself and led to the ongoing translation of and prosecution of claims as those of culturally distinct communities—in short, an 'identity politics'.

While this policy direction is sound, it is now insufficient. The explosion of community-based ethnic video networks demonstrates that policies designed to develop additional and diverse kinds of television service are now necessary. Further, governments are increasingly recognising social and cultural disadvantage in fine-grained socio-economic and geo-demographic terms. This is driving 'regional' ways of managing and thinking about services and amenities to disadvantaged and marginal populations which are clustered together and often consist of a variety of ethnicities. The consequences of this return of social class and geography to our understandings of marginal audiences are only now beginning to be worked through.

Taking these issues into account, then, it is clear that there are still areas where policy development is required. Free-to-air television providers are still to fully accept that they have responsibilities for implementing, at the very least, the codes of advisory practice, Equal Employment Opportunity (EEO) policies and anti-discrimination and racial vilification laws. These are both specific industry standards and broad legal obligations that, if implemented, would result in a greater representation of marginal groups behind and before the cameras on Australian screens and related media. On the other hand, while mass-market free-to-air television will rarely meet all the needs of culturally pluralistic societies, there is some economic evidence (see Noam 1991: 51–57) that the addition of further broadcast stations ensures a greater chance of 'outlying (audience) preferences' being met and that 'viewers find closer substitutes for their favoured program pitches' (1991: 52). Some marginal audience needs are therefore likely to be met through more free-to-air services.

There is also the environment established for pay TV. Subscription television services can help regularise and develop what we have referred to here as the 'informal television' services which are currently being provided by rental video. This requires the reducing of barriers to entry for regional and ethnic minority participation in pay TV services. Pay TV policy-making could perform a useful role in encouraging a shift in audience dynamic from the informal to the formal and from the illegal to the legal. Instead of envisaging new media as a threat to cultural diversity and public provision, it could instead be seen, as it is elsewhere, as a means 'to open the electronic marketplace, encourage diversity and allow the audience to realize television's full potential' (Webster 1989: 192).

Finally, many would agree that stronger community-based media, better controlled by minority communities themselves but supported by the state, are needed to meet the needs currently serviced through diasporic cinema and video circuits and the other methods outlined through this book (see, for example, Husband 1992; Thussu 1998). However, the future for enhanced community broadcasting services is complicated strongly by the increasingly complex mix of technologies, and subscription-based as well as free-to-air terrestrial services emerging in most countries—and Australia is no exception.

References

ABA Update 1998 Sydney, February.

——1999 'New ABA Australian content Standard from 1 March', March, p. 6.

Adair, D. and Vamplew, W. 1997, *Sport in Australian History*, Oxford University Press, Melbourne.

AdNews 1999a 'Pay TV Update', 12 March, pp. 27–34.

——1999b 'Top 100 Magazines', 10 September, pp. 25–31

Allen, R.C. 1985 (1975), 'The Guiding Light: Soap Opera as Economic Product and Cultural Document' in H. Newcomb (ed.) *Television: The Critical View*, 4th edn, Oxford University Press, New York.

——1992, 'Audience-Oriented Criticism and Television', in R.C. Allen (ed.), *Channels of Discourse, Reassembled: Television and Contemporary Criticism*, 2nd edn, Routledge, London.

Anderson, B. 1991, *Imagined Communities*, 2nd edn, Verso, London.

Andersen, Robin 1995, *Consumer Culture and TV Programming*, Westview Press, Boulder.

Ang, I. 1985, *Watching Dallas: Soap Opera and the Melodramatic Imagination*, Methuen, London.

——1991, *Desperately Seeking the Audience*, Routledge, London.

——1997, *Living Room Wars: Rethinking Media Audiences for a Postmodern World*, Routledge, London.

Appleton, G. 1997, 'Converging and Emerging Industries: Video, Pay TV and Multimedia', in S. Cunningham and G. Turner (eds), *The Media in Australia: Industries, Texts, Audiences*, Allen & Unwin, Sydney.

AUSTAR 1999, *Productivity Commission Submission*, <www.pc.gov.au/inquiry/broadcst/subs/sub082.pdf>, accessed 22/7/99.

Austin, K. 1999, 'The Knives are Out', *Sydney Morning Herald*, *The Guide*, 28 June–4 July, pp. 4–5.

Australian, The 1999, 'ABC Report: Predictable but Irrational', 27 May, p. 10.

Australian Broadcast Standard 1999, <www.aba.gov.au/what/program/newozst.htm>.

Australian Broadcasting Authority (ABA) 1997a, *Australian Content on Pay TV*. Report to the Minister for Communications and the Arts, ABA, Sydney.

——1997b, *Inquiry into the Future Use of the Sixth Television Channel. Report to the Minister for Communications and the Arts*, ABA, Sydney.

——1997, *Investigation into Control: CanWest Global Communications Corporation/The Ten Group Ltd Second Investigation*, ABA, Sydney, April.

——1999a '[Television] Revenue and Expenditure for Australia' and 'Program Expenditure—Australia', Broadcasting Financial Results disk, ABA, Sydney.

——1999b, *Investigation into Control: Mr Brian Powers, Mr Kerry Packer and Mr James Packer/John Fairfax Holdings Ltd*, ABA, Sydney, March.

——1999c *Trends and Issues No. 6*, August, ABA, Sydney.

——1999d, 'Only Four Pay TV Channels Meet Australian Content Standard', *ABA Update*, June.

Australian Broadcasting Tribunal 1982, *Cable and Subscription Television Services for Australia. Report*, Vol. 1, Part A, AGPS, Canberra.

——1983, *A Country Practice and the Child Audience—A Case Study*, Children's Program Committee, Melbourne.

——1985, *Remote Commercial Television Services. First Report*, AGPS, Canberra.

——1990, *Television Violence in Australia*, vol. 1, AGPS, Canberra.

——1998, *1997 Time Use on Culture/Leisure Activities*, ABS Catalogue No. 4173.0, AGPS, Canberra.

——1999a, *Use of the Internet by Householders*, Commonwealth of Australia, ABS Catalogue No. 8147.0, AGGPS, Canberra.

——1999b, *Australian Social Trends 1999*, Commonwealth of Australia, ABS Catalogue No. 4102.0, AGPS, Canberra.

——1999c, 'Internet and Internet Purchases Continue to Grow', media release, 20 December.

Australian Caption Centre 1999, Caption Centre Website: <*www.auscap.com.au/captions/index.html*>, accessed 22/11/99.

Australian Competition and Consumer Commission 1997, 'ACCC to Oppose Foxtel/Australis Media Merger', media release 133/97, 14 October.

Australian Film Commission (AFC) 1996, *Get the Picture: Essential Data on Australian Film, Television, Video and New Media*, 4th edn, Australian Film Commission, Sydney (5th end, 1998).

Bacon-Smith, C. 1992, *Enterprising Women: Television Fandom and the Creation of Popular Myth*, University of Pennsylvania Press, Philadelphia.

Bale, J. 1998, 'Virtual Fandoms: Futurescapes of Football', in A. Brown (ed.), *Fanatics! Power, Identity and Fandom in Football*, Routledge, London, pp. 265–77.

Barnett, S. 1990, *Games and Sets: The Changing Face of Sport on Television*, British Film Institute, London.

Barnett, S. and Curry, A. 1994, *The Battle for the BBC: A British Broadcasting Conspiracy*, Aurum Press, London.

Baudrillard, J. 1980,'The Implosion of Meaning in the Media and the Information of the Social in the Masses' in K. Woodward (ed.), *Myths of Information: Technology and Post-Industrial Culture*, Coda Press, Madison, Wis., pp. 137–48.

Bausinger, H. 1984, 'Media, Technology and Everyday Life', *Media, Culture and Society* vol. 6, no. 4.

Beazley, Kim 1991, 'The New Broadcasting Services Bill', address to the Communications

Law Centre and the Communications and Media Law Association Conference, Sydney, 29 November.

Bednall, David 1988, 'Television Use by Melbourne's Greek Community', *Media Information Australia* no. 47, pp. 44–48.

Bennett, Tony, Emmison, Michael and Frow, John 1999, *Accounting for Tastes*, Cambridge University Press, Melbourne.

Best, Bruce 1993, Producer, *GP*, interview, Sydney, October.

Bibby, A., Denford, C. and Cross, J. 1979, *Local Television: Piped Dreams? A Critique of Community TV in Britain*, Redwing Press, Milton Keynes.

Birt, John 1998, 'Towards the Millennium—What will the Public Expect of Public Service Broadcasters?', Keynote Speech to the PBI Conference, Biarritz, October, <*www.bbc.co.uk/info/news/biarritz.htm*>.

Blomfield, J. 1999, Address to 'The Future of TV Networks' seminar papers forthcoming, RMIT Media and Telecommunications Policy Group, Sydney.

Bolton, Geoffrey 1967, *Dick Boyer, an Australian Humanist*, Australian National University, Canberra.

Bonner, Frances 1994, 'Representations of the Female Cook', in K. Ferres (ed.), *Coastscripts: Gender Representations in the Arts*, Griffith University, Brisbane.

Bonner, Frances and du Gay, Paul 1991, '*thirtysomething* and Contemporary Consumer Culture: Distinctiveness and Distinction', in R. Burrows (ed.), *Consumption and Class: Divisions and Change*, Macmillan, London.

Bottomley, Gil 1994, 'Post-multiculturalism? The Theory and Practice of Heterogeneity', *Culture and Policy* vol. 6, no. 1, pp. 139–52.

Bourdieu, Pierre 1989, *Distinction: A Social Critique of the Judgement of Taste*, Routledge, London.

Branigan, T. 1999, General Manager, Federation of Australian Commercial Television Stations, personal interview, 25 June.

Brown, M. 1994, *Soap Opera and Women's Talk: The Pleasure of Resistance*, Sage, London.

BRS Media 1999, *Web-Radio. Radio Stations Broadcasting on the Net!* <*www.web-radio.com*> accessed 22/7/99.

Brunsdon, C. 1997, *Screen Tastes: From Soap Opera to Satellite Dishes*, Routledge, London.

——1998, 'What is the "Television" of Television Studies?' in Christine Geraghty and David Lusted (eds), *The Television Studies Book*, Arnold, London.

Brunsdon, C. and Morley, D. 1978, *Everyday Television: Nationwide*, BFI, London.

Buckingham, D. 1987, *Public Secrets: EastEnders and Its Audience*, BFI Publishing, London.

Budde, P. 1999, 'Foxtel—the Cracks are Starting to Appear', *Information Superhighways*, vol. 4, no. 6.

Bulbeck, P. 1998, 'Pay Television in Australia', in *Get the Picture; Essential Data for Australian Film, Television and Video*, 5th edn, Australian Film Commission, Sydney.

——1999a, 'AUSTAR Adds Third Tier with Foxtel, Seven Channels . . . as it Eyes Possible Local IPO', *Australian Pay TV News*, 25 March, pp. 1–2.

——1999b, 'Foxtel Now a Billion Dollar Outfit as Red Ink Corner Turned', *Australian Pay TV News*, 10 February, pp. 1–2.

——1999c, 'PBL moves on Foxtel', *Australian Pay TV News*, 12 November, pp. 2–3.

Burbury, R. 1999, 'Boom Year Sees the Industry Scale Dizzy Heights', *Australian Financial Review*, 22 June, p. 41.

Bureau of Transport and Communications Economics 1995, *Australian Content on Pay TV*, BTCE Working Paper 31, AGPS, Canberra.

——1996, Australian *Commercial Television 1986–95: Structure and Performance*, AGPS, Canberra.

Burns, Maureen 1997, 'From Dix to Mansfield: 15 Years of Policy', in E. Jacka, H. Wilson, G. Hawkins and M. Burns (eds), *Australian Public Service Broadcasting in Transition: 1986–1996 Working Papers*, UTS, Sydney.

Burton L. 1998, *The Media Report* <*www.abc.net.au/rn/talks*>.

Carey, Gabrielle 1995, 'The Sum of Us', the *Age Good Weekend Magazine*, 25 March, pp. 30–32.

Cashman, R. 1995, *Paradise of Sport: The Rise of Organised Sport in Australia*, Oxford University Press, Melbourne.

Casimir, John 1998, 'The Big Turn-Off', *The Sydney Morning Herald*, *The Guide*, 22–28 June, pp. 4–5.

CEASA (Commercial Economic Advisory Service of Australia) 1999, *Advertising Expenditure in Main Media Year ended 31 December 1998: The CEASA Report*, CEASA, Sydney.

CEPU Database 1999, <*fbeu.labor.net.au/unions/cepu/toa/toa415htm*> downloaded 2 June.

Chadwick, P. 1989, *Media Mates: Carving Up Australia's Media*, Sun Books, Melbourne.

Clarke, Michael 1952, 'Television Prospect: Some Reflexions of a Documentary Film-maker', in Roger Manvell and R.K. Neilson Baxter (eds), *The Cinema 1952*, Penguin, Harmondsworth, pp. 174–87.

Clifford, J. and Marcus, G.E. (eds) 1986, *Writing Culture: The Poetics and Politics of Ethnography*, University of Berkeley Press, Berkeley.

Collins, J. 1992, 'Postmodernism and Television' in R.C. Allen (ed.), *Channels of Discourse, Reassembled*, Routledge, London, pp. 327–53.

Collins, L. 1999a, 'Advertisers Switch off TV Networks', *Australian Financial Review*, 21 April, p. 21.

——1999b, 'Packer Axes "Up to 200 Jobs"', *Australian Financial Review*, 23 April, p. 3.

Collins, R. 1990, *Television: Policy and Culture*, Unwin Hyman, London.

Commonwealth of Australia 1995, *Our ABC*, Report of the Senate Select Committee on ABC Management and Operations Department of the Senate, Canberra.

Communications Law Centre 1992, *The Representation of Non-English Speaking Background People in Australian Television Drama*, Discussion Paper, Communications Law Centre, Kensington, Sydney, March.

——1999, *Submission to the Productivity Commission Review of the* Broadcasting Services Act *1992 and Associated Licence Fees Acts* <*www.pc.gov.au/inquiry/broadcst/subs/sub109.pdf*> accessed 22 July 1999.

Communications Update 1992, 'Pay TV? No, Thanks', no. 80, August, p. 4.

——1999 'Media Ownership Update', no. 151, February.

Comstock, G. 1991, *Television in America*, Sage, Newbury Park.

Cook, J. and Jennings, K. 1995, 'Live and Sweaty: Australian Women Re-cast Australian Sports Television', *Media Information Australia* no. 75, February, pp. 5–12.

Cox, P. 1989, *Network Television Stations: What Are They Really Worth?* Peter J. Cox and Associates, Double Bay, Apps 2.3.3, 2.3.4.

Craig, G. 2000, 'Perpetual Crisis: The Politics of Saving the ABC', *Media International Australian incorporating Culture and Policy* no. 94, February, pp. 105–60.

Craik, J., James-Bailey, J. and Moran, M. 1995, *Public Voices, Private Interests: Australia's Media Policy*, Allen & Unwin, Sydney.

Crofts, S. 1994, 'Global *Neighbours*?' in K. Bowles and S. Turnbull (eds), *Tomorrow Never Knows: Soap on Australian Television*, AFI, Melbourne.

Cunningham, S. 1984, 'The Dismissal and Australian Television', in Stuart Cunningham et al., *The Dismissal: Perspectives*, Australian Film and Television School, Sydney.

——1992, *Framing Culture: Criticism and Policy in Australia*, Allen & Unwin, Sydney.

——1993, 'Television', in S. Cunningham and G. Turner (eds), *The Media in Australia*, Allen & Unwin, Sydney.

——1997, 'Influences on the Idea of Media "Influence"', *Metro*, no. 111, pp. 31–34.

Cunningham, S. and Jacka, E. 1996, *Australian Television and International Mediascapes*, Cambridge University Press, Cambridge.

Cunningham, S. and Miller, T. 1993/94, 'Tomorrow's Television', *Metro*, no. 96, pp. 19–25.

——1994, *Contemporary Australian Television*, University of New South Wales Press, Sydney.

Cunningham, S. and Nguyen, T. 1999, 'The Popular Media of the Vietnamese Diaspora', *Media International Australia*, no. 91, pp. 125–47.

——2000, 'Popular Media of the Vietnamese Diaspora', in S. Cunningham and J. Sinclair (eds), *Floating Lives: the Media and Asian Diasporas*, University of Queensland Press, Brisbane.

Cunningham, S. and Ritchie, J. 1994, 'An Ersatz Asian Nation? The ABC in Asia', *Media International Australia* no. 71, pp. 46–55.

Cunningham, S. and Turner, G. (eds) 1997, *The Media in Australia: Industries, Texts, Audiences*, 2nd edn, Allen & Unwin, Sydney.

Cupitt, M. and Stockbridge, S. 1986, *Families and Electronic Entertainment*, Australian Broadcasting Authority and the Office of Film and Television Classification, Sydney.

Curthoys, A. 1986, 'The Getting of Television: Dilemmas in Ownership, Control and Culture 1941–56', in A. Curthoys and J. Merritt (eds), *Better Dead than Red: Australia's First Cold War 1945–1959*, Volume Two, Allen & Unwin, Sydney.

——1991 'Television Before Television', *Continuum* vol. 4, no. 2, pp. 152–70.

Curtis, R. and Gray, C. 1998, *Get the Picture: Essential Data on Australian Film, Television, Video and New Media*, 5th edn, Australian Film Commission, Sydney.

Dale, David 1999, 'The Kiss or Death of Ratings Land' *Sydney Morning Herald*, 25 June, p. 13.

Darling, J.R. 1964, Speech to the Asian Broadcasting Union dinner, 13 November, ABC archives.

Davies, A. and Spurgeon, C. 1992, 'The *Broadcasting Services Act*: A Reconciliation of Public Interest and Market Principles of Regulation?', *Media Information Australia*, no. 66, November, pp. 85–92.

Davis, Glyn 1988, *Breaking Up the ABC*, Allen & Unwin, Sydney.

——1997, 'The Mansfield Vision for the ABC', *Media International Australia*, no. 84, pp. 81–86.

Deleuze, Gilles 1979, 'The Rise of the Social', in Jacques Donzelot, *The Policing of Families*, Pantheon Books, New York.

Department of Aboriginal Affairs 1984, *Out of the Silent Land: Report of the Task Force on Aboriginal and Islander Broadcasting and Communications*, AGPS, Canberra.

Department of Communications and the Arts 1998, 'Digital Broadcasting—QandA', <*www.dca.gov.au/mediarel/98/digitalqa.html*>, accessed 29/3/98.

Department of Communications, Information Technology and the Arts (DoCITA) 1999, *Review of the Retransmission of Digital Television Broadcasting Services: Discussion of Options*, DoCITA, Canberra, 1 June.

Department of Transport and Communications 1988, *Review of National Broadcasting Policy— Discussion Papers—Australian Broadcasting Corporation*, AGPS, Canberra.

Derriman, P. 1999, 'Strangled by Cable', *Sydney Morning Herald*, 29 April, p. 11.

Docker, John 1991, 'Popular Culture versus the State: An Argument Against Australian Content Regulation for Television', *Media Information Australia*, no 59, February, pp. 7-26.

Dodd, A. 1999, 'Testing Times at Local TV', *The Australian—Media*, 20 May, pp. 12–13.

Dodson, Pat 1991, *Royal Commission into Aboriginal Deaths in Custody: Regional Report of Inquiry into Underlying Issues in Western Australia*, AGPS, Canberra.

duBose, M. 1977, 'Days of Our Lives', *Nation Review*, 13–19 January, pp. 302–4.

Dwyer, T. 1995, 'Pay TV Policies: Are Audiences the 'Users' Who Will Pay?', in J. Craik, J.J. Bailey and A. Moran (eds), *Public Voices, Private Interests: Australia's Media Policy*, Allen & Unwin, Sydney.

Eco, U. 1986, 'Sports Chatter' in *Travels in Hyperreality*, Harcourt Brace Jovanovich, Sydney.

Emy, Hugh 1993, *Remaking Australia: The State, the Market and Australia's Future*, Allen & Unwin, Sydney.

Encore 1986, interview with James Davern, 8–21 May, pp. 9–10.

Ettema, J.S. and Whitney, D.C. (eds) 1994, *Audiencemaking: How the Media Create the Audience*, Sage, Thousand Oaks.

Featherstone, Mike 1991, *Consumer Culture and Postmodernism*, Sage, London.

Feldman, T. 1997, *An Introduction to Digital Media*, Routledge, London.

Feuer, Jane 1983, 'The Concept of Live Television: Ontology as Ideology', in E. Ann Kaplan (ed.), *Regarding Television: Critical Approaches—An Anthology*, University Publications of America/American Film Institute, Frederick, MD.

Film Finance Corporation (FFC) 1999, at <*www.ffc.gov.au/*>.

Fiske, J. 1983, 'Cricket/TV/Culture' *Metro* no. 62, pp. 21–26.

——1987, *Television Culture*, Methuen, London.

——1989, *Reading the Popular*, Unwin Hyman, Boston.

——1992, 'British Cultural Studies and Television', in R.C. Allen (ed.), *Channels of Discourse, Reassembled*, Routledge, London.

Fiske, J. and Hartley, J. 1978, *Reading Television*, Methuen, London.

Fist, S. 1996, 'Cable Fiasco', *Pipe Dreams*, <*www.abc.net.au/http/sfist/cabfiasc.htm*> accessed 22/7/99.

Flew, T. 1994, *Financing, Programming and Diversity in Australian Television*, Communications Law Centre Occasional Paper no. 8, Sydney.

——1995, 'Pay TV and Broadcasting Diversity in Australian Television', *Media International Australia*, no. 77, August, pp. 130–38.

Franklin, Bob 1998, *Newszak and News Media*, Arnold, London.

Freeman, J. 1999, 'Drama's Darkest Hour', *The Sydney Morning Herald: The Guide*, 21–27 June, pp. 4–5.

Geraghty, C. 1991, *Women and Soap Opera: A Study of Prime Time Soaps*, Polity Press, London.

Geraghty, C. and Lusted, D. (eds) 1998, *The Television Studies Book*, Arnold, London.

Giddens, Anthony 1991, *Modernity and Self-Identity: Self and Society in the Late Modern Age*, Stanford University Press, Stanford.

Gilder, G. 1994, *Life After Television*, W.W. Norton and Co., New York.

Gilmore, H. 1999, 'Clean Sweep' *The Sun Herald—TV Now*, 28 February, p. 6.

Given, J. 1998a, *The Death of Broadcasting? Media's Digital Future*, University of New South Wales Press, Sydney.

——1998b, 'Being Digital: Australia's Television Choice', *Media and Arts Law Review*, vol. 3, no. 1, March, pp. 38–51.

——1999, 'High Price of Better Definition', *The Australian*, 22 December.

Glasgow Media Group 1976, *Bad News*, Routledge and Kegan Paul, London.

Goethals, Gregor T. 1981, *The TV Ritual: Worship at the Video Altar*, Beacon Press, Boston.

Goldlust, J. 1987, *Playing for Keeps: Sport, the Media and Society*, Longman Cheshire, Melbourne.

Gordon, S. and Sibson, R. 1998, 'Global Television: The Atlanta Olympics Opening Ceremony', in D. Rowe and G. Lawrence (eds), *Tourism, Leisure, Sport: Critical Perspectives*, Hodder Education, Sydney.

Grainger, G. 1996, 'The *Broadcasting Services Act* 1992: Present and Future Implications', in R. Lynch, I. McDonnell, S. Thompson and K. Toohey (eds), *Sport and Pay TV: Strategies for Success*, School of Leisure and Tourism Studies, UTS, Sydney.

Grant, Barry K. (ed.) 1986, *Film Genre Reader*, University of Texas Press, Austin.

Gray, A. 1992, *Video Playtime: The Gendering of a Leisure Technology*, Routledge, London.

Green, Lelia 1998a, 'Not Using the Remote Commercial Television Service to Dispel Distance in Rural and Remote Western Australia', *Media International Australia incorporating Culture and Policy*, no. 88, August, pp. 25–38.

——1998b, Communications and the Construction of Community: Consuming the Remote Commercial Television Service in Western Australia, PhD Thesis, Division of Social Sciences, Humanities and Education, Murdoch University.

Gripsrud. J. 1995, *The Dynasty Years: Hollywood Television and Critical Media Studies*, Routledge, London.

Gwenllian-Jones, Sara and Pearson, Roberta E. (eds) forthcoming, *Worlds Apart: Essays on Cult Television*, Minnesota University Press, Minneapolis.

Habermas, J. 1974, 'The Public Sphere', *New German Critique*, vol. 1, no. 3, pp. 49–55.

Hage, Ghassan 1995, 'The Limits of "Anti-racist Sociology"', *UTS Review*, vol. 1, no. 1, pp. 59–82.

Hall, Sandra 1976, *Supertoy: Twenty Years of Australian Television*, Sun Books, Melbourne.

Hall, Stuart 1980, 'Encoding/Decoding' in D. Hobson et al. (eds), *Culture, Media, Language*, Hutchinson, London.

——1982, 'The Rediscovery of "Ideology": The Return of the Repressed in Media Studies', in Michael Gurevitch, Tony Bennett, James Curran and Janel Woollacott (eds), *Culture, Society and the Media*, Methuen, London.

——1986, 'Cultural Studies: Two Paradigms', in R. Collins, J. Curran, N. Garnham, P. Scannell, P. Schlesinger and C. Sparks (eds), *Media, Culture and Society: A Critical Reader*, Sage, London.

Hall, S., Critcher, C., Jefferson, T., Clarke, J. and Roberts, B. 1978, *Policing the Crisis: Mugging, the State, and Law and Order*, Macmillan, London.

Harding, Richard 1979, *Outside Interference*, Sun Books, Melbourne.

Harrington, C.L. and Bielby, D.D. 1995, *Soap Fans: Pursuing Pleasure and Making Meaning in Everyday Life*, Temple University Press, Philadelphia.

Harris, K. 1988, 'What Do We See When We Watch the Cricket?' *Social Alternatives*, vol. 7, no. 3, pp. 65–70.

Harriss, I. 1990, 'Packer, Cricket and Postmodernism', in D. Rowe and G. Lawrence (eds), *Sport and Leisure: Trends in Australian Popular Culture*, Harcourt Brace Jovanovich, Sydney.

Hartley, J. 1987, 'Invisible Fictions: Television Audiences, Paedocracy, Pleasure', *Textual Practice*, vol. 1, no. 2, pp. 121–38.

——1992a *Tele-ology: Studies in Television*, Routledge, London.

——1992b *The Politics of Pictures: The Creation of the Public in the Age of Popular Media*, Routledge, New York and London.

——1996 *Popular Reality: Journalism, Modernity, Popular Culture*, Arnold, London.

——1999, *Uses of Television*, Routledge, London.

Hartley, J. and McKee, A. (eds) 1996, *Telling Both Stories: Indigenous Australia and the Media*, Arts Enterprise, Edith Cowan University, Mt Lawley, WA.

Hartley, J. and O'Regan, T. 1992, 'Quoting Not Science but Sideboards' in J. Hartley (ed.), *Tele-ology: Studies in Television*, Routledge, London.

Haskell, M. 1974, *From Reverence to Rape: The Treatment of Women in the Movies*, Holt, Rinehart and Winston, New York.

Haverfield, Robert and Haverfield, Margaret M. 1998, *TV Across Australia: The Caravaner's Guide to Television Reception*, 2nd edn, Australian Broadcasting Directories, Canberra.

Hawke, J. 1995, 'Privatising the Public Interest: The Public and the *Broadcasting Services Act 1992*', in J. Craik, J.J. Bailey and A. Moran (eds), *Public Voices, Private Interests: Australia's Media Policy*, Allen & Unwin, Sydney.

Hawkins, Gay 1996, 'SBS: Minority Television', *Culture and Policy*, vol. 7, no. 1, pp. 45–64.

——1997, 'The ABC and the Mystic Writing Pad', *Media International Australia*, no. 83, pp. 11–17.

Heath, Stephen and Skirrow, Gillian 1977, 'Television, a World in Action', *Screen*, vol. 18, no. 2, pp. 7–59.

Herman, Edward S. and McChesney, Robert W. 1997, *The Global Media: The New Missionaries of Corporate Capitalism*, Cassell, London and Washington.

Herzog, H. 1941, 'On Borrowed Experience: An Analysis of Listening to Daytime Sketches', *Studies in Philosophy and Social Science*, vol. 9, pp. 65–95.

Hobson, D. 1982, *Crossroads: The Drama of a Soap Opera*, Methuen, London.

Hodge, B. 1989 'Children and Television', in J. Tulloch and G. Turner (eds), *Australian Television: Programs, Pleasures and Politics*, Allen & Unwin, Sydney.

Hodge, B. and Tripp, D. 1986, *Children and Television*, Polity Press, Cambridge.

Hoggart, R. 1958, *The Uses of Literacy*, Penguin, London.

House of Representatives Standing Committee on Transport, Communications and Infrastructure 1989, *To Pay or Not to Pay? Pay Television and Other New Broadcasting-related Services*, The Parliament of the Commonwealth of Australia, Canberra.

Husband, Charles 1992, *Minorities, Mobility and Communication in Europe*, Race Relations Research Unit Research and Policy Papers, Bradford.

Inglis, Ken 1983, *This is the ABC: The Australian Broadcasting Commission 1932–1983*, Melbourne University Press, Melbourne.

——1997, 'ABC Shock Crisis', *Media International Australia*, no. 83, pp. 5–10.

Jacka, E. 1991, *The ABC of Drama: 1975–1990*, Australian Film Television and Radio School, Sydney.

——1994, 'Researching Audiences: A Dialogue between Cultural Studies and Social Science', *Media Information Australia*, no. 73, August, pp. 45–51.

Jakubowicz, Andrew 1987, 'Days of Our Lives: Multiculturalism, Mainstreaming and "Special" Broadcasting', *Media Information Australia*, no. 45, pp. 18–32.

——(ed.) 1994, *Racism, Ethnicity and the Media*, Allen & Unwin, Sydney.

Jameson, Frederic 1981, *The Political Unconscious: Narrative as a Socially Symbolic Act*, Cornell University Press, Ithaca, NY.

Jamrozik, A., Boland, C. and Urquhart, R. 1995, *Social Change and Cultural Transformation in Australia*, Cambridge University Press, Melbourne.

Jenkins, H. 1992, *Textual Poachers: Television Fans and Participatory Culture*, Routledge, London and New York.

Jones, C. and Bednall, D. 1980, *Television in Australia: Its History Through the Ratings*, ABT, January.

Joyrich, L. 1996, *Re-viewing Reception: Television, Gender and Postmodern Culture*, Indiana University Press, Bloomington and Indianapolis.

Keneally, T. 1999, 'Sydney's Big Night Out', *The Sunday Telegraph*, 7 March, p. 2.

Kerr, Graham 1973, *The Complete Galloping Gourmet Cookbook*, W.H. Allen, London.

Kilmurray, R. 1998, 'Digital TV—Lost in Space', Law and Bills Digest Group, Parliament of Australia, Parliamentary Library, Current Issues Brief 19, 1997–98, <*wopared.aph.gov.au:80/library/pubs/cib/1997–98/98cib19.htm*>, accessed 23/6/98.

Kingsley, H. 1989, *Soap Box: The Australian Guide to Television Soap Operas*, Sun Books, Melbourne.

Kitses, Jim 1969, *Horizons West: Anthony Mann, Budd Boetticher, Sam Peckinpah: Studies of Authorship Within the Western*, Thames and Hudson/BFI, London.

Klinger, B. 1994, *Melodrama and Meaning: History, Culture, and the Films of Douglas Sirk*, Indiana University Press, Bloomington, IN.

Kneale, Nigel 1959, 'Not Quite So Intimate', *Sight and Sound*, Spring.

Kolar-Panov, D. 1997, *Video, War and the Diasporic Imagination*, Routledge, London.

Langer, John 1998, *Tabloid Television: Popular Journalism and the 'Other' News*, Routledge, London.

Lawe Davies, Chris 1998, 'SBS-TV and its Amazing World', *Media International Australia incorporating Culture and Policy*, no. 89 pp. 87–108.

Le Moignan, M. 1974, 'Climactic Endless Middles', *The Australian*, 29 June, n.p.

Lewis, Jon E. and Stempel, Penny 1993, *Cult TV: The Essential Critical Guide*, Pavilion Books, London.

Liebes, T. and Katz, E. 1990, *The Export of Meaning: Cross-Cultural Readings of Dallas*, Oxford University Press, New York and Oxford.

Lindlof, T. (ed.) 1987, *Natural Audiences: Qualitative Research of Media Uses and Affects*, Ablex, Norwood, NJ.

Long, Malcolm 1995, 'Representing SBS and Australia to the World', *Media Information Australia*, no. 76, pp. 18–21.

Lotman, Yuri 1990, *The Universe of the Mind: A Semiotic Theory of Culture*, Indiana University Press, Bloomington.

Lowery, S. and de Fleur, M. 1983, *Milestones in Mass Communication Research*, Longman, New York.

Lull, J. 1990, *Inside Family Viewing: Ethnographic Research on Television's Audiences*, Routledge, London.

Lumby, C. 1997 *Bad Girls: The Media, Sex and Feminism in the '90s*, Allen & Unwin, Sydney.

——1999, *Gotcha! Life in a Tabloid World*, Allen & Unwin, Sydney.

Malor, Deborah 1991, 'From the Sublime to the Ridiculous: Edmund Burke's Bucolia—Don Burke's Backyard', *Not My Department*, no. 1, pp. 57–70.

May, P. 1998, 'A Sexual Revolution on the Net', *San Jose Mercury News*, 28 June.

McConnell, Bill 1999, 'FCC Weighs Aid for the Blind', *Broadcasting and Cable*, 8 November 1999, p. 16.

McGuigan, Jim 1992, *Cultural Populism*, Routledge, London.

McKay, J. and Miller, T. 1991, 'From Old Boys to Men and Women of the Corporation: The Americanization and Commodification of Australian Sport', *Sociology of Sport Journal*, vol. 8, no. 1, pp. 86–94.

McKee, A. 1996, 'Do You Believe in Fairies? Creating Fictional Identities in Bent TV', *Media International Australia*, no. 79, February, pp. 115–18.

——1997 '"The Aboriginal version of Ken Done . . ." Banal Aboriginal Identities in Australia', *Cultural Studies*, no. 112, pp. 191–206.

——1999 '"Suck on that Mate!": Perverse Centres in Australia' in Deb Verhoeven (ed.), *Twin Peeks: Australian and New Zealand Feature Films*, Damned Publishing, Melbourne.

McKnight, D. 1998, 'Broadcasting and the Enemy Within: Political Surveillance and the ABC, 1951–64', *Media International Australia incorporating Culture and Policy*, no. 87, May, pp. 35–48.

McLuhan, M. 1967, *The Mechanical Bride: Folklore of Industrial Man*, Routledge and Kegan Paul, London.

McQuail, D. 1972, *Sociology of Mass Commmunication*, Sage, London.

——1991, *Mass Communication Theory: An Introduction*, 2nd edn, Sage, London.

McQuire, S. 1997, *Crossing the Digital Threshold*, Australian Key Centre for Cultural and Media Policy and Australian Film Commission, Sydney.

Meade, A. and McKenzie, A. 1999, 'Pay TV Captures a Rating of 7.3 Per Cent', *The Australian*, 3 August, p. 6.

Meadows, M. 1999, 'The Indigenous Broadcasting Sector', in Productivity Commission, *Broadcasting Issues Paper*, Productivity Commission, Melbourne, C1–C18.

Michaels, E. 1986, *The Aboriginal Invention of Television in Central Australia 1982–86*, Australian Institute of Aboriginal Studies, Canberra.

——1994, *Bad Aboriginal Art: Tradition, Media, and Technological Horizons*, Allen & Unwin, Sydney.

Mickler, Steve 1998, *The Myth of Privilege: Aboriginal Status, Media Visions, Public Ideas*, Fremantle Arts Centre Press, Fremantle.

Miller, T. 1998, *Technologies of Truth: Cultural Citizenship and the Popular Media*, University of Minnesota Press, Minneapolis.

Modleski, T. 1984, *Loving with a Vengeance: Mass-produced Fantasies for Women*, Methuen, New York.

Molloy, Simon and Burgan, Barry 1993, *The Economics of Film and Television in Australia*, Australian Film Commission, Sydney.

Moores, S. 1993, *Interpreting Audiences: The Ethnography of Media Consumption*, Sage, London.

Moran, A. 1982, *Making a TV Series: The Bellamy Project*, Currency Press, Sydney.

——1985, *Images and Industry: Television Drama Production in Australia*, Currency Press, Sydney.

——1989, 'Crime, Romance, History: Television Drama', in Albert Moran and Tom O'Regan (eds), *The Australian Screen*, Penguin, Ringwood.

——1993, *Moran's Guide to Australian TV Series*, Australian Film, Radio and Television School, North Ryde.

Morley, D. 1980, *The 'Nationwide' Audience*, British Film Institute, London.

——1981, 'The *Nationwide* Audience: A Critical Postscript', *Screen Education*, no. 39.

——1986, *Family Television: Cultural Power and Domestic Leisure*, Comedia, London.

——1992, *Television Audiences and Cultural Studies*, Routledge, London and New York.

Morley, D. and Robins, K. 1995, *Spaces of Identity, Global Media, Electronic Landscapes and Cultural Boundaries*, Routledge, London.

Morris, Meaghan 1988 'Tooth and Claw: Tales of Survival and *Crocodile Dundee*', in *The Pirate's Fiancée: Feminism, Reading and Postmodernism*, Verso, London.

——1993 'Panorama: The Live, the Dead and the Living', in Graeme Turner (ed.), *Nation, Culture, Text: Australian Cultural and Media Studies*, Routledge, London.

Mulgan, Geoff 1990, 'Television's Holy Grail: Seven Types of Quality', in Geoff Mulgan (ed.), *The Question of Quality*, BFI Publishing, London.

Murdock, Graham and Golding, Peter 1973, 'For a Political Economy of Mass Communications', in R. Miliband and J. Saville (eds), *The Socialist Register*, Merlin.

Naficy, Hamid 1993, *The Making of Exile Cultures: Iranian Television in Los Angeles*, University of Minnesota Press, Minneapolis.

Neale, Steve 1990, 'Questions of Genre', *Screen*, vol. 31, no. 1, Spring, pp. 45–66.

Negroponte, N. 1995, *Being Digital*, Hodder and Stoughton, Sydney.

New Idea 1998, 'A Peek Behind Politics', *New Idea*, 1 August 1998, pp. 20–21.

Newcastle Herald 1999, 'Sterlo Defends Tirade', 6 March, p. 4.

Nightingale, V. 1989, 'What's Ethnographic About Ethnographic Audience Research?' *Australian Journal of Communication*, no. 16, pp. 50–63.

——1992, 'Contesting Domestic Territory: Watching Rugby League on Television', in A. Moran (ed.), *Stay Tuned: An Australian Broadcasting Reader*, Allen & Unwin, Sydney.

——1994, 'Improvising Elvis, Marilyn and Mickey Mouse', *Australian Journal of Communication*, vol. 21, no. 1, pp. 1–20.

Noam, Eli 1991, *Television in Europe*, Oxford University Press, New York.

Noble, K. 1999, Director of Drama, Nine Network, personal interview, 7 July.

Nochinson, Martha 1992, *Soap Opera and the Female Subject*, University of California Press, Berkeley.

Noriega, Chon 1987, 'Godzilla and the Japanese Nightmare—When Them! is U.S.' *Cinema Journal*, vol. 27, no. 1.

Nye, J., Zelikow, P. D. and King, D.C. (eds) 1997, *Why People Don't Trust Government*, Harvard University Press, Cambridge, Mass.

Olson, Scott Robert 1999, *Hollywood Planet: Global Media and the Competitive Advantage of Narrative Transparency*, Lawrence Erlbaum Associates, Mahwah, NJ and London.

O'Regan, T. 1989, 'The Converging of Film and Television', in John Tulloch and Graeme Turner (eds), *Australian Television: Programs, Pleasures and Politics*, Allen & Unwin, Sydney.

——1993, *Australian Television Culture*, Allen & Unwin, Sydney.

——1994, 'Introducing Critical Multiculturalism', *Continuum*, vol. 8, no. 2, pp. 7–19.

——1996a, *Australian National Cinema*, Routledge, London and New York.

——1996b, 'Television Futures in Australia', *Prometheus*, vol. 14, no. 1, pp. 66–79.

O'Regan, T. and Batty, P. 1993, 'An Aboriginal Television Culture: Issues, Strategies and Politics', in T. O'Regan (ed.), *Australian Television Culture*.

O'Regan, T. and Kolar-Panov, D. 1993 'SBS-TV: Symbolic Politics and Multicultural Policy in Television', in T. O'Regan, *Australian Television Culture*, Allen & Unwin, Sydney.

Organisation for Economic Co-operation and Development, Committee for Information, Computer and Communications Policy 1997, *Webcasting and Convergence: Policy Implications*, OECD, Paris.

Palmer, P. 1986a, *The Lively Audience: A Study of Children Around the TV Set*, Allen & Unwin, Sydney.

——1986b, *Girls and Television*, Social Policy Unit, NSW Ministry of Education, Sydney.

Paterson, Richard 1998, 'Drama and Entertainment' in A. Smith (ed.), *Television: An International History*, 2nd edn, Oxford University Press, Oxford.

Patterson, Rosalind 1992, 'SBS-TV: Forerunner of the Future', *Media Information Australia*, no. 66, pp. 43–52.

PBL 1999, 'PBL announces $173.9 million Profit after Tax and Abnormals', media release, 24 August.

Peach, Bill 1992, *TDT: How Australian Current Affairs TV Came of Age*, ABC Books, Sydney.

Peters, B. 1999, Presentation to Media and Telecommunications Policy Group seminar, 'Is There a Future for TV Networks?' Sydney, 27 July.

Peters, B. and Leigh, P. 1993, *Broadcasting Bounces Back—A Financial Evaluation of Australian Commercial Metropolitan Television Part One—Industry Overview*, ANZ McCaughan Corporate and Financial Services, Melbourne, June.

Pilger, J. 1989, *A Secret Country*, Jonathan Cape, London.

Pringle, P. 2000, 'Obscenely Profitable', *The Australian*, 10 January.

Productivity Commission 1999, *Broadcasting*, Draft Report, Ausinfo, Canberra.

Putnam, R.D 1995, 'Tuning In, Tuning Out: The Strange Disappearance of Social Capital in America', *PS: Political Science and Politics*, no. 24, pp. 664–83.

Raymond, Robert 1999, *Out of the Box: An Inside View of the Coming of Current Affairs and Documentaries to Australian Television*, Seaview Press, Henley Beach.

Rayson, C. 1998, *Glued to the Telly*, Elgua Media, Redhill, South Australia

Reeves, Jimmie L., Rodgers, Mark C. and Epstein, Michael 1996, 'Rewriting Popularity: the Cult Files', in David Lavery, Angela Hague and Marla Cartwright (eds), *Deny All Knowledge: Reading* The X-Files, Syracuse University Press, Syracuse, NY, pp. 22–35.

Richards, D. 1999, Presentation to Media and Telecommunications Policy Group seminar, 'Is There a Future for TV Networks?' Sydney, 27 July.

Robins, K. and Webster, F. 1988, 'Cybernetic Capitalism: Information, Technology, Everyday Life', in V. Mosco and J. Wasko (eds), *The Political Economy of Information*, University of Wisconsin Press, Madison.

Rosenberg, Howard 1999, 'Man Commits Suicide—Live!' *Media Studies Journal*, no. 132, pp. 70–71.

Rowe, D. 1996, 'Taming the "Media Monsters": Cultural Policy and Sports TV', *Metro*, vol. 105, pp. 57–61.

——1998, 'If You Film It, Will They Come? Sports on Film', *Journal of Sport and Social Issues*, vol. 22, no. 4, pp. 350–59.

——1999a, 'Helter Skelter': A Screen Sex and Violence Reprise', *Metro Education*, no. 19, pp. 7–8.

——1999b, *Sport, Culture and the Media: The Unruly Trinity*, Open University Press, Buckingham.

SBS 1999, 'Submission of the SBS Corporation to the Review into Multi-channelling by the National Broadcasters', DoCITA Website <*www.dca.gov.au*>.

Scannell, Paddy 1996, *Radio, Television and Modern Life*, Blackwell, London.

Schatz, Thomas 1981, *Hollywood Genres: Formulas, Filmmaking and the Studio System*, Temple University Press, Philadelphia.

Schiller, H. 1989, *Culture Inc: The Corporate Takeover of Public Expression*, Oxford, New York.

Schramm, W. et al. 1961, *Television in the Lives of our Children*, Stanford University Press, Stanford, CA.

Schultz, Julianne 1998, *Reviving the Fourth Estate: Democracy, Accountability and the Media*, Cambridge University Press, Melbourne.

Seiter, E. 1990, 'Making Distinctions in TV Audience Research: A Case Study of a Troubling Interview, *Cultural Studies* vol. 4, no. 1, January, pp. 61–84.

——1999, *Television and New Media Audiences*, Clarendon Press, Oxford.

Seneviratne, Kalinga 1992, 'Multicultural Television: Going Beyond the Rhetoric', *Media Information Australia*, no. 66, pp. 53–57.

Seven Network Limited 1999, *Annual Report*, Seven Network, Sydney.

Silverstone, R. and Hirsch, E. 1992, *Consuming Technologies*, Routledge, London.

Simper, E. 1999, 'Julian Mounter's Tough Test', *The Australian—Media*, p. 1.

——1994, 'His Own Worst Enemy', *The Weekend Australian*, 5–6 November, p. 23.

——1999 'The Boys are Back in Town', *The Weekend Australian*, 1–2 May, p. 21.

Sinclair, John, Yue, Audrey, Hawkins, Gay, Kee Pookong and Fox, Josephine 2000, 'Chinese Cosmopolitanism and Media Use', in S. Cunningham and J. Sinclair, *Floating Lives: The Media and Asian Diasporas*, University of Queensland Press, Brisbane, pp. 36–90.

Southern Star 1998, *Annual Report 1998*, no publication details.

Special Broadcasting Services 1999, Marketing Pages, <*www.sbs.com.au/*>, accessed 19/11/99.

Spigel, L. 1992, *Make Room for TV: Television and the Family Ideal in Postwar America*, University of Chicago Press, Chicago.

Spurgeon, C. 1989, 'Challenging Technological Determinism: Aborigines, AUSSAT and Remote Australia', in H. Wilson (ed.), *Australian Communication and the Public Sphere*, Macmillan, Melbourne.

——1994 'Black White and Blue: Program Classifications for Pay TV', *Media Information Australia*, no. 72, pp. 55–61.

Stapledon, Ross 1993, 'The Mouth from the South', *The Australian Magazine*, 24–25 July, pp. 28–34.

Steel, Alex 1997, 'Mansfield's ABC?' *Media International Australia*, no. 84, pp. 74–80.

Sterling, P. 1999, 'Why I Blew my Stack', *Newcastle Herald*, 6 March, p. 4.

Stern, Lesley 1982, 'The Australian Cereal: Home Grown Television', in Susan Dermody, John Docker and Drusilla Modjeska (eds), *Nellie Melba, Ginger Meggs, and Friends: Essays in Australian Cultural History*, Kibble Books, Malmsbury.

Sternberg, Jason 1995, 'Children of the Information Revolution: Generation X and the Future of Journalism', *CQU Working Papers in Communications and Cultural Studies*, no. 2, pp. 45–59.

Stockbridge S. 1994, *Looking at the Eighties: The Australian Video Music Clip Industry*, AFTRS, Sydney.

Stoddart, B. 1986, *Saturday Afternoon Fever: Sport in the Australian Culture*, Angus & Robertson, Sydney.

Strange, Niki 1998, 'Perform, Educate, Entertain: Ingredients of the Cookery Programme Genre', in C. Geraghty and D. Lusted (eds), *The Television Studies Book*, Arnold, London.

Stutchbury, M. 1999, 'Meaningless Distinctions Driven by Rent-seeking', *The Australian*, 9 March.

Surgeon General's Scientific Advisory Committee on Television and Social Behaviour 1972, *Television and Growing Up: The Impact of Televised Violence*, US Government Printing Office, Washington DC.

Thomas, C. 1980, 'Girls and Counter School Culture', in D. McCallum and U. Ozolins (eds), *Melbourne Working Papers in Sociology*, Research Group in Cultural and Educational Studies, University of Melbourne.

Thussu, Daya Kishan (ed.) 1998, *Electronic Empires: Global Media and Local Resistance*, Edward Arnold, London.

Tiffen, Rodney 1994, 'The Media and Democracy: Reclaiming an Intellectual Agenda', in Julianne Schultz (ed.), *Not Just Another Business: Journalists, Citizens and the Media*, Pluto, Sydney.

Timberg, B. 1985 (1975), 'The Rhetoric of the Camera in Television Soap Opera' in H. Newcomb (ed.), *Television: The Critical View*, 4th edn, Oxford University Press, New York.

Tracey, Michael 1992, 'Our Better Angels: The Condition of Public Service Broadcasting', *Media Information Australia*, no. 76, pp. 18–21.
——1997, *Decline and Fall of Public Service Broadcasting*, Oxford University Press, Oxford.
Tulloch, J. 1990, *Television Drama: Agency, Audience and Myth*, Routledge, London.
Tulloch, J. and Alvarado, Manuel 1983, *Doctor Who: The Unfolding Text*, Macmillan, London.
Tulloch, J. and Jenkins, H. 1995, *Science Fiction Audiences: Watching 'Doctor Who' and 'Star Trek'*, Routledge, London.
Tulloch, J. and Moran, A. 1986, *A Country Practice: 'Quality Soap'*, Currency Press, Sydney.
Tulloch, J. and Turner, G. (eds) 1989, *Australian Television Programs, Pleasures and Politics*, Allen & Unwin, Sydney.
Turnbull, S. 1993a, 'Accounting for Taste: The Moral and Aesthetic Dimensions of Media Practice', in L. Yates (ed.), *Melbourne Studies in Education*, La Trobe University Press, Melbourne.
——1993b, 'The Great Australian Theme Park', *Melbourne Report*, vol. 8, no. 6, pp. 17–19.
——1997, 'On Looking in the Wrong Places: Port Arthur and the Media Violence Debate', *Australian Quarterly*, vol. 69, no. 1, pp. 41–49.
——1998, 'How Australia Entertained Itself This Week', *Sydney Morning Herald*, 14 August 1998, p. 17.
Turner, G. 1990 and 1996 *British Cultural Studies: An Introduction*, Unwin Hyman and Routeledge, London.
——(ed.) 1993, *Nation, Culture, Text: Australian Media and Cultural Studies*, Routledge, London.
——1996a, 'Post-journalism: News and Current Affairs Programming from the Late 1980s to the Present', *Media International Australia*, no. 82, November.
——1996b, 'Current Affairs Hits the Off Button', *The Australian*, 13 November, p. 17.
——1996c 'Maintaining the News', *Culture and Policy*, vol. 7, no. 3.
——1997, 'First Contact: Coming to Terms With the Cable Guy', *UTS Review*, no. 32, pp. 109–21.
——1999, 'Tabloidisation, Journalism and the Possibility of Critique', *International Journal of Cultural Studies*, vol. 2, no. 1.
Turrow, J. 1997, *Breaking Up America: Advertisers and the New Media World*, University of Chicago Press, Chicago.
TV Week 1998, 'Xena: a Mum, a Wife and a Superhero', *TV Week*, 11–16 July, pp. 8–9.
University of Technology, Sydney 1990, *Racism, Cultural Pluralism and the Media*, Office of Multicultural Affairs, Canberra.
Vogel, H.L. 1998, *Entertainment Industry Economics: A Guide for Financial Analysis*, Cambridge University Press, Cambridge.
Walkerdine, V. 1986, 'Video Replay: Families, Films and Fantasy', in V. Burgin et al. (eds), *Formations of Fantasy*, Methuen, London.
Wark, McKenzie 1994, *Virtual Geography: Living with Gobal Media Events*, Indiana University Press, Bloomington.
——1999a, *Celebrities, Culture and Cyberspace: The Light on the Hill in a Postmodern World*, Pluto Press, Sydney.
——1999b, 'Writers Run the Gamut from Plato to Porn', *The Australian*, 26 May, p. 38.
Webster, James 1989, 'Television Audience Behavior: Patterns of Exposure in the New Media Environment', in Jerry L. Satunggio and Jennings Bryant (eds), *Media Use in the Information Age: Emerging Patterns of Adoption and Consumer Use*, Lawrence Erlbaum Associates, New Jersey.

Wenner, L. (ed.) 1998, *MediaSport: Cultural Sensibilities and Sport in the Media Age*, Routledge, New York.

Whannel, G. 1992, *Fields in Vision: Television Sport and Cultural Transformation*, Routledge, London.

White, P., Segall, P. and Hoad, I. 1982, *Public Television in Melbourne. The Preview Broadcasts and Beyond*, Open Channel Co-operative Limited, Melbourne.

Williams, Raymond 1974, *Television: Technology and Cultural Form*, Fontana/Collins, London.

Willis, P. 1977, *Learning to Labour: How Working Class Kids Get Working Class Jobs*, Saxon House, London

Wilson, H. 1998, 'Television's *tour de force*: The Nation Watches the Olympic Games', in D. Rowe and G. Lawrence (eds), *Tourism, Leisure, Sport: Critical Perspectives*, pp. 135–45.

Windschuttle, K. 1988, *The Media*, 2nd edn, Penguin, Melbourne.

Winton, K. 1998, 'Pay-per-view Channels Box Clever', *Communications Update*, no. 143, May, pp. 8–9.

——1999a, 'The Online Advertising Proposition', *Communications Update*, no. 157, August, pp. 18–19.

——1999b, 'Pay TV Finally Gets a Rating', *Communications Update*, no. 157, August, p. 9.

Wober, J.M. and Fazal, S. 1994, '*Neighbours* at Home and Away: British Viewers' Perceptions of Australian Soap Operas', *Media Information Australia*, no. 71, pp. 78–87.

Woodley, B. 1999, 'Nine's Kingpin', *The Australian—Media*, 25–31 March, pp. 3–4.

Woods, Mark 1998, 'Booming Oz Nervy', *Encore*, no. 1621, 2 December, p. 10.

Index

THE AUSTRALIAN TV BOOK